Race and the Jury

Racial Disenfranchisement and the Search for Justice

THE PLENUM SERIES IN CRIME AND JUSTICE

Series Editors:
James Alan Fox, *Northeastern University, Boston, Massachusetts*
Joseph Weis, *University of Washington, Seattle, Washington*

DELINQUENCY CAREERS IN TWO BIRTH COHORTS
Paul E. Tracy, Marvin E. Wolfgang, and Robert M. Figlio

RACE AND THE JURY: Racial Disenfranchisement and the Search for Justice
Hiroshi Fukurai, Edgar W. Butler, and Richard Krooth

RAPE LAW REFORM: A Grassroots Revolution and Its Impact
Cassia Spohn and Julie Horney

Race and the Jury

Racial Disenfranchisement and the Search for Justice

Hiroshi Fukurai

University of California, Santa Cruz
Santa Cruz, California

Edgar W. Butler

University of California, Riverside
Riverside, California

and

Richard Krooth

University of California, Berkeley
Berkeley, California and
Sonoma State University
Rohnert Park, California

Springer Science+Business Media, LLC

Library of Congress Cataloging-in-Publication Data

Fukurai, Hiroshi, 1954-
Race and the jury : racial disenfranchisement and the search for justice / Hiroshi Fukurai, Edgar W. Butler, and Richard Krooth.
p. cm. -- (The Plenum series in crime and justice)
Includes bibliographical references and index.
ISBN 978-1-4899-1129-2
1. Jury selection--United States. 2. Race discrimination--Law and legislation--United States. I. Butler, Edgar W. II. Krooth, Richard. III. Title. IV. Series.
KF8979.F84 1992
347.73'0752--dc20
[347.307752] 92-29611
CIP

ISBN 978-1-4899-1129-2 ISBN 978-1-4899-1127-8 (eBook)
DOI 10.1007/978-1-4899-1127-8

Originally published by Plenum Press, New York in 1993
Softcover reprint of the hardcover 1st edition 1993

Preface

The study of the jury and race has preoccupied social psychologists and other behavioral scientists, who have examined the intertwining relationship of the attitudes and the psychological characteristics of jurors and their inclination to reach particular verdicts. Such sociopsychological concerns tended, for many years, to crowd out a consideration of macrolevel issues about the selection of racially unbalanced juries that have indicted and convicted members of racial minorities.

Reductionist and psycholegal approaches have negated a critical examination of the structural mechanisms that have maintained and perpetuated racial discrimination in the jury system. For example, a variety of informal mechanisms in the jury selection process identify prospective minority jurors and exclude them from serving on juries. Such structural and institutional discrimination includes (1) gerrymandered judicial districts that exclude minority-dominated neighborhoods from the jurisdictional boundaries; (2) the use of registered-voter rolls (ROV) as a source list to identify the candidates for jury service, as low registration rates by racial and ethnic minorities systematically exclude minority populations from jury service; and (3) juridical discrimination, including blue ribbon juries, less-than-unanimous verdicts, and small-size juries, all of which have the propensity to be empowered by the racial majority.

The book is divided into two parts. Part I contains four introductory chapters that examine the institutional and structural mechanisms that have maintained the underrepresentation of racial and ethnic minorities on juries. Chapter 1 considers two specific cases that illustrate the relationship between the racial backgrounds of jurors and their verdicts. Chapters 2 and 3 examine the use of structural and macro approaches to evaluate the racial inequality in the jury system and in jury selection. Chapter 4 examines U.S. Supreme Court reviews that dealt with the underrepresentation of minority populations on juries between 1880 and 1980. The minorities discussed are blacks, Hispanics, women, and the poor.

Part II presents a sample of substantive problems in the methodological application of various statistical techniques to evaluate racial representation on juries. Chapter 5 examines economic excuses, which are the often-used excuses in voluntary self-exclusion from jury service. This chapter examines the extent to which organizational resources and company supports influence racial and ethnic representation. Chapter 6 presents an in-depth analysis of scientific jury selection in *voir dire*. A number of sophisticated statistical models, such as Markov chains and multiple regression, are used to evaluate jury representation and the selection of minority populations in *voir dire* to create racially balanced juries. Chapter 7 offers the optimal statistical design for obtaining a racially representative jury. The chapter examines the application of the cluster-sampling method with probability proportionate to size (PPS) to jury selection procedures. The technique is of great importance because it has the potential to eliminate the effect of gerrymandered judicial districts on the racial and ethnic composition of jury panels.

In light of the theoretical analyses of racial disenfranchisement presented in Part I and the methods for creating more egalitarian juries presented in Part II, Chapter 8 examines the *voir dire* jury selection by the defense in the *McMartin* child-molestation trial, one of the most notorious jury trials in American history. The chapter examines the trial background, the pretrial publicity and its influence on people's perceptions, the importance of race on the screening of prospective jurors, the verdict, and the aftermath of the trial. We were involved in the trial as jury consultants and helped the defense attorneys, Dean Gits and Danny Davis, to select the most impartial jurors to try the unpopular defendants, Raymond Buckey and Peggy McMartin Buckey. Jo-Ellan Huebner Dimitrius, our collaborator in the *McMartin* and many other jury trials, was a principal contributor to Chapter 8.

Thus the book is organized on a discussion of basic problems in the theory of race, law, and the jury. It does not seek to provide additional support to previous psychoelegal research that has established the close relationship between the racial and ethnic backgrounds of jurors and their perceptions of trial outcomes. Rather, the book is designed to address macrolevel problems of racial disenfranchisement and judicial inequality. We will demonstrate throughout the book the utility of this macro approach. For the moment, let us offer two justifications.

First, all research entails both theoretical and empirical issues. By orienting our thinking around these two kinds of issues, we hope to provide a more systematic understanding of race and the jury than could be obtained from the psycholegal literature.

Second, factual knowledge in the expanding investigation of relations between race and the jury has often proved highly elusive. The knowledge of this topic of just a decade ago has been superseded by recent, more thorough analyses (see Butler, Fukurai, Huebner-Dimitrius, & Krooth, 1992; Fukurai, 1985; Fukurai & Butler, 1987, 1991, 1992a, 1992b; Fukurai, Butler, & Huebner-Dimitrius, 1987; Fukurai, Butler, & Krooth, 1991a, b). Thus, it seems far more important to present a *theoretical framework* for and an *analytical approach* to how social scientists evaluate racial representativeness on juries and the legitimacy of the resulting verdicts. Therefore, the theory of racial disenfranchisement in Chapter 2, the step-by-step evaluations of racial representation in Chapter 3, and the statistical techniques applied to the evaluation in Chapters 5, 7, and 8 provide the critical sociological and methodological perspectives on this topic.

Finally, we hope that this book will help provide both theoretical and methodological frameworks within which to examine the structural causes of racial disenfranchisement on juries, to eliminate the sources of such nonegalitarian social structures, and to help in the search for justice and equality in the jury system in the United States.

Acknowledgments

This book is based on a review of historical and contemporary court cases, research literature, and our actual experience in a vast number of capital punishment trials, mainly involving racial and ethnic minorities as the defendants. So far, at least one of these cases has reached the Supreme Court of the United States; others have failed to go beyond the local superior court level.

Over the years, we have been fortunate, while participating in these endeavors, to come into contact with many dedicated people involved in the jury system. Thus, in writing this book, we came to appreciate the great contributions made by several specific individuals. Specifically, we thank Jo-Ellan Huebner-Dimitrius, our coauthor in another book on jury selection in the *McMartin* child-molestation case in Los Angeles County, California. We appreciate her contribution to our general education on the jury selection process and her helpful comments on many aspects of this book.

Raymond Arce, of the Jury Commissioner's Office, Los Angeles County, California, was one of our primary adversaries. Much of the information reported in this book has come from his office in Los Angeles over the years. We are thankful for his recognition that our opposition was based not on personalities but on our mutual commitment to both democratic and egalitarian principles in regard to the jury system. Our contacts with other jury commissioners and their representatives were also favorable, and we came to appreciate a number of jury commissioners, their staffs, and the efforts they go through to bring jurors to the courtroom.

In the process of carrying out research and testimony involving the underrepresentation of racial and ethnic minorities on juries, we have worked closely with a host of defense attorneys—too many to mention by name here. We found them to be outstanding attorneys who have a serious and abiding interest in the law and justice. On the whole, we felt that the defense attorneys were more interested in pursuing social justice than the vast majority of prosecuting attorneys, many of whom probably knew that jury selection laws were being systematically violated but appeared to be uninterested in judicial reform, social justice, or administration of the laws as written. For the most part, their focus was more on getting the "jury challenges" out of the way than on diligently applying the law. There were several prosecuting attorneys, however, who have won our great respect and who in a very real sense advanced our knowledge of the jury selection process by forcing us to pursue a greater depth in our jury research. To them, we express our sincere admiration.

Finally, once again, we wish to convey our indebtedness to everyone who contributed to the research effort. Here we wish to recognize the help and contributions of others.

At various stages of completion, discussions about the manuscript were held with Jon Alston and Letitia Alston of the Sociology Department at Texas A & M University, and a number of undergraduate and graduate students at Texas A & M University and the University of California, Riverside, also worked closely on the research reported in this book; to them, we offer our congratulations for a job well done.

We would also like to thank those who contributed their expert knowledge in the period before this particular manuscript took form. Notable here are Mary Zey, Thomas Glass, Karen Wilson, Gail Thomas, and Ben Aguirre of the Sociology Department at Texas A & M University; Dean Gits and Danny Davis, defense attorneys in the *McMartin* child-molestation trial in Los Angeles; Glenda Jones of the Sociology Department at the University of California, Riverside, and Jim Pick at the University of Redlands; and Troy Duster, Robert Bellah, and office staffs in the Sociology Department at the University of California, Berkeley.

We also appreciate the support, encouragement, and assistance of Jerry Gaston, Rogelio Saenz, Jim Burk, and Howard Kaplan of the Sociology Department, Harlow Landpahir of the Center for Urban Affairs, Jaan Laane of the Koriyama-Japan Office, and Lori Cheatham and other office staff of the Sociology Department at Texas A & M University; the late Elizabeth M. Humbargar at the University of the Pacific; Alex Ramirez and Larry Sautter of Computing and Communications; Wanda Clark, Marge Souder, and the office staff of the Sociology Department at the University of California, Riverside; John Kitsuse, Dane Archer, John Childs, Marcia Millman, Dana Hagler, Susan Curtis, and other office staff of the Board of Studies in Sociology, and Bill Hyder and Jim Mulherin of the Computing and Telecommunication Services at the University of California, Santa Cruz; Jack Curtin in Interdisciplinary Studies at San Francisco State University; and Alan Stacy of the Psychology Department at the University of Southern California.

Funding for this study came from a number of sources. We thank, in particular, the following groups: the Faculty Senate at the University of California, Santa Cruz; the College of Liberal Arts, the Center for Urban Affairs, the Institute of Pacific Asia, and the Office of International Coordination at Texas A & M University; the Faculty Senate and the Mexican Data Base Project at the University of California, Riverside; and superior courts in various California counties, including Los Angeles, Riverside, San Bernardino, San Diego, Orange, Sonoma, and Sacramento.

We also appreciate the assistance of Plenum Press and anonymous reviewers for their helpful comments and suggestions. Finally, the book would not have been completed if it had not been for the outstanding efforts, dedication, and continued support and encouragement from our collaborators: Letitia Alston of the Sociology Department at Texas A & M University; Millie Almy of the Education Department at the University of California, Berkeley; and oral historian and essayist Ann B. Krooth in Berkeley.

Needless to say, we accept full responsibility for the contents, the facts presented, and the elaboration of the relationship between race and the jury in this book.

HIROSHI FUKURAI
EDGAR W. BUTLER
RICHARD KROOTH

Contents

I. INTRODUCTION TO RACE AND THE JURY

1. *Race and the Jury* 3

Introduction 3
Race and Jury Verdicts 5
  Greensboro Trials 5
  Vincent Chin Trials 7
Race and the Jury 8
Organization of the Following Chapters 10
Notes 11

2. *The Structural Approach to Racial Inequality in the Jury System and Jury Selection* 13

Introduction 13
A Structural Theory of Racial Disenfranchisement 17
  Procedural Anomalies and Racial Inequities in Jury Selection ... 18
  Residential Mobility and Undeliverables 21
  Judicial Discrimination against Racial and Ethnic Minorities as Jurors 26
  Gerrymandered Judicial Districts 29
Conclusions 34
Notes 35

3. *Jury Selection Procedures: An Overview* 39

Introduction 39
Racial Inequality in the Jury Selection Process 40

Stage 1: Geographic Areas and the Population 42
Stage 2: Source Lists 44
Stage 3: The Master File 47
Stage 4: Qualified-Juror Files 51
Stage 5: Jury Impanelment Lists 56
Stage 6: Jury Panels 63
Stage 7: *Voir Dire* 68
Stage 8: The Jury Box 71
Conclusions 75
Notes 78

4. *The U.S. Supreme Court, the Constitutional Background of Jury Selection, and Racial Representation* *81*

Introduction 81
Substantive Guidelines 83
Blacks' Rights before 1880 86
The Rights of Blacks between 1880 and 1934 88
The New Era of Jury Challenges: 1935 to 1948 89
The Criterion of "A Fair Cross Section of the Community" 91
Cross-Sectionality and Juror Representation 92
Jury Representation: 1965 to 1967 95
Institutional Racism 97
Statistical Indices as Evidentiary Proof of Discrimination 100
A White Defendant and Black Underrepresentation 102
Discrimination and Jury Forepersons 103
Discrimination against Hispanics 104
Discrimination against Women 107
Economic Discrimination 110
Conclusions and Unresolved Questions 113
Notes 115

II. ANALYSES OF RACIAL INEQUALITY ON JURIES: EMPIRICAL ISSUES

5. *Anatomy of Economic Excuses: Organizational Resources and Company Support for an Egalitarian Jury System* *119*

Introduction 119

Anatomy of Economic Excuses: Structural Determinants of Inequality in Jury Representation 121
Judicial Inequality 123
Hypotheses 124
Research Design 125
The Sample 125
Methods 126
Measurement 126
Results 129
Organizational Structure and Labor Market Characteristics 129
Labor Market Structures 129
Authority and Class Measures 134
Extralegal Variables 135
Legal Variables 135
Discussion 136
Conclusions 138
Notes 140

6. *Scientific Jury Selection in* Voir Dire: *The Hidden Structure of Jury Selection* *141*

Introduction 141
By What and Whose Standard? 142
Scientific Defense *Voir Dire* Jury Selection 143
Trial Background of *People v. Harris* 144
Defense *Voir Dire* Jury-Selection Strategies 145
Jury Profile in *Harris* Retrial 147
Scientific Defense *Voir Dire* 148
Surviving Trend: Markov Chain 150
Voir Dire and Its Social Significance 154
Research on Biases in Scientific Jury Selection 156
Conclusions 160
Notes 162

7. *The Optimal Design to Obtain a Racially Representative Jury: Cluster-Sampling Methods with the Probability Proportionate to Size Applied to Jury Selection* *165*

Introduction 165
Residential Factors and Jury Selection 166

Cluster Sampling with the Probability Proportionate to Size 168
The Empirical Model of Jury Representation 170
Data 172
Methods 173
Covariance Structure Analysis 173
Computer-Generated Graphics Analysis 173
Results 174
Cluster-Sampling Methods 178
The First Stage 178
The Second Stage 182
Discussion and Policy Implications 187
Conclusions 189
Notes 190

8. The McMartin *Trial: Race and Scientific Jury Selection* *193*

Introduction 193
The Trial Background 194
Prepublicity and Political Motives 196
Jury Selection: Community Cross Section and Biases 197
Pretrial Publicity and Its Influence on People's Perceptions 198
Analyses for Developing Juror Profiles 200
Comparisons of Eligibles in the Central District and Impaneled Jurors 205
Importance of Race in Screening Prospective Jurors 208
The Verdict 210
Media Event and the Aftermath 211
Recipe for Reform 213
Conclusions 214
Notes 217

References *221*

Table of Cases *233*

Index *235*

I

Introduction to Race and the Jury

Our Hope

*Justice and an egalitarian jury
and jury selection system for all,
regardless of race, ethnicity, gender,
or social class*

1

Race and the Jury

Introduction

The jury is one of our most democratic institutions. A random sample of the community is asked to render an impartial verdict in a case after hearing evidence from both sides. The notion that ordinary men and women of good will can and will exercise good judgment is basic to our tradition of government by the people. Furthermore, a jury's verdict is assumed to reflect the collective sentiments and conscience of the community and therefore carries a legitimacy that cannot be attained by experts, no matter how intelligent and skillful they may be.

In the United States, the foundation for the criminal jury's composition is contained in the Sixth Amendment to the Constitution. It states that defendants have the right to a trial "by an impartial jury of the States and district wherein the crime shall have been committed." A similar guarantee for the civil jury appears in the Seventh Amendment. From these amendments and subsequent U.S. Supreme Court decisions involving the jury and its representativeness, three general guidelines and principles have emerged for the selection and the makeup of the jury. First, the jury must be drawn from a representative cross section of the community. Second, the trial should be held in the district in which the crime has been committed. Third, the jurors must be impartial; that is, potential jurors unable to judge the facts with an impartial mind may be rejected from the jury.

In recent years, however, inequities in the jury system and in jury selection have challenged the ideal of a representative jury and a fair trial by one's peers.[1] Although the jury is required to be composed of a fair cross section of the community, racial and ethnic minorities are consistently underrepresented in the vast majority of both federal and state courts (Butler, 1980a, b, 1981; Carp, 1982; Fukurai, 1985; Fukurai & Butler, 1991a; Fukurai *et al.*, 1991a, b; Hans & Vidmar, 1986; Hastie, Penrod, & Pennington, 1983; Kassin & Wrightsman, 1989; Wishman, 1986; Wrightsman, 1987). The underrepresentation of racial and ethnic minorities is particularly important because the majority of defendants in criminal cases are, in fact, members of racial minorities. A trial by a jury that includes persons with the same racial background as the defendants offers strong legitimacy to the basic premise of a jury trial by one's peers. Historically, however, the jury in America has been dominated by white males.[2] The persistent underrepresentation of racial minorities has contributed to public distrust and lack of faith in the legal system.

Our ability to maintain the jury as an institution in the future depends on our commitment to its democratic principles. The jury is the embodiment of the belief that only by gathering together persons from all sectors of society can we be sure that all relevant perspectives have been considered and that the verdict represents the community's collective judgment on the controversial issue. Any other source of these decisions undermines their legitimacy in the eyes of citizens.

Up until the last few decades, however, jury participation was largely reserved for the majority, reflecting societal insensitivity to the rights of minorities. Even though some changes have taken place, a system still exists in which the legal and judicial structures continuously reproduce, maintain, and perpetuate the subordination of racial and ethnic minorities. Historically, they have been discouraged, if not prevented, from full participation in political structures, courts, and the judicial decision-making process. Labor-market and other socioeconomic inequalities have served to reinforce poor representation.

Specific mechanisms of discrimination still exist. We examine an array of factors that affect racially disproportionate participation in the judicial decision-making process: specific procedural anomalies in jury selection; socioeconomic barriers that undermine the inclusion of racial minorities; and gerrymandered judicial districts. For example, potential sources of institutional biases in jury selection include the legal structures that prevent full-community jury participation, thereby perpetuating and maintaining racially demarcated juries. Labor market characteristics also set limits on the selection of minorities for jury duty. Members of these minorities are more likely to be in secondary labor markets with high residential mobility, so that their call to jury service is impeded. They are more likely to be classified as "undeliverables," and residents who do not respond to the jury summons are more likely to become defined as "recalcitrants." In addition, a different court and judicial strategy regulates the degree of minority participation on juries through gerrymandered judicial districts.

A jury speaking for the community is an essential element in a democratic government that derives its power from the people. The jury shows that harmony is possible if we listen to each other and seek a unified judgment from a diversity of viewpoints. But these benefits of democracy can be attained only if the assembled jury is *representative of a cross section of the community,* so that the persons deliberating can legitimately claim to speak on behalf of the community. Thus, racially nonrepresentative juries are detrimental to our commitment to democratic solutions. The jury is the institution of the people rather than of the government, and it is the body that expresses the people's collective conscience rather than expert opinions or racially motivated views. In other words, it is the essence of democracy. Consistent biases toward nonrepresentative juries, therefore, need to be rectified, and the sources of this disproportionate representation need to be critically examined and eliminated.

This book examines the relationship between race-ethnicity and the jury and sheds light on the legal, socioeconomic, and geopolitical factors that lead to racially unbalanced juries.

Race and Jury Verdicts

The problem of the effect of racial composition on a jury and its verdict is most noticeable when the trial involves a blatantly racial issue. A large number of jury litigations have examined the equality of the jury system, the fairness of the jury selection process, and the racial representativeness of jury panels. Although there are large variations in the nature of trials, social milieus, and legal or statutory factors that affect juries' composition and verdicts, the following two jury trials provide clear evidence of the social mechanisms that allow jury verdicts to perpetuate racial inequality. The cases reviewed here are the trials in Greensboro, North Carolina, and the Vincent Chin case in Michigan. The two cases are typical examples of racial disenfranchisement and judicial discrimination against members of racial minorities in the jury system.

Greensboro Trials

In late 1979, racial tension was building in Greensboro, North Carolina. The local police and the FBI had been alerted that the Ku Klux Klan had planned to arm against any attempt to criticize their operations in the city. Greensboro was a segregated town that did not take kindly to those who advocated integration.

On November 3, 1979, in a predominantly black city neighborhood in Greensboro, the stage was set for bloody confrontations. Demonstrators were singing folk songs as they prepared for an anti–Ku Klux Klan rally scheduled by the Workers Viewpoint Organization (WVO) of the Communist Workers' Party (CWP). A Ku Klux Klan motorcade appeared and drove through a street lined with protestors. The lead car suddenly stopped, and the Klansmen and members of the American Nazi Party opened fire on the demonstrators, picking off the five leaders of the CWP organization. Four were killed instantly, a fifth died two days later, and seven others were injured. None of the Klan supporters was hit. All these events were documented in television news film taken by crews at the scene, so there were many witnesses.

In 1980, five gunmen were tried for the murder of these five members of the CWP in a state court in Greensboro, North Carolina. Approximately 25% of the state's population was nonwhite. However, no black juror served on the jury that tried the case. During the jury selection, eligible blacks were peremptorily stricken by the defense. Only white jurors were accepted, including one who said, "It's less of a crime to kill communists" (DiPerna, 1984, p. 171). All defendants were subsequently acquitted of all charges by the all-white jury.

A second trial began in January 1984 for the nine accused Klansmen and neo-Nazis for conspiring to violate the victims' civil rights. The prosecution introduced videotapes to support its claim that the defendants had attacked a peaceful and lawful anti–Ku Klux Klan demonstration. An FBI investigation of the videotape substantiated that the first 11 shots had been fired by Klansmen, contrary to the defendants' testimony (Kassin & Wrightsman, 1988). The defendants had argued that they had shot the demonstrators in self-defense and that their motive for attending the rally was to save Greensboro from a communist takeover.

Jury selection started in a clandestine manner, with the judge questioning prospective jurors *in camera,* behind closed doors. This was done because the U.S. Supreme Court had ruled in *Press-Enterprise Co. v. Superior Court of California* in 1984 that the press could not be barred from *voir dire* except for "good cause." Though questioning of the jurors was conducted in private, the exercise of peremptory challenges was conducted in open court. Of 69 jurors who survived prescreening questions, 11 were black. Every black was stricken by the defense attorneys who represented members of the Ku Klux Klan, the American Nazi Party, or both (DiPerna, 1984, pp. 171–173). Again, no black juror served on the jury. In April 1984, the all-white jury acquitted the defendants entirely.

The Greensboro trials challenge the most cherished ideal of the jury system, that the case be tried by an impartial jury and that the case not be predisposed to favor a particular verdict. Though the two North Carolina juries might very well have been impartial, the fact that the defense was twice able to manage to achieve an all-white jury in this North Carolina jurisdiction raises questions about the fairness of the jury decision and the racial representativeness of the jury. Defendants of the jury selection process could protest that this case is not representative of jury selection elsewhere in the country. The South has a long history of discrimination against blacks, and even there, sensitivity to civil rights issues has increased in recent years. The next case, however, suggests that the Greensboro trials are not an anomaly.

Vincent Chin Trials

In 1982, Vincent Chin, a 27-year-old Chinese-American, was about to be married. Chin was a draftsman for an engineering company in a Detroit suburb. One night, he was with three friends at his bachelor party at the Fancy Pants Lounge, a bar in the Detroit suburb of Highland Park, a blue-collar enclave. Two men, Ronald Ebens and his stepson Michael Nitz, arrived and exchanged words with Chin and his friends. A fight broke out, and the two men were injured. Chin later left the bar. About 20 minutes later, Ebens spotted Chin in front of a nearby restaurant. He immediately retrieved a baseball bat from Nitz's car, chased Chin through the streets, and clubbed him repeatedly. The incident was witnessed by a number of people, including two off-duty police officers. One officer, Gardenhire, said that Nitz was holding Chin as Ebens swung the bat at him: "Chin broke away, ran into the street and fell. Ebens caught up, swung the bat at the prone Chin, just like you are hitting a golf ball; he hit him four times in the head." Chin died four days later from a head injury (Locin, 1984).

Race and economic conditions both contributed to the incidents because the killing was motivated not only by the race of the victim but also because it occurred when Michigan was gripped by an economic recession. Factories were being closed, workers were being laid off, and many middle westerners were blaming Japanese imports for the problems in the American automobile industry. According to Boyce Maxwell, the owner of the club, the killing was the result of the ill feeling against the Japanese that he saw as endemic to Detroit because of the losses the auto industry was taking from Japanese imported cars. He said, "We got 16 percent unemployment in town . . . There's lots of hard feelings. In my opinion, these people come in, they see a man, supposedly Japanese. They look at this guy and see Japan—the reason all my buddies are out of work" (Cummings, 1983).

Ebens pled guilty in a Michigan state court to a reduced charge of manslaughter. Judge Charles Kaufman then sentenced Ebens to three years' probation and a $3,780 fine. The sentence prompted angry demonstrations by Asian-Americans across the country. It was later revealed that Judge Kaufman had been a Japanese-held prisoner of war in World War II, but he denied that any antioriental feelings guided his ruling (Wilderson, 1987). The sentence led federal officials to reopen the criminal case as a civil rights matter, and in 1984, Ebens was convicted of violating Chin's civil rights. Nitz was found not guilty. The U.S. Court of Appeals for the Sixth Circuit overturned Mr. Ebens's conviction in September 1986 on the ground that the trial judge, Anna Diggs Taylor, had erred in refusing to admit as evidence tapes of some eyewitnesses being interviewed shortly after the killing (Wilderson, 1987).

The second federal trial opened for federal *civil charges* in the death of Vincent Chin in 1987 ("Second rights trial opens in 1982 beating death," 1987). The case gained so much notoriety in Detroit that the trial was moved to Cincinnati, a conservative community where there is a small Asian population. In the eight-day trial in the federal district court, the jury did not include any Asian; it was composed of 10 whites and 2 blacks. It deliberated for eight hours before finding Ebens not guilty ("Autoworker acquitted at rights violation in Asian's death," 1987; Wilderson, 1987).

This story also challenges the ideal of trial by an impartial jury. The crime had been committed in a community that shared widespread negative feelings toward Asians, particularly the Japanese, who were seen as causing massive unemployment in the community. While the final trial was held in Cincinnati, the jury had no Asian members, although to be fair, the Asian community in the city was small. James Tso, president of the Washington-based Organization of Chinese-Americans, said that "the case pointed up what many Asian-Americans saw as a growing problem of violence and bigotry aimed at them, largely because of the nation's burgeoning trade deficit" (Wilderson, 1987).

Race and the Jury

Two examples, the Greensboro and the Vincent Chin cases, illustrate jury trials in which the crimes were racially motivated and the juries that tried the defendants did not include any members who shared the race-ethnic or ideological characteristics of the victims. Those two cases also offer evidence of the intertwined relationship among race, the composition of juries, and verdicts. The race of victims, of defendants, and of the accused played a crucial role in influencing trial outcomes.

The degree of racial disharmony and social conflict in the American court system has long been recognized by historians. In 1880, 12 years after the 14th Amendment added the equal protection clause to the U.S. Constitution, applying the Bill of Rights to the states, the U.S. Supreme Court declared unconstitutional a West Virginia statute that explicitly limited jury service to "all-white male persons" and thus overtly discriminated against all blacks and other nonwhites (*Strauder v. West Virginia*, 1880). The Court indicated that some standards could be erected to exclude persons from jury service, and that such standards would limit service to educated male property holders. More recent Supreme Court decisions, however, have stated that virtually all of these standards serve to discriminate unconstitutionally against protected groups in society. But the road away from the *Strauder* decision has been slow. The Court did not, for example, finally rule unconstitutional overt discrimination against Hispanic jurors until 1954 and against women until 1975.

Numerous U.S. Supreme Court decisions have examined the domination and racial supremacy of the majority in both judicial and political spheres. In 1970, *Carter v. Jury Commission of Greene County* became the first class-action suit reviewed by the Supreme Court; it was brought by a group of citizens to question the legitimacy of the entire court system and jury selection process in Alabama. Previously, only defendants arguing that their right to a fair trial had been denied were allowed to raise jury challenges. The petitioner claimed that the entire state apparatus, which included the county jury commissioners, their clerks, the local circuit judges, and even the governor of Alabama, was in conspiracy in perpetuating racial inequality in jury selection. Further, in *Turner v. Forche* (1970), the petitioner alleged that the state-run system of jury selection was rooted in explicit racial discrimination and argued that the county board of education, which was composed of only five white freeholders, had been selected by an all-white grand jury, which in turn had been drawn from a jury list selected by an all-white six-member body of county jury commissioners.

The notion of a racially biased jury system is also reported elsewhere. In many trials of political activists in the late 1960s, a large number of minority defendants were tried by juries composed of the majority (Barkan, 1985; Becker, 1971; Danielski, 1971; Keating, 1970; O'Rourke, 1972). In the trial of Huey Newton, a cofounder of the Black Panthers, for instance, ethnographic research suggested the notion of racial supremacy in the criminal court system. He was tried for the murder of a police officer. The study noted:

> A black man like Huey Newton is tried under a system of law developed by white Western European jurists. He is confronted in the black ghetto by white police officers, then indicted by an all-white, or predominantly white, grand

> jury, prosecuted by a team of all-white district attorneys, tried by a white judge, convicted by a predominantly white jury, and denied bail on appeal by white state appellate courts and a white federal judge. It is not simply the color of the principles that is at issue, but the more profound point that the various officials and processes in the system represent institutions that reflect and are responsive to values and interests of the white majority—a power structure and a community that benefit from keeping black people in "their place," namely, in the ghetto and without power. (Blauner, 1972; p. 253)

The examples illustrate that race and the jury are inescapably interdependent, and that the relationship between them needs critical examination. The questions should include the extent of the interrelationship between race and the jury, the extent to which racial representativeness affects the legitimization of a jury trial by one's peers and the resulting verdicts, and whether the jury reflects a fair cross section of the community. This book offers a critical examination of those questions and discusses a number of legal, socioeconomic, and geopolitical factors that influence jury composition and the resulting legitimacy of the jury trial. The book also helps us to understand that the 1992 verdict of Rodney King's beating trial in acquitting four white police officers in Los Angeles was not simply an anomaly but a consequence of the jury system in which the position of racial minorities in the social system in general and the court system in particular was molded by socio-historical factors of subordination.

Organization of the Following Chapters

The following outline shows the organization of the remainder of this study. Chapter 2 provides the basic background and information for a structural approach to racial inequality in the jury system. Chapter 3 specifically examines various stages of the jury selection process and offers insights into both legal and extralegal variables that affect jury selection and the resulting jury composition. Chapter 4 provides an overview of cases reviewed by the U.S. Supreme Court involving the inequities of the jury system and racial participation.

Section II of the book focuses on empirically related aspects of racial representativeness and its evaluations. Chapter 5 examines the anatomy of economic excuses in jury representation and identifies the sociodemographic and economic variables that significantly influence the composition of the jury. Chapter 6 focuses on a number of key variables that affect the decision-making process of selecting prospective jurors during *voir dire*. We provide insight into the identification of extralegal variables affecting the racial composition of juries and show how scientific jury-selection techniques can be effectively used in jury selection to design racially representative juries. Specifically, we provide in-depth analyses of *Harris v. California* (1985), the jury-challenge case that set the standard and made the significant pronouncement on the evaluation of racial representation in California. In Chapter 7, we examine the feasibility of applying the cluster-sampling strategy to jury selection and evaluate the extent to which the selected jury reflects a racial and socioeconomic cross section of the community.

In the final chapter, we offer a summary of the *McMartin* child-molestation trial. The *McMartin* trial became the longest and costliest criminal trial in American history. In 1987, the scientific jury-selection method was used by the authors to evaluate the assigned jury pool and to select the least biased jurors to try two defendants, Raymond Buckey and Peggy McMartin Buckey. Our statistical analyses revealed that race and ethnicity were keys to screening prospective jurors for an impartial final panel.

Race and ethnicity exercise a significant impact on the outcome of trials. The racial backgrounds of prospective jurors have become a crucial factor in selecting the final jury in many well-publicized trials that have touched on sensitive racial and ideological issues. We offer a summary of the intertwined relationship between race and a jury and examine a number of factors that lead to race-ethnic inequality in the jury and judicial-decision mechanism. Finally we hope to contribute to the intense debate concerning the present search by both legal and academic researchers for an egalitarian jury system.

Notes

1. See Alker, Hosticka, and Mitchell (1976); Brady (1983); Carp (1982); Chevigny (1975); De Cani (1974); Diamond (1980); Finkelstein (1966); Fukurai and Butler (1987, 1991, 1992a, 1992b); Hans and Vidmar (1986); Heyns (1979); Kairys (1972); Kairys, Kadane, and Lehoczky (1977); Mills (1969); Robinson (1950); Staples (1975); Summers (1961, pp. 35–42); *U.S. 90th Congress Senate Report No. 891* (1967); and *U.S. 90th Congress House Report No. 1076* (1968).
2. For various court trials in the Federal Supreme Court, see *Alexander v. Louisiana* (405 U.S. 625 1972); *Peters v. Kiff* (407 U.S. 493 1972); *Taylor v. Louisiana* (419 U.S. 522 1975); *Duren v. Missouri* (439 U.S. 357 1979); *City of Mobile, Ala. v. Bolden* (466 U.S. 55 1980). In California, see *People v. White* (43 Cal. 3d 740 1954), *People v. Newton* (8 Cal. App. 3d 359, 87 Cal. Rptr. 294 1970); *People v. Breckenridge* (52 Cal. App. 3d. 913, 125 Cal. Rptr. 425 1975); *People v. Lewis* (74 Cal. App. 3d. 633, 141 Cal. Rptr. 614 1977); *People v. King* (49 Cal. Rptr. 562, 1966); *People v. Sirhan* (7 Cal. 3d 258 1978); *People v. Wheeler* (148 Cal. Rptr. 890 1978); *People v. Estrada* (155 Cal. Rptr. 731 1979); *People v. Grahm* (160 Cal. Rptr. 10 1979); and *People v. Harris* (36 Cal. 3d 36, 201, Cal. Rptr. 782 679 P. 2d 433 1984).

2

The Structural Approach to Racial Inequality in the Jury System and Jury Selection

Introduction

The primary influence on the contemporary jury system in the United States is derived from early English colonists who brought their legal institutions to North America. Subsequently, the jury system evolved as an essential ingredient of America's judicial framework.

The law is clear; every citizen has the right to participate in court as a juror. Indeed, federal law currently specifies panel selection procedures for a jury *venire,* according to two key concepts: There must be (1) *random selection* of jurors and (2) inclusion of the special geographic district in which a particular court convenes (U.S. 1968, Section 1961). The logic is that all qualified residents of a given geographic area should be part of the pool from which a jury is selected, and the opportunity to serve should be on an *equal-chance-opportunity* basis.[1]

In recent years, however, the traditional reverence accorded to the American jury has been brought into question. Since the early 1980s particularly, inequities in the jury selection process have become important issues in the minds of those questioning the impartiality of the U.S. justice system. The center of the controversy over the justice system's lack of fairness has focused on blacks, Hispanics, women, and the poor.[2]

Racial minorities have gained their rights in the courtroom only through a long and tortuous process. Until recently, racial minorities seldom appeared as judges. They were usually the accused and had limited rights as witnesses and jurors. Although there were no general disqualifications regarding witnesses before the Civil War, blacks were allowed to testify only against other blacks, not whites, and in the South, this system continued with the demise of Reconstruction (Avins, 1967, p. 256). It still persists in many places in our time (Benokraitis, 1975).

There were some high points in the steps taken to legally recognize rights for blacks. Through recognition of the rights to freedom and citizenship by the 13th, 14th, and 15th Amendments to the Constitution, slavery was formally ended, and black males finally acquired the right to participate in jury service. By passage of the Civil Rights Act of March 1, 1875, Congress made it a crime to exclude or to fail to summon a qualified citizen for jury service for reasons of race. The 14th Amendment to the Constitution further guaranteed such equality in state courts and extended equal protection to all citizens in the selection of grand and petit juries, without distinctions of race, color, or previous condition of servitude. However, the first case involving the underrepresentation of black jurors was not brought to the attention of the Supreme Court until 1880 (*Strauder v. West Virginia*, 100 U.S. 303).

Over the next 100 years, litigated cases overwhelmingly viewed blacks as inferior, and this inferiority was ensured by structural conditions imposed in the jury selection process to limit the number of black jurors. Both implicit and explicit discriminatory mechanisms were used to set limits on jury participation by racial minorities.

A number of factors played an important part in setting the limit on judicial participation by black jurors. Personnel functionaries involved in the jury selection process, for example, played an important role in fostering black underrepresentation on juries. Systematic underselection of blacks by jury clerks proved to be a significant factor in maintaining disproportionate jury representation. In *Avery v. Georgia* (345 U.S. 559 1953), the federal Supreme Court found that jury panels in Georgia were drawn from a *jury box* that contained the county tax returns, with names of prospective white jurors printed on white tickets and names of potential black jurors printed on yellow tickets. Using this system of racial identification, jury clerks consciously sought white jurors for trials, excluding potential black jurors from serving on juries.

Jury commissioners have also played a crucial role in limiting full-community participation by black jurors. A review of litigated cases by the U.S. Supreme Court revealed an implicit view of blacks as inferior. This view is demonstrated by limitations imposed to manipulate the jury selection process. In *Akins v. Texas* (325 U.S. 398 1954), for example, testimony demonstrated that all three jury commissioners in Dallas County *consciously* sought only one black grand juror, severely limiting black participation on grand juries. In *Cassell v. Texas* (339 U.S. 282 1950), the U.S. Supreme Court further discovered evidence of systematic selection in that jury commissioners chose only those whom they knew for grand jury service, and in that they knew no eligible blacks in a county where blacks made up approximately one seventh of the eligible jury population.

Systematic selection by jury commissioners was further compounded by the setting of a proportional limit on black jury participation. In *Smith v. Texas* (311 U.S. 128 1940), the U.S. Supreme Court found that, between 1931 and 1938, grand jurors' lists had 512 white and only 18 black names. Of them, 13 black jurors were placed at the bottom of the list; 4 were numbers 13, 14, and 15; and only 1 was put among the first 12. Further, only 5 blacks had ever participated on a grand jury during this period, and the same individual had served in three separate instances. In the same period, 379 whites had served as grand jurors. In *Patton v. Missouri* (332 U.S. 463 1947), the Court found that no blacks "had served on a criminal court grand or petit jury for a period of thirty years." Out of a total adult population of 34,821 in the county and an adult black population of 12,511, only about 25 blacks met the basic jury requirement of being a qualified elector (332 U.S. 465 467, 1947). Other U.S. Supreme Court decisions have also focused on jury commissioners' systematic exclusion of potential black jurors (see, for example, *Hill v. Texas*, 316 U.S. 400, 1942; *Patton v. Mississippi*, 332 U.S. 463 1947).

The racial composition of juries has also been affected by lawyers using peremptory challenges in *voir dire* (Blauner, 1972; Saltzburg & Powers, 1982; Silas, 1983). Because so many different persons are allowed to use their own individual discretion in deciding who should be excused and who should serve, the possibility that individual prejudice will influence excuses and exemptions is great (Van Dyke, 1977, p. 391). Some of the uncharted consequences may be corrected by recent U.S. Supreme Court rulings (see *Baston v. Kentucky*, 1986), but the replacement of peremptory challenges with required reasons for all challenges will still not guarantee that the parties challenged will give the real reasons of racism, as well as sexism, xenophobia, and ageism.

Underrepresentation of black jurors has also been accentuated by discrimination against black jury forepersons. *Rose v. Mitchell* (433 U.S. 574 1979) revealed racial discrimination against black jury forepersons in a case demonstrating that no black had ever served as a grand jury foreperson in at least 50–76 years in Tipton County, Tennessee.[3]

Two 1970 U.S. Supreme Court decisions examined the judicial domination and racial supremacy of the majority in both judicial and political spheres. The Supreme Court, for the first time, permitted a group of citizens to bring suit, charging that they had been denied the right to serve on juries. In *Carter v. Jury Commission of Greene County* (396 U.S. 332 1970), the petitioner claimed that the entire state apparatus—which included the county jury commissioners, their clerks, the local circuit judge, and even the governor of Alabama—was in conspiracy in perpetuating racial inequality in jury selection. The appellants sought three goals in the case: (1) a declaration that qualified blacks had been systematically excluded from grand and petit juries in Greene County and thus that the Alabama statutes were unconstitutional, and that the jury commissioner had operated illegally through his deliberate segregation of a governmental agency; (2) a permanent injunction forbidding the systematic exclusion of blacks from juries, thereby requiring all eligible blacks to be placed on the jury roll; and (3) an order to vacate the appointment of the current jury commissioners and to compel the Alabama governor to select new members without racial discrimination (*Carter v. Jury Commission of Greene County*, 396 U.S. 322 1970).[4]

Further, *Turner v. Fouche* (396 U.S. 346, 1970) also argued the notion of institutional discrimination against potential black jurors. The appellants, a black schoolchild and the father, lived in Taliaferro County, Georgia, where approximately 60% of residents were black.

The county school system consisted of a grammar school and a high school. Before the fall of 1965, Taliaferro County used one school building for black students and the other for whites. In that year, after 87 black students sought transfers to a desegregated school, the superintendent arranged for the transfer of white students, at the public expense, to public schools in adjoining counties. Consequently, the populations of these schools became entirely black. Efforts to combine Taliaferro with other adjacent counties to prevent an all-black school system, however, were unsuccessful. The petitioners alleged that the county board of education, which consisted of five freeholders, had been selected by the grand jury, which in turn had been drawn from a jury list selected by the six-member county jury commission. The commissioners had been appointed by the judge of the state superior court for the circuit in the county. The petitioners, however, pointed out that all board-of-education members were white, having been selected by all-white grand juries, which in turn had been selected by all-white jury commissioners. Because of racial oppression against blacks, the petitioners alleged that "the board of education had deprived the Negro schoolchildren of textbooks, facilities, and other advantages" (*Turner v. Fouche*, 396 U.S. 349 350 1970).

Although the first case of systematic underrepresentation of black jurors was brought to the U.S. Supreme Court in 1880 (*Strauder v. West Virginia*, 100 U.S. 303), it has proved to be more difficult for other minority groups to gain the status of legally defined "cognizable groups" and to be protected against discrimination by the court. After *Strauder v. West Virginia*, it took an additional 74 years for Hispanics to raise the question of discrimination against them in jury representation. Until 1954, the U.S. Supreme Court did not recognize Hispanics as a group that required protection against discrimination. *Hernandez v. Texas* (347 U.S. 475 1954) changed this by reversing the conviction of a Hispanic who had been tried before a jury from which Hispanic persons had been systematically excluded.

A Structural Theory of Racial Disenfranchisement

U.S. Supreme Court decisions that have reviewed racial discrimination in jury selection reveal that, in addition to historical discrimination, various structural and individual factors account for the underrepresentation of racial minorities on juries.

Many studies by criminologists, psychologists, and sociologists have focused on "supply-side" determinants of racially and ethnically imbalanced juries (Alker & Barnard, 1978; Erlanger, 1970, pp. 345–370; Fukurai & Butler, 1991; Fukurai *et al.*, 1991b; Horowitz, 1980). In the late 1970s and early 1980s, sociologists and criminologists argued that "human-capital" factors, such as race, socioeconomic origins, educational investments, and occupational standings of jurors, generated differences in jury representation (Alker *et al.*, 1976; Brady, 1983; Carp, 1982; Chevigny, 1975; De Cani, 1974; Diamond, 1980, Heyns, 1979; Kairys, 1972; Kairys *et al.*, 1977; Staples, 1975). For instance, potential jurors with specific human-capital factors, such as higher income, higher education, and white background, were more likely to be represented on juries than others because they were more inclined to register to vote and could afford to take time off from work to serve on juries (Hastie *et al.*, 1983; Starr & McCormick, 1985).

Psychologists have further argued that microdimensions of individuals influence jury composition. For example, the "inherent criminality" of some racial groups and the "impaired intelligence" of some potential jurors have meant voluntary self-exclusion or being screened out by the selection process ("The case for black juries," 1970). Authoritarian personalities among those responsible for jury composition and decisions also contribute to selectivity in jury composition (Benokraitis & Griffin-Keene, 1982; Hans & Vidmar, 1986; Hastie *et al.*, 1983; Kassin & Wrightsman, 1988; Kerr & Bray, 1982; Nietzel & Dillehay, 1986; Wishman, 1986; Wrightsman, 1987).

In an attempt to balance the "supply-side" explanation of the human-capital thesis, we concentrate on a structural explanation of judicial inequality that focuses on the factors that determine the position of potential jurors in society and that consequently affect their chances of serving on juries. These structural factors include the following four dimensions: (1) specific procedural anomalies in jury selection; (2) socioeconomic structural barriers, such as residential mobility and its impact on the delivery of summons and jury qualification questionnaires; (3) discrimination against racial and ethnic minorities by the court and judicial system; and (4) gerrymandered judicial districts. Thus, this chapter examines an array of institutional and structural factors that systematically discriminate against racial minorities and prevent their full jury participation.

Procedural Anomalies and Racial Inequities in Jury Selection

There is a long-established mechanism for maintaining majority domination in jury participation. Those mechanisms especially discriminate against blacks, Hispanics, and other racial minorities. One of the specific discriminatory mechanisms includes the use of registered-voters' rolls (ROV) as source lists. Because minorities are less likely to register to vote, jury pools consist primarily of whites, and thus, underrepresentation of racial minorities on juries is ensured. The exclusive use of voter registration lists thus provides a legal mechanism effectively enforcing the "rule of exclusion" (Fukurai, 1985; Fukurai *et al.*, 1991b).

A lower voter-registration rate among minority groups is found in both past and recent congressional and presidential elections. Research shows that Hispanic populations are most likely to be underrepresented in jury pools because of their lower registration rates. Hispanic political participation is even lower than that of black populations. For instance, whereas 67.9% of whites registered for the 1988 presidential election, only 35.5% of the Hispanic-origin population registered (see Table 2–1). In the

TABLE 2-1

Reported Registration by Race and Hispanic Origin (Percentages)[a]

	Presidential Election						*Congressional Election*				
Race	*1988*	*1984*	*1980*	*1976*	*1972*	*1968*	*1986*	*1982*	*1978*	*1974*	*1970*
Total voting registration	66.6	68.3	66.9	66.7	72.3	74.3	64.3	64.1	62.6	62.2	68.1
White	67.9	69.6	68.4	68.3	73.4	75.4	65.3	65.6	63.8	63.5	69.1
Black	64.5	66.3	60.0	58.5	65.5	66.2	64.0	59.1	57.1	54.9	60.8
Hispanic origin[b]	35.5	40.1	36.3	37.8	44.4	NA[c]	35.9	35.3	32.9	34.9	NA[c]

[a]From U.S. Bureau of the Census, Current Population Reports, Series P-20, No. 359, 440, "Voting and Registration in the Election of November, 1980," "Voting and Registration in the Election of 1988," U.S. Government Printing Office, Washington, D.C., 1981, 1989.
[b]Persons of Hispanic origin may be of any race.
[c]Not Available.

1986 congressional election, 65.3% of whites registered, but only 35.9% of Hispanic-origin adults registered. Although the registration rate of black voters was higher than that of Hispanics, it was consistently lower than the overall registration of white populations in both presidential and congressional elections between 1968 and 1988.[5]

Similar trends exist among different jurisdictions. For example, voting patterns for selected minority groups are shown for both California and Los Angeles County (see Table 2–2). In California, less than one fourth of the Hispanic-origin population registered (24.4%), whereas 60.7% of whites registered for the November 1988 presidential election. In Los Angeles County, moreover, less than 19% of the Hispanic-origin population registered, whereas 54% of whites registered in 1980. This finding suggests that, if voter registration lists are used as the sole jury source list, 81% of all the potential Spanish-origin population are systematically and legally excluded from jury service.[6] Thus, the use of voter rolls does not lead to a jury drawn from a representative cross section of the community.

In some states, multiple source lists have been used to rectify the shortcomings of using voter registration lists. In California, for example, a 1981 law mandates the use of lists for both voter registration (ROV) and driver registration (Department of Motor Vehicles, DMV) lists in an attempt to rectify voter registration bias (CA. 1981, section 16.204.7). In California, the use of both ROV and DMV lists yielded an approximate 71% increase of potential jurors over using ROV lists alone (see Fukurai, 1985). In a number of states, however, drivers' lists are used instead of voter rolls. For example, in the Eighth Judicial District of Nevada (serving Las Vegas and surrounding Clark County), county drivers' lists have been the sole source for selecting potential jurors since 1980 (Lowman, 1981).

TABLE 2-2

Reported Registration in California and Los Angeles County by Race and Hispanic Origin in November 1980 and 1988 Elections[a]

	1988 California		*1980 California*		*1980 Los Angeles*	
Race	*Percentage*	*Standard error*	*Percentage*	*Standard error*	*Percentage*	*Standard error*
Total voting age	59.1	0.9	60.0	0.6	53.7	1.2
White	60.7	1.0	62.1	0.7	54.7	1.3
Black	69.5	4.2	61.5	2.7	65.1	4.0
Hispanic origin[b]	24.4	2.1	27.0	2.4	18.8	3.4

[a]U.S. Bureau of the Census, Current Population Reports, Series P-20, No. 370, 440, "Voting and Registration in the Election of November, 1980," "Voting and Registration in the Election of November, 1988," U.S. Government Printing Office, Washington, D.C., 1981, 1989.
[b]Persons of Hispanic origin may be of any race.

Despite the obvious advantages of using multiple source lists, the majority of states as well as all federal courts still exclusively rely on the voter registration list to identify eligible jurors. Because the source list constitutes the beginning of jury selection procedures, the impact of the exclusive use of ROV lists on racial representativeness becomes cumulative and even more severe in the subsequent stages of jury selection.

Persistent procedural anomalies of jury selection procedures suggest that minorities have to operate within the framework of a racially biased institutional system. As a result, blacks and other racial minorities have learned to mistrust the fairness of most racially dominated institutions of power, such as law enforcement agencies and courts making decisions via racially disproportionate juries (see *Baston v. Kentucky*, 1986; Van Dyke, 1977, p. 32). One dominant ideological underpinning is the suggestion that criminality is inherent in minority groups, and that they need to be controlled by the legal system (Cullen & Link, 1980; Hepburn, 1978; Kramer, 1982). In modern phraseology, the "black community takes a permissive view of crime within its borders. As a result, the black community is vulnerable to its own criminal element as well as to the criminal element of the white community ("The case for black juries," 1970, p. 534). Given such permissiveness, blacks' jury participation needs to be both supervised and minimized.

Those accused of crimes are allowed to defend themselves, but courts, judges, and juries may still be locked into legal structures handed down from a history of discrimination. This past has in fact contoured the underrepresentation of minorities on jury panels in our time, and such racial prejudgment generates different outcomes in various trials. In one Black Panther murder trial, there was a contention that the race of the defendant predisposed certain jurors to a negative verdict (Rokeach & McLellan, 1970). Studies covering the "psychology of juries" provide numerous examples of the influence of race on verdicts ("Grigsby vs. Mabry" a new look at death-qualified juries, 1980; Hans & Vidmar, 1986; Kassin & Wrightsman, 1988; Lipton, 1979; Starr & McCormick, 1985; Wishman, 1986).

A 1986 California survey also revealed that a large proportion of minority members believe that, under the current jury selection procedure, blacks and Hispanics are more likely to receive the death penalty than white defendants (see Table 2–3).[7] Whereas 34% of whites agreed that the death penalty is affected by defendants' racial identification, a larger proportion of minority groups believed that racial identity is one of the most important dimensions in influencing the likelihood of receiving the death penalty (40.0%, 40.8% and 42.1% of blacks, Asians, and Hispanics, respectively). Mock studies that examined jurors' psychologi-

TABLE 2-3
Likelihood of Blacks/Hispanics' Receiving the Death Penalty

Response[a]	*White*	*Black*	*Asian*	*Hispanic*	*Total*
Strongly agree	7.1%	0.0%	18.1%	10.5%	32 (5.3%)
Agree	26.9	40.0	22.7	31.6	159 (26.4)
Disagree	54.0	40.0	54.6	42.1	286 (47.5)
Strongly disagree	11.9	20.0	4.6	15.8	124 (20.6)
Total	99.9[b]	100.0	100.0	100.0	99.8[b]

[a]Subjects responded to the question, "A minority person (Black, Hispanic) is more likely to receive the death penalty than an Anglo (White)."
[b]Due to rounding errors.

cal characteristics and related behavioral patterns provide numerous examples of the impact of racial prejudice on different verdicts in criminal trials (Hastie *et al.*, 1983; Lipton, 1979). The racial composition of juries and the resulting verdicts become a larger problem in many states where the defendants are routinely sentenced by a jury. In Texas, the jury carries decision-making power in both the conviction and the sentencing phases. Once the jury convicts the defendants, the jury can also decide the severity of the penalties. Because the racial identification of the defendants is likely to predispose some jurors to particular verdicts, the perception of racially demarcated juries may have negative effects on the legitimacy of the jury trial itself.

A wall of racial tensions may have been built between black and white populations, despite—and because of—structured practices like the underrepresentation of minority jurors and their ideological justification (Kairys, 1974). Without jury participation by racial and ethnic minorities, racial dominance is structurally reinforced and perpetuated by individual racism and the withdrawal of support by minorities. In fact, the large proportion of blacks who do not respond to jury qualification questionnaires or summonses have been classified as "recalcitrants" and eliminated from subsequent jury selection procedures (Fukurai *et al.*, 1991b; Van Dyke, 1977).

Residential Mobility and Undeliverables

The exclusive use of ROV lists and the prejudicial actions of personnel involved in jury selection are not the only determinants of racially imbalanced participation in jury service. Occupations and positions in the labor market affect residential mobility, and those factors in turn influence the degree of jury representation. Because jury summonses and qualification questionnaires are generally sent by mail, a permanent residence is essential if one is to participate in the process. One's labor-market position as a migrant enhances the probability of being excluded from a jury pool, as those who move and fail to receive jury summonses ("undeliverables") or to return jury qualification questionnaires ("recalcitrants") cannot qualify for selection. In fact, such persons are systematically eliminated. Thus, a potential juror who has just entered the job market, and/or who is placed in a less stable, secondary labor market, is likely to be eliminated long before being called into the courthouse. Even if he or she makes it into the courthouse, he or she is likely to be excused for reasons of economic hardship (Fukurai & Butler, 1991a).[8]

Three principal factors explain high residential mobility and a high incidence of economic hardship among unskilled laborers. First, home ownership influences residential mobility and consequently influences jury participation. Because nonwhite minorities are more likely to be renters and to move frequently, they are more likely to be classified as undeliverables and thus to be eliminated from jury selection procedures. Second, minorities' positions in the labor market often involve low wages, seasonal work, and thus a high degree of occupational instability (Butler & Kaiser, 1971; Butler, Chapin, Hemmens, Kaiser, Stegman, & Weiss, 1969; Newman, 1985; Sabagh, Van Arsdol, & Butler, 1969). Third, an unstable job market and economic shifts in production locations and volumes are conducive to a high level of geographic mobility in search of steady employment. As a result, residential and short-distance geographical mobility is generally higher in minority groups than in their white counterparts (Clark, 1986; Featherman & Hauser, 1978; Lipset & Bendix, 1959).

Residential mobility obviously affects the size of the population of undeliverables and is also closely tied to home-ownership status (Johnson, 1981; Newman, 1985; Pollakowski, 1982). For example, a 1986 community survey in California indicated that only 22.4% of whites lived in an apartment or residence that they rented, whereas 55.6 and 38.5% of blacks and Hispanics, respectively, lived in a transient residence (see Table 2–4). Whites showed the highest home ownership (68%), compared with minority groups (44.4%, 60.7%, and 49.9% for black, Asian, and Hispanic eligible jurors, respectively).

This difference in ownership status is also associated with the residential mobility of minorities and is closely tied to their jury participation. For example, for whites, the average length of stay at the current address was 118.9 months (approximately 10 years), compared with 30.8 months for blacks and 85.9 months for Asian jurors. Although Hispanics showed the lowest incidence of residential mobility (126.9 months), their mobility pattern was highly influenced by a few outliers (i.e., a skewed-

TABLE 2-4
Home Ownership

Housing status	*White (%)*	*Black (%)*	*Asian (%)*	*Hispanics (%)*	*Others (%)*
Rent	22.35	55.56	29.51	38.54	36.36
Own	67.98	44.44	60.66	49.88	45.45
Others	5.45	0.00	9.84	7.29	9.09
No answer	4.13	0.00	0.00	7.29	9.09
Total	100.01[a]	100.00	100.01	100.00	99.99[a]
N	1,065	9	61	98	11

[a]Due to rounding errors.

ness index of 1.7). When the top 6% of the Hispanic jurors who had lived in the same residence for more than 35 years was eliminated, the average shrank to 99.7 months. The greater skewedness and departure from a normal symmetrical distribution was also observed for black populations (a skewedness index of 2.5).

Such residential mobility is closely linked to the socioeconomic status of prospective jurors. Although the relationship is not a perfect one, there is a tendency for a shorter length of residence to be found in conjunction with lower income and lesser occupational prestige, particularly in minority groups. For example, both black and Hispanic residents showed the lowest income levels (5.4 and 5.2, indicating the range between $20,000 and $29,999) and occupational prestige (37.4 and 37.3) and were more likely to move and become undeliverables. On the other hand, white jurors were more likely to have a higher income (6.6, indicating the range between $25,000 and $39,999) and occupational prestige (51.7) and were less likely to move and become undeliverables (see Table 2–5).

Home ownership and its influence on mobility is also closely tied to the labor market position of racial minorities and has similar effects on jury representation. For example, temporary or seasonal work makes a sedentary life impossible for minority labor. The migratory search for jobs is the lifebread of the nation's poorest groups, with their large proportions of blacks, Hispanics, and females (McAllister, Kaiser, & Butler, 1971; Palen & London, 1984). These highly mobile minorities constitute the largest segment of those designated as undeliverables (Fukurai *et al.*, 1991b). Jury commissioners typically do not track down the undeliverables, though such follow-up is required by law.[9]

Home ownership also increases feelings of community identification and a greater willingness to participate in social activities (Fukurai & Butler, 1987). For example, a lower level of residential mobility leads to higher levels of social integration and hence higher rates of community participation and greater feelings of belonging to the community

TABLE 2-5
Residential Mobility, Income, and Occupation

Variables	*White*	*Black*	*Asian*	*Hispanics*	*Others*
Length at current address[a]					
Mean	118.65	30.75	85.87	126.89	90.72
SD	101.27	42.02	73.95	136.10	99.52
Skewness[b]	0.99	2.54	1.06	1.73	1.56
Income[c]					
Mean	6.58	5.44	5.86	5.24	6.30
SD	2.55	3.16	2.71	2.65	2.83
Skewness	–0.46	–0.40	–0.16	0.21	–1.00
Occupational prestige					
Mean	51.66	37.37	48.86	37.34	46.80
SD	20.89	29.29	22.41	22.47	25.19
Skewness	–0.26	0.67	0.02	0.60	–0.04
N	1,065	9	61	98	11

[a]A number of months.
[b]Skewness index is calculated in the following equation: $n/(n-1)(n-2)\Sigma(Xi-X)^3/S^3$
[c]Income breakdowns: (1) < $5,000; (2) $5,000–9,999; (3) $10,000–14,999; (4) $15,000–19,999; (5) $20,000–24,999; (6) $25,000–29,999; (7) $30,000–39,999; (8) $40,000–49,999; (9) $50,000–74,999; and (10) > $75,000.

(Fukurai & Alston, 1990; Shelton, 1987). The greater sense of social integration thus leads to higher incidence of jury participation.

The relationship between the pattern of residential mobility and the determinants of jury representation are examined in Table 2–6. Age is the single most important indicator of residential mobility for all groups examined: the older the resident, the longer the residence at the current address, a finding suggesting that the undeliverables are not only more likely to be poor but also more likely to be younger.[10] The findings also indicate other significant exceptions to this finding when ethnicity is introduced into the model. For whites, greater seniority, as measured by length of employment in companies, also leads to lower residential mobility ($p < .01$). Because occupational prestige is associated with home ownership, we would expect that white potential jurors with higher job status are more easily contacted for jury summonses than whites with lower-status jobs.

Although the relationship is not statistically significant, this causal direction is reversed for blacks and Hispanics. The finding suggests that the greater job prestige, the more likely they are to move (–.001 and .009 for whites and blacks/Hispanics, respectively). Thus, minority groups with high-status jobs are less likely to receive jury qualification questionnaires and/or jury summonses.

The same inverse relationship is found in the effect of employment status. Full-time minority workers are more likely to move, and full-time

TABLE 2-6
Unstandardized (Standardized) Coefficients Obtained from Regression of (Log) Length of Residency on Determinants

	Race/Ethnic Groups		
Variables	*White*	*Black/Hispanics*	*Others*
Age	.030 (.368)****	.031 (.355)***	.048 (.488)***
Education	−.029 (−.061)*	−.048 (−.135)	.015 (.042)
Marital status[a]	−.059 (−.021)	.109 (.038)	−.122 (−.044)
Income[b]	.015 (.029)	−.141 (−.278)**	.061 (.122)
Ownership[c]	−.199 (−.046)	−.510 (−.102)	−.261 (−.087)
Occupation[d]	−.001 (−.010)	.009 (.159)	.004 (.076)
Length of employment[e]	.001 (.120)***	.001 (.111)	.001 (.126)
Employment status[f]	−.029 (−.011)	.032 (.011)	.262 (.080)
Ownership[g]	.707 (.245)****	.926 (.343)***	.491 (.197)
Constant	2.196	3.075	.450
R^2 (adj)[h]	.351	.490	.395
R^2 (adj)[i]	.289	.409	.309
N	700	63	44

[a](1) Unmarried; (2) married.
[b]Income breakdowns: (1) < $5,000; (2) $5,000–9,999; (3) $10,000–14,999; (4) $15,000–19,999; (5) $20,000–24,999; (6) $25,000–29,999; (7) $30,000–39,999; (8) $40,000–49,999; (9) $50,000–74,999; and (10) > $75,000.
[c]Ownership of their own business: (1) yes (2) no.
[d]Measured in Duncan SEI (Socio-Economic Index).
[e]Measured in months.
[f]Employment status: (1) full-time; (2) not full-time.
[g]Ownership of the residence: (1) yes; (2) no.
[h]Length of current residency with natural log-transformation.
[i]Length of current residency without natural log-transformation.
*$p < .10$
**$p < .05$
***$p < .01$
****$p < .001$

white workers are more likely to stay at their current residence (−.029 and .032 for whites and blacks/Hispanics). Occupational security for racial minorities often requires a change in residence (Fukurai *et al.*, 1987, 1991b). In fact, higher income is associated with a higher degree of residential mobility for blacks and Hispanics (−.141). These socioeconomic factors, then, affect racial groups in the labor market and in residential mobility. Thus, racial minorities become a larger proportion of those who fail to receive jury qualification questionnaires and/or jury summonses, even among those steadily employed. The problem of "undeliverables" among racial and ethnic minorities is further compounded because there are no follow-ups.

Prospective jurors who work in large companies are likely to be reimbursed by their employers for jury service. Firm size, employment duration, and the employment status of potential jurors are all related to company reimbursement (see Table 2–7). Large firms are almost uniformly able to support their workers while they are on jury duty. Whereas only 28% of the self-employed are able to absorb the cost of jury service, 52.9% of those working for firms are paid for jury service.

With respect to the effect of organizational resources on jury representation, senior workers (i.e., employees with longer length of employment) are more likely to be employed in a firm that pays for jury duty (Table 2–8). Further, 57.3% of full-time workers are employed in firms that pay for jury service. The majority of jurors supported by their employers work for large firms, whereas workers in smaller firms are not supported for jury service. Consequently, potential jurors from small firms have fewer chances of surviving the jury selection process, and in the world of job-structured benefits, those who ask to be excused from jury duty are predominantly members of racial minorities (Fukurai & Butler, 1991a; Van Dyke, 1977).

Judicial Discrimination against Racial and Ethnic Minorities as Jurors

In addition to socioeconomic barriers, various types of institutional mechanisms in the court and the judicial system set the limit on racial and ethnic participation on juries. Echoes of such institutionalized inequality appear as three judicial dimensions that influence the racial and ethnic composition of juries. First, there is the "blue-ribbon jury" which systematically and disproportionately excludes minorities. Second, juries of unusually small size undercut minority participation. Third, jurors may be empowered to enforce less-than-unanimous decisions, so that minority opinions may be disregarded.

Under the blue-ribbon system, based on perceived special qualifications, special jurors are selected from a general panel to hear important and intricate cases (Starr & McCormick, 1983, pp. 23–29). The blue-ribbon or "elite" jury has a long tradition. In the early days of the Republic, a

TABLE 2-7
Organizational Characteristics of Prospective Jurors (%)

	Company size[a]						*Self-ownership*[a]	
Company reimbursement	*10 >*	*11–50*	*51–100*	*101–1000*	*1001–10,000*	*> 10,000*	*Yes*	*No*
Yes	19.1	43.2	63.6	73.6	82.2	98.3	28.0	52.9
No	80.9	56.8	36.4	26.4	17.8	1.7	72.0	47.1
Total	100.0	100.0	100.0	100.0	100.0	100.0	100.0	100.0

[a]The number of employees in the firm.

TABLE 2-8
Labor Market Characteristics of Prospective Jurors (%)

Company reimbursement	Length of employment[a,b]					Employment status[b]				Supervisory responsibility	
	1 yr >	1–5	5–10	10–20	> 20	Full time	Part time	Retired	Student	Yes	No
Yes	33.1	43.9	54.9	62.9	75.3	57.3	25.0	26.3	21.6	53.5	48.5
No	66.9	56.1	45.1	37.1	24.7	42.7	75.0	73.7	78.4	46.5	51.3
Total	100.0	100.0	100.0	100.0	100.0	100.0	100.0	100.0	100.0	100.0	100.0

[a]Measured in years.
[b]Differences are statistically significant at .001 level.

property qualification existed for jury duty. The limitation of jury duty to males was consistent with the complete exclusion of women from the voter rolls. In many states, jurors were chosen by the sheriff, who tended to select large landowners. Blue-ribbon or elite panels have been and still are permitted in some state courts, although the U.S. Rules of Civil Procedures forbid them at present in the federal courts, where litigants are guaranteed a random selection of jurors.

Narrowly qualified blue-ribbon jurors present an insurmountable barrier to fairness. Jury studies indicate that such homogeneous panels, selected by certain criteria, may be less adept at reaching reasonable verdicts than are heterogeneous panels (Mills, 1969, pp. 338–339). The latter bring to the decision-making process a mix of various points of view and of life experiences and are more likely than homogeneous juries to recognize and offset individual biases (Van Dyke, 1977).

Although the blue-ribbon juries have not met the criterion of being a "fair cross section of community" demanded by the Sixth Amendment (*Fay v. New York*, 332 U.S. 261 1947), in the past the U.S. Supreme Court has nevertheless given constitutional sanction to them. Blue-ribbon juries are therefore still empowered to parade their constitutionality and to give judicial justification to the systematic exclusion of racial minorities from juries.

Nor does the U.S. Constitution require a jury of 12. The U.S. Supreme Court declared in *Williams v. Florida* (406 U.S. 356 1972) that a state may use a jury of 6 in criminal trials, even when the sentence is as severe as life imprisonment. Jury research shows that, without an adequate theory of group dynamics, the Supreme Court was in error in assuming that there are no differences in the behavior of 12- and 6-member juries (Cocke, 1979; Kaye, 1980; Roper, 1980).[11] The fact is that smaller juries have a great propensity to be controlled by a dominant group or person. A change of verdict may sometimes be attributed to an authoritarian personality, such a person can more easily control and influence small groups than large groups (Hastie *et al.*, 1983). Distinct or authoritarian personality traits are often characterized by the dominant ideology that shapes perceptions and affects everyday interactions (Goffman, 1959; Steiner, 1992). Because the prevailing ideology is likely to reflect the interests of the dominant group in society, the minority's alternate view—once formulated—may be sidestepped by the control of minority members' participation in judicial decision-making processes or by a disregard of their opinions.

A clear pattern of racial discrimination is found in death penalty cases. Blacks have been more likely to receive the death sentence than whites, particularly if the victim was white. Such perceptions are shared by both jurors and judges. In Florida, one study showed that if a black person killed a white person, the chances of receiving a death sentence were about 1 in 5; if a white killed a white, the chances were about 1 in 20; if a black killed a black, the chances were about 1 in 167; and if a white killed a black, the probability of a death sentence was zero (Bowers & Pierce, 1980). When a large number of compounding factors that may have explained the difference in sentencing (e.g., crime severity, past criminal record, and the number of charges) was controlled, the basic pattern of racial discrimination still remained (Baldus, Pulaske, & Woodsworth, 1983). One explanation is simple racism: a white life is more important than a black life. Another explanation is that whites are much more supportive of the death penalty than blacks, and that the white community thus may pressure the prosecutor to ask for the death penalty when a white victim is killed. Given the prevalence of white overrepresentation on juries and the impact on the jury decision-making process, a smaller jury exhibits a greater propensity to be controlled by society's dominant ideology, which is shared and reflected by the racial majority.

Less-than-unanimous decisions also pose problems for minorities. In 1972, in *Johnson v. Louisiana* (406 U.S. 356 1972), the U.S. Supreme Court voted by a narrow margin not to apply the unanimity rule to state jury cases, concluding that the rule lacked constitutional authority.[12] Rejecting previous pronouncements on unanimity requirements as inconclusive, the Court majority upheld verdicts in which the juries had voted 11 to 1, 10 to 2, 9 to 3 for conviction. One study shows that the elimination of the unanimity rule favors the prosecution in the bulk of the cases, as it increases the conviction rate (Kalven & Zeisel, 1966, p. 466; Nemeth, 1977). It is clear that relaxing the unanimity rule deemphasizes any opposing opinion expressed by a minority of jurors. There is some evidence that racial and ethnic minorities have a high probability of expressing dissenting opinions (*Harris v. People of California*, 36 Cal. 3d. 36 1984) and that members of small factions express themselves less fully under majority decision rules than under unanimity rules (Hastie *et al.*, 1983, p. 230).

Relaxing the unanimity rule thus has a greater propensity to disregard the opinions of racial and ethnic minorities and undermines the nature of justice and fairness in the judicial system. Because such a rule disregards disproportionate deliberation votes by jury members, it becomes a special problem in cases of possible hung juries. In some capital punishment cases, for instance, the discrepant initial vote on the verdict, which eventually led to a final unanimous decision, was racially demarcated (e.g., *Harris v. People of California*, 36 Cal. 3d. 36 1984).[13] Thus, frequent incidents of racially disproportionate voters in deliberation can ultimately be used ideologically to empower the racial majority.

Racially demarcated points of view are also found in cases involving interracial sexual encounters. One study found that white jurors were more likely to find a defendant culpable of rape when he was black and the victim was white than in other racial combinations. Blacks, on the other hand, were more likely to judge that a white defendant was guilty when the victim was black (Ugwuegbu, 1979). In a rape simulation study, black defendants were treated more harshly than white defendants (Feild, 1979). Further, race remains a significant factor even when evidence has been clear-cut in favor of guilt or innocence. Less-than-unanimous votes thus become a particular problem because relaxing the unanimity rule is likely to disregard the opinion of racial minorities, and racially demarcated votes in deliberation can be used to negate the expressive power of racial and ethnic minorities in the judicial decision-making process.

Gerrymandered Judicial Districts

Residential mobility, socioeconomic barriers, and judicial discrimination by the court are not the only determinants of racial participation in jury service. Another important mechanism that limits the participation of racial and ethnic minorities is the systematic representation of geographic units in defining judicial districts. Such a racially discriminatory district is called a *gerrymandered judicial district.*

Examples of the gerrymandered judicial district are found in several judicial districts, including Los Angeles County in California (Fukurai *et al.*, 1991a; Kairys, 1972). The Sixth Amendment to the Constitution has vicinity requirements, and following these, the legislature in California long ago defined the judicial districts in Los Angeles County as being within a 20-mile radius of each courthouse. The Los Angeles County Board of Supervisors adopted this rule in the early 1970s because Los

Angeles County is so large that its geographic boundaries placed prospective jurors beyond reasonable reach of getting to court. The State Senate approved the bill, A.B. 1454, which added the 20-mile rule to the *California Code of Civil Procedure*. But, in fact, the 20-mile rule for judicial districts has not been followed. Rather, a systematic inclusion and exclusion of certain neighborhoods has led to a significant underrepresentation of racial minorities on jury panels. Particular neighborhoods with high concentrations of blacks and other minorities have been systematically excluded from the defined boundaries of the judicial districts. By regulating the degree of minority participation on jury panels, an effective mechanism for gerrymandering judicial districts was created and enforced. For example, a three-month study of jury representation in Los Angeles in 1985 revealed that, although there was a defined judicial district within which jurors were supposed to be selected and called to serve on juries, areas with high concentrations of racial and ethnic minority residents were systematically excluded from jury service.

Figure 2–1 shows spatial representations of jurors in the Long Beach Superior Court district in 1985 and indicates the specific neighborhoods from which jurors were selected. The Pacific Ocean lies on both the west and the south sides of the map. Orange County is located on the southeast side of Los Angeles County.

According to the 1980 U.S. Census, Orange County had 1.14% black and 12.50% Hispanic populations. The residents were predominantly white and of at least middle-class status. The Long Beach judicial district in Los Angeles County, on the other hand, had 16.4% black and 20.8% Hispanic populations.

The map indicates that the racial and residential characteristics of neighborhoods were closely associated with the opportunity to serve on juries. Note that the neighborhoods adjacent to economically prosperous Orange County had far greater chances of placing jurors on panels. Some areas in the judicial district had no jurors on panels. Nonrepresented areas primarily included the areas of downtown Los Angeles and Long Beach with high concentrations of racial minorities. The analysis further suggests racially disproportionate representations among impaneled jurors within the neighborhoods (see Table 2–9). Potential jurors from one census tract were represented 22 times, whereas 117 census tracts (21.7% of the district) were represented fewer than 4 times, and 326 tracts (60.6%) had not a single juror on the panels. Half the potential jurors came from 35 census tracts of the 538 census tracts that made up the Long Beach judicial district. That is, 6.5% of the entire judicial district constituted the majority of the jury pool for the Long Beach Superior Court.

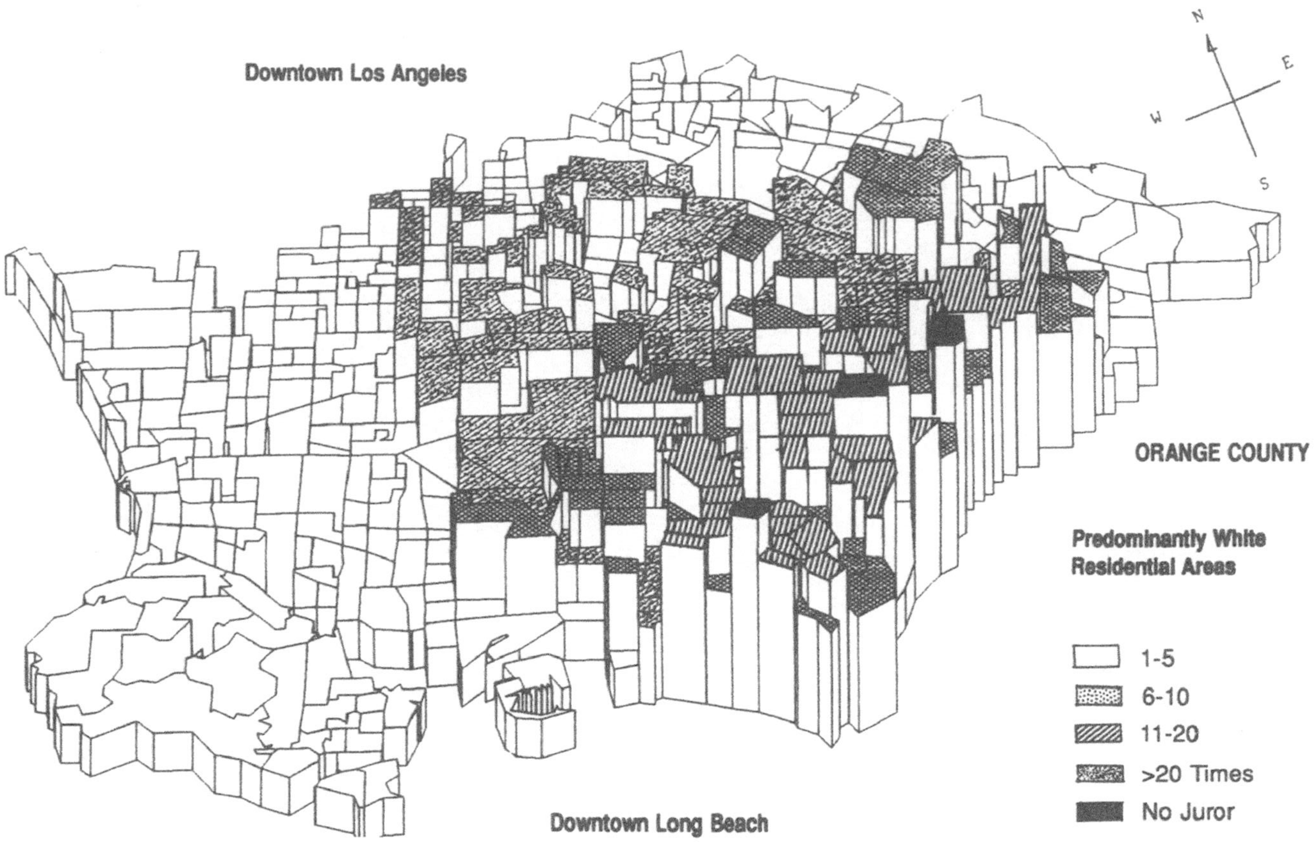

FIGURE 2-1. Long Beach Superior Court Judicial District, 1985.

TABLE 2-9
Census Tracts Represented on 10 Panels: The Long Beach Judicial District

				Minority composition	
Number of times census tracts represented	*Frequency*	*Percentage*[a]	*Cumulative percentage*	*Black percentage*	*Hispanic percentage*
				16.4	20.9
0	326	—	—	16.6	35.0
1	53	24.2	24.2	31.7	35.7
2	25	11.4	35.6	34.8	21.1
3	21	9.6	45.2	19.5	29.0
4	18	8.2	53.4	7.7	20.8
5	14	6.4	59.8	5.1	28.5
6	17	7.8	67.6	10.6	28.8
7	14	6.4	74.0	5.6	23.1
8	9	4.1	78.1	5.0	11.1
9	9	4.1	82.2	11.8	17.1
10	1	0.5	82.6	0.6	8.1
11	3	1.4	84.0	3.6	9.6
12	6	2.7	86.8	5.6	10.8
13	3	1.4	88.1	0.9	3.9
14	4	1.8	90.0	4.2	9.0
15	5	2.3	92.2	0.9	12.7
16	5	2.3	94.5	2.2	6.9
17	6	2.7	97.3	4.8	10.2
19	2	0.9	98.2	6.8	9.2
20	1	0.5	98.6	0.3	3.6
21	2	0.9	99.5	4.5	13.5
22	1	0.5	100.0	0.2	5.9

Median = 4
Mean = 10.28

[a]Percentage is computed by the represented census tracts.

Racial participation is also influenced by the systematic representation of census tracts. The proportion of black and Hispanic jurors in nonrepresented areas (326 tracts) was higher than that of the Long Beach judicial district as a whole. Further, the census tract with the highest representation had only 0.2% black and 5.9% Hispanic residents, far below the average in the jurisdiction.

Neighborhoods with below-average jury-service representation also had far greater percentages of minority residents than the above-average neighborhoods with incidence of jury service (19.3% and 26.6%, respectively, for black and Hispanic residents). The neighborhood based on the median also substantiates disproportionality of jury representation. Since the distribution of racial compositions in census tracts is highly skewed, the median is a better statistical index than the average in showing the disproportionality of racial representation in the community. For instance, 26.1% of the residents in neighborhoods with below-median jury representation were black, in contrast to 6.0% of the residents in above-median neighborhoods (see Table 2–10). The same disproportionality was found for Hispanics as well (28.4% and 18.0% above and below the median, respectively). Similar observations have been made in other superior courts in Los Angeles County (Butler, 1981; Fukurai, 1985; Fukurai *et al.*, 1991a; Heyns, 1979).

It is possible, of course, that nondiscriminatory factors were at work; that is, did underrepresented census tracts have a significantly lower percentage of qualified jurors? Jury qualification criteria, such as U.S. citizenship, language proficiency, residency requirement, and no prior felony conviction, would have eliminated a large number of minority individuals and may have affected overall representation on jury impanelment lists. However, when qualification criteria were introduced into the analysis, disqualifying certain jurors did not explain the geographical biases found here. For instance, while 19.0% of the potential jurors in the Long Beach district were qualified, and similarly, 19.8% of the potential jurors who resided in the impaneled neighborhoods (212 tracts) were also qualified (see Table 2–11) the proportions of black and Hispanic jurors in the selected neighborhoods, however, diminished drastically from 16% and 20% to 9% and 6%. Juror qualification thus does not explain the true extent of racially demarcated representation.

Nevertheless, the jury selection process eliminated such areas as downtown Los Angeles and Long Beach from the defined boundary of the judicial district. Subsequently, a large number of racial and ethnic minorities were simply excluded, an exclusion that accounts for their significant underrepresentation on juries. The gerrymandered judicial district thus systematically represented geographic units in the jurisdiction

TABLE 2-10
Average Representation of Census Tracts on 10 Panels: Black and Hispanic Potential Jurors (%)[a]

			Mean		*Median*	
Race/ ethnicity	*Judicial district*	*Not represented*	*10 times or less*	*11 times or more*	*4 times or less*	*5 times or more*
Black	16.40	16.62	19.36	3.60	26.16	6.01
Hispanic	20.90	35.02	26.67	9.59	28.49	18.04

[a]96 out of 538 census tracts in the judicial district had at least one Hispanic juror in the impanelment lists; during the 10-week period, 136 out of 1,250 impaneled jurors had Hispanic surnames (11.0%).

TABLE 2-11
Potential and Qualified Jurors[a]

District	Potential jurors N	Potential jurors %	Qualified jurors N	Qualified jurors %	Race (%) Black	Race (%) Hispanic
Judicial district	243,274	100.00	46,436	19.08	16.4	20.9
Impaneled district	62,758	100.00	12,459	19.85	9.7	6.7

[a]96 out of 538 census tracts in the judicial district had at least one Hispanic juror in the impanelment lists; during the 10-week period, 136 out of 1,250 impaneled jurors had Hispanic surnames (11.0%).

with specific racial and ethnic characteristics. Gerrymandering is found in other judicial districts as well (Fukurai *et al.*, 1991a; Kairys, 1972).

Conclusions

What broad conclusions can be drawn from this critical analysis of jury selection? Until the last few decades, jury participation was largely reserved for the majority. Even though some changes have taken place, a system still exists in which the legal and judicial structures continuously reproduce, maintain, and perpetuate the subordination of racial and ethnic minorities. Historically, these minorities have been discouraged, if not prevented, from full participation in political structures, courts, and the judicial decision-making process. Labor-market and other socioeconomic inequalities serve to reinforce the poor representation of minority jurors.

Today, specific mechanisms of discrimination still exist. We have examined four factors that affect racially disproportionate representation in jury selection: (1) specific procedural anomalies in jury selection; (2) socioeconomic barriers that undermine the occupational and residential resources of racial minorities; (3) various forms of discrimination in the court system; and (4) gerrymandered judicial districts. For example, the potential sources of institutional biases in jury selection include structural and individual racism that prevents full-community jury participation, thereby perpetuating and maintaining racially demarcated juries. Labor market characteristics also set limits on the selection of minorities for jury duty. Members of ethnic and racial minorities are more likely to be in less stable secondary markets and to be characterized by high residential mobility, so that the call to jury service is impeded. They are more likely to be classified as "undeliverables," and residents who do not respond to the call are more likely to become defined as "recalcitrants." In addition, a different court and judicial strategy regulates the degree of minority participation on juries through gerrymandered judicial districts.

In the next chapter, we evaluate a number of legal and extra-legal determinants of racial participation by examining the different stages of the jury selection process. That is, we focus on various institutional and structural factors pertinent in *each specific stage* of the jury selection process. Every stage of jury selection plays an important role in identifying and filtering out specific segments of racial and ethnic minorities from jury service. For example, the first stage of the jury selection process defines the population and the geographic boundaries of the judicial district. The gerrymandering of the district effectively eliminates minority-dominant neighborhoods from jury service. The second stage of jury selection then defines the source list, such as registered voter rolls, that identifies the potential candidates for jury duty. Our analysis suggested that a large proportion of racial and ethnic minorities fail to register to vote. Thus, although some minority jurors live within the defined boundaries of a judicial district, they become subject to systematic exclusion from subsequent stages of jury selection.

There are eight distinctive stages in jury selection. A detailed analysis of the different stages of jury selection is important in an examination of the cumulative exclusionary effects of the many filtering techniques that shape and determine the ultimate composition of a jury. Further, because jury verdicts are less likely to reflect the opinions of a cross section of the community, analyses of jury representation also enable us to evaluate the social biases shaping jury verdicts and the legitimacy of jury trials. A critical examination of the institutional and structural mechanisms that influence racial representation is thus of great importance, as the analyses shed light on both structural and individual factors that lead to racial discrimination in the judicial decision-making process.

Notes

1. See *U.S. 90th Congress Senate Report No. 891* 1967, and *U.S. 90th Congress House Report No. 1076* 1968. See also U.S. 1968, Section 1961.
2. For more detailed discussions, see Boags and Boags (1971); Fukurai and Butler (1991a,b); Fukurai *et al.* (1991a,b); Hans and Vidmar (1986); "Jury-mandering: federal jury selection and the generation gap" (1973); Levine and Schweber-Koren (1976); Nietzel and Dillehay (1986); and Wrightsman (1987).
For various court trials in the U.S. Supreme Court, see *Alexander v. Louisiana* (405 U.S. 625 1972); *Peters v. Kiff* (407 U.S. 493 1972); *Taylor v. Louisiana* (419 U.S. 522 1975); *Duren v. Missouri* (439 U.S. 357 1979); and *City of Mobile, Ala. v. Bolden* (466 U.S. 55 1980). In California, see *People v. White* (43 Cal.3d 740 1954); *People v. Newton* (8 Cal.App.3d 359, 87 Cal. Rptr. 294 1970); *People v. Breckenridge* (52 Cal.App.3d. 913, 125 Cal. Rptr. 425 1975); *People v. Lewis* (74 Cal.App.3d. 633, 141 Cal. Rptr. 614 1977); *People v. King* (49 Cal. Rptr. 562 1966); *People v. Sirhan* (7 Cal.3d 258 1978); *People v. Wheeler* (148 Cal. Rptr. 890 1978); *People v. Estrada* (155 Cal. Rptr. 731 1979); *People v. Grahm* (160 Cal. Rptr. 10 1979); and *People v. Harris* (36 Cal. 3d 36, 201 Cal. Rptr. 782 679 P.2d 433 1984).

3. The U.S. Supreme Court ruled, however, that respondents failed to make out a *prima facie* case of discrimination in violation of the equal protection clause of the 14th Amendment with regard to the selection of the grand jury forepersons. As a result, the judgment of the court of appeals, which initially concluded that the respondents had made out a *prima facie* case, was reversed (*Rose v. Mitchell* 433 U.S. 545, 1979).
4. Before 1970, only individual defendants who argued that their right to a fair jury trial had been denied were allowed to raise jury challenges. *Carter* thus became the first class-action suit to challenge a jury selection process and to be reviewed by the U.S. Supreme Court.
5. The terms *Hispanic* and *Spanish-origin population* are used interchangeably by the authors in this book. The 1980 and 1990 U.S. Census definition is as follows: Persons of Spanish origin or descent are those who classified themselves in one of the specific Spanish-origin categories listed on the questionnaire—Mexican, Puerto Rican, or Cuban—as well as those who indicated that they were of other Spanish or Hispanic origin. Persons reporting "Other Spanish/Hispanic" origin are those whose origins are from Spain or the Spanish-speaking countries of Central or South America, or they are Spanish-origin persons identifying themselves generally as Spanish, Spanish American, Hispano, Latino and so on. Origin or descent can be viewed as the ancestry, nationality group, lineage, or country in which the person or the person's parents or ancestors were born before their arrival in the United States. Persons of Spanish origin may be of any race.
   In our analyses, Spanish surnames defined by the Census Bureau were used to determine the Hispanic population. Jury lists prepared by jury commissioners do not provide racial identifications. Self-identification is used to identify racial and ethnic backgrounds when questionnaires are administered in the jury assembly room (for more detailed discussion on the procedure and the administration of the questionnaires, see Fukurai, 1985).
6. The likelihood of registering to vote is also influenced by registration laws. Arizona, for instance, has a 50-day residency requirement for registering to vote, whereas Arkansas, Hawaii, Indiana, and many other states do not impose any residency requirement. The residency criterion often imposes a restriction on racial participation on juries, particularly for those with high degrees of geographic and residential mobility. Their high degree of residential mobility makes it less likely that they will register to vote, particularly if there is a strict residency requirement.
7. Survey questionnaires were sent to potential jurors who were randomly selected from a California County master key list for a period of three months in 1985. The data identified the socioeconomic and demographic profiles of those who were on the master list. More than 1,000 potential jurors were asked various questions about their eligibility to serve on juries. Their step-by-step status in jury selection was carefully monitored, computerized, and analyzed.
8. Doeringer and Poire (1968) first attempted to explain the persistent unemployment among racial minorities and argued that there are two kinds of labor market, a primary labor market (stability, security, and good pay) and a secondary labor market (with characteristics opposite those of the primary labor market). Specifically, laborers in the secondary labor market are characterized as being the following: (1) racial and ethnic minorities; (2) less educated; (3) lower income earners; (4) youth and the elderly; and (5) women (Edward, Reich, & Gordon, 1975). Edward *et al.* later incorporated a Marxian flavor into their analysis of the primary and secondary labor markets and posited that, in the late 19th century, because of the growing proletarianization and proliferation of labor conflicts, employers devised an elaborate system of job satisfaction, involving the

proliferation of job categories and the ranking of those jobs in a status hierarchy (Edward *et al.*, 1975). Further, Gordon (1972) identified two types of discrimination present in the labor market exercised by employers: (1) simple discrimination (pure prejudice) and (2) statistical discrimination (not instrumental racism, but prejudice based on statistical inferences from past experiences). Thus, racial discrimination is used to sort the pool of potential workers into primary and secondary labor markets.

9. For a three-year interval, using national data, one study found that 48.0% of blacks had moved, whereas 25.2% of whites had moved (McAllister *et al.*, 1971). During a one-year time period, in Los Angeles County, 49.8% of the age group between 15 and 29 had moved, whereas only 12.8% of those 60 and over had moved. And those mobile groups were predominantly members of racial minorities (Van Arsdol, Maurice, Sabagh, & Butler, 1968).
10. The length of the current residency was transformed into natural logarithms in order to satisfy the statistical assumption of performing multiple-regression analyses, that is, multivariate normal distributions. For all racial groups, a log-transformed variable of residency increased the proportion of explained variance. It suggested a better fit of linear relationships with an array of independent variables.
11. See the following for detailed discussions of the size of petit and grand juries in relation to the Sixth Amendment's right to trial by jury: Robert T. Roper in *Law and Society Review* (1980, pp. 977–995) and Peter W. Sperlich in *Judicature* (1980, pp. 262–279).
12. Rulings in both *Johnson v. Louisiana* (406 U.S. 356 1972) and *Apodaca v. Oregon* (406 U.S. 404 1972) were by five-to-four votes.
13. Postverdict interviews revealed that the first vote on the penalty was 9 to 3 in favor of death. The three jurors who voted against the death penalty were three black jurors. The second vote resulted in a unanimous decision in favor of a life sentence without possibility of parole. For more detailed descriptions of the case, see Chapter 6, "Scientific Jury Selection in *Voir Dire:* The Hidden Structure of Jury Selection." Empirical analyses of *People v. Harris* (36 Cal.3d 36 201, Cal. Rptr. 782 679 P.2d 433 1984) were performed at the University of California, Riverside. In *People v. Harris,* the motion of the respondent for leave to proceed *in forma pauperis* was granted; however, the writ of *certiorari* by the prosection to the U.S. Supreme Court was denied on October 29, 1984. Another example of racially demarcated verdicts is the *Jackson* case in Long Beach, California. Don Jackson was a police sergeant in the Los Angeles suburb of Hawthorne. The Long Beach case attracted national attention on January 14, 1989, when an NBC crew secretly videotaped a police officer apparently pushing Jackson through a plate glass window after a routine traffic stop. The two defendants in the trial were officers Mark Ramsey, 31, and Mark Dickey, 29. Both were white. These two defendants, who retired at half-pay on stress disability after the arrest, said that they had stopped Jackson because his car was weaving and that he had deliberately provoked them.

The jury for the trial consisted of 9 whites, 2 Hispanics, and 1 black. The jury deliberated 3½ days before reporting itself deadlocked 11 to 1 in favor of a verdict of not guilty. The jurors accepted the explanation of the officers that they had not purposely pushed Jackson through the window and concluded that Jackson had broken the fall with his elbows, instead of with his head. The jurors also apparently believed a psychologist and former Long Beach police officer, who testified that the two policemen had filed a false report of the incident because they were suffering from posttraumatic stress syndrome (Cannon, 1991).

Judge James Wright of the municipal court declared a mistrial and granted a defense motion for a dismissal of the misdemeanor charges against the two defendants. Charles Woolery, the only black juror and the juror who voted in favor of conviction, said that the other jurors "didn't see it like I saw it, you know? . . . I saw excessive force" ("Mistrial in officers' beating of motorist in '89," 1991). After the trial, the two defendants, the defense attorneys, and most of the jurors celebrated the verdict together at a long lunch at a waterfront restaurant. The black juror, however, did not join the festivities (Cannon, 1991).

3

Jury Selection Procedures

An Overview

Introduction

The starting point in jury selection is sending a jury summons, which calls prospective jurors to the courthouse. Yet relatively few eligible citizens are successful in finally entering the jury box. Before they reach the courthouse, most prospective jurors are screened out by a variety of legal and extralegal factors.

This chapter examines the variety of legal and nonlegal factors at every stage of jury selection that play a significant role in the minority representativeness of both petit and grand juries. Legal variables include various statutes (at both state and federal levels) requiring racial and ethnic judicial participation, particular types of prospective-juror source lists, specific procedural techniques (random selection or key-man selection), excuses, subjective qualifications, exemptions, legal disqualifications, and follow-up procedures for nonreturned qualification questionnaires. Extralegal variables cover a broad range of political and economic factors reflecting the social climate of a particular epoch, including the presence of racism or prejudice operating at both individual and structural levels, as well as the socioeconomic and demographic status of potential jurors.

Detailed structural and institutional analysis of every stage of the jury selection process is an essential ingredient in extending our knowledge of the degree and quality of justice. The questions asked must include: (1) How are jurors selected? (2) To what extent do juries actually represent the community? And (3) by what methods has racial discrimination been perpetuated and maintained? These questions are especially important because most psycholegal research focuses on determinants of final jury verdicts and their relation to the psychological and attitudinal characteristics of the jurors in the jury box. As we have discussed in the previous chapters, important dimensions of racial and judicial inequities are more likely to exist long before the impaneling of final jurors in the jury box. Thus, psycholegal research fails to address the social and/or institutional dimensions of racial and judicial discrimination and *how* and *why* such inequities have emerged and been maintained.

The step-by-step analysis of jury selection procedures presented here elucidates the restrictions and barriers to participation at each selection stage, specifying important dimensions of racial and judicial inequality and assessing their impact on racial representativeness.

Racial Inequality in the Jury Selection Process

The general overall jury-selection process used in both federal and state courts is summarized in the schematic, step-by-step process shown in Figure 3–1 (U.S. 1968). In the figure, each of the eight boxes represents a single stage in the jury selection system:

1. A given population in a specified geographical area is defined as eligible for jury service.
2. Source lists are obtained and/or generated that will allow the selection of potential jurors.
3. A master file (or wheel) is constructed, which contains a list of names compiled randomly from the source lists.
4. Jury qualification questionnaires are sent to (presumably) randomly selected candidates; from the returned questionnaires, a qualified-jurors file is constructed, which contains the names of those who have met various requirements for jury service, such as residency, citizenship, and English-language proficiency.
5. From this juror list, potential jurors are assigned to impanelment lists and to various courts.
6. Jury panels are brought together, composed of those potential jurors who actually show up at the courthouse.
7. After assignment to a courtroom and a trial, the *voir dire* screening process begins. It is designed to eliminate potential jurors who may be biased and unacceptable to the plaintiff or to the prosecuting and defense attorneys.
8. Specific jurors are selected for the jury box and the alternates.[1]

The logic of the entire selection process is based on screening, from the target population to those who finally enter the jury box. According to the law, the purpose of the selection procedure is to choose a jury that

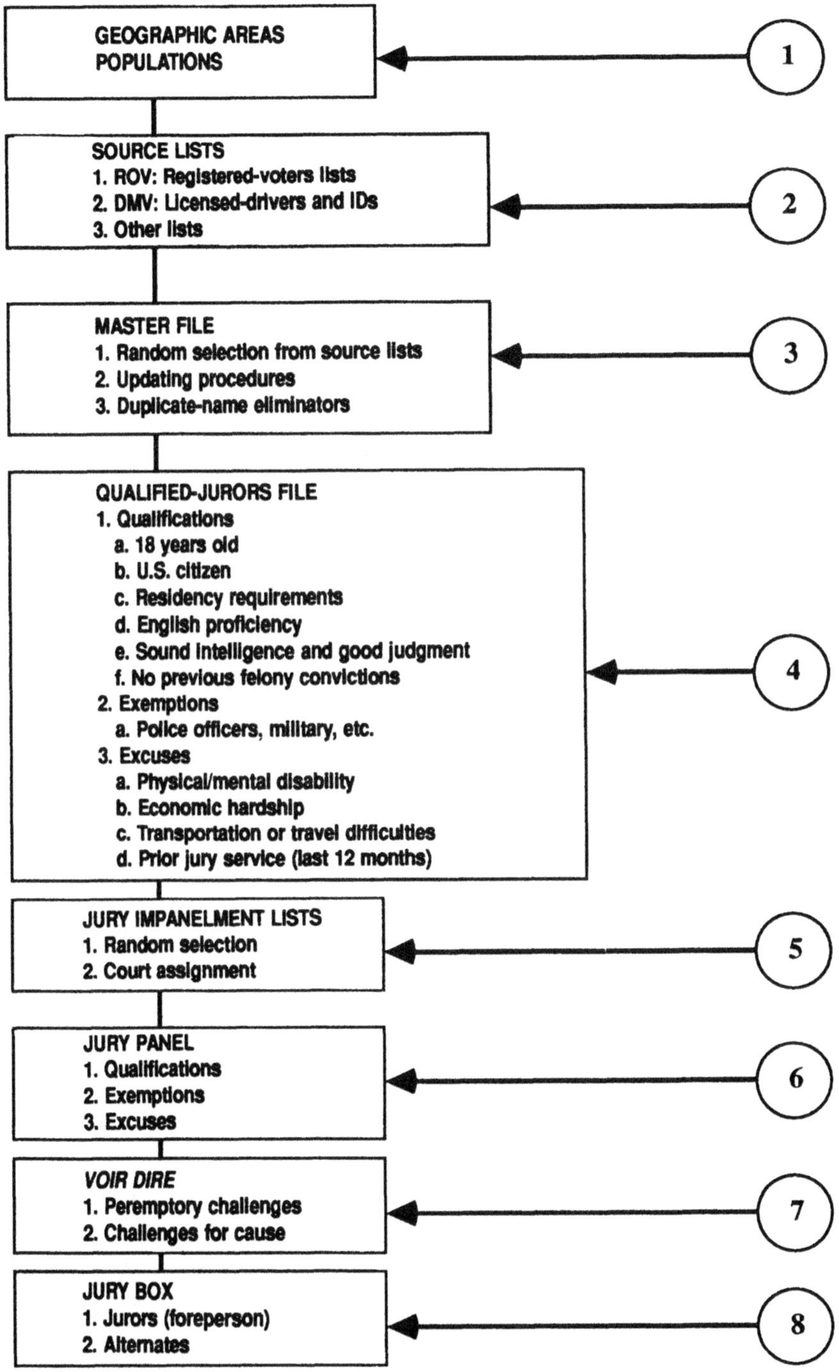

FIGURE 3-1. Jury selection procedures.

reflects a cross section of the community. The chosen jurors are then viewed as being impartial and qualified to represent the community.

Some of the shortcomings of the process are known. How closely juries reflect a cross section of the community depends on the success of the procedures by which jurors are chosen. For instance, the representation of whites, blacks, and Hispanics in a master file and source list, as well as their qualifications for jury service, are considered the most direct determinants of balanced racial participation on jury panels (Benokraitis, 1975; Huebner-Dimitrius, 1984; Scott, 1984). In each of the selection stages, however, many other factors influence egalitarian participation, and these have a *cumulative effect* on the racial and ethnic composition of jury panels. Moreover, in the various stages of jury selection, a series of informal filtering techniques shape and determine the racial, ethnic, and class balance of prospective jurors.

Stage 1: Geographic Areas and the Population

The first stage in the jury selection process is defining the geographic area from which the population for jury service is to be chosen, which is defined by the jurisdiction and geographic area served by the court.

A court of general jurisdiction is a trial court of unlimited original jurisdiction within the legal bounds of rights and remedies, whereas a special or limited jurisdiction covers only a particular class of cases, cases in which the amount in controversy is below a prescribed sum, or cases subject to specific exceptions (Black, 1990). The different levels of court structure define jurisdictional boundaries. There are two main levels of court jurisdiction: state and federal. For example, each court has the power to implement and legislatively define criminal conduct, to evaluate civil rights and liabilities within its own boundaries, and to provide appropriate punishment. However, limitations are imposed by the U.S. Constitution: (1) no state can criminally punish conduct sanctioned by the Constitution as this document is interpreted by the U.S. Supreme Court; (2) criminal conduct must be brought to trial in the state where the crime was committed; and (3) the courts of one state may not interfere with those of its sister states. A civil action, however, can be brought in a state other than the one where the events giving rise to it took place.

The federal judicial system has been superimposed on the 50 states through a network of federal courts. The need for such a court is trifold: (1) it supervises the broad jurisdiction of the state courts; (2) it enforces federal law; and (3) it creates uniformity in the decisions throughout the nation on questions of federal law (Karlan, 1964, pp. 11–20). It has been up to the federal courts, for example, to give meaning to the Sixth Amendment in deciding jury challenges. The U.S. Supreme Court has developed certain guidelines by which to judge jury challenges: A litigant must show that (1) "the group alleged to be excluded is a 'distinctive' group in the community"; (2) "the representation of this group in venires from which juries are selected is not fair and reasonable to the number of such persons in the community"; and (3) "this underrepresentation is due to systematic exclusion of the group in the jury selection process" (*Duren v. Missouri*, 439 U.S. at p. 364, 99. S.Ct. at p. 668 1979). Under this test, the Supreme Court has ruled that blacks, Hispanics, and women are "cognizable classes" for jury challenges.[2]

Various factors influence the social and racial makeup of what constitutes the general population for jury service in a given jurisdiction. Age, for instance, is an important dimension of defining an eligible population for jury service. There is an age requirement in every state. The minimum age limit ranges from 18 to 21. Alabama, Connecticut, Mississippi, Missouri, New Jersey, New York, Rhode Island, South Carolina, and Utah have the lowest minimum limit, 18 years. At the federal level, all citizens over 18 are eligible for jury service [U.S., 1968, Section 1865(b)]. Some states also set an upper age limit. In Alabama, South Carolina, and West Virginia, no one over 65 can serve as a juror. In Nebraska and South Dakota, 70 is the limit, and the limit is 72 in Wyoming and most of the counties of New York, and 75 in New Jersey. Other states, including California, do not have an upper age limit (Van Dyke, 1977, pp. 258–262).

Another important dimension in defining jurisdiction is the delineation of the geographic boundaries of the judicial district. In the past, jury practitioners have relied on counties, cities, and census tracts to define the judicial district. In California, as in most of the states, counties and census tracts are used for the selection and evaluation of judicial representation (*People v. Harris*, 36 Cal. 3d 36, 201 Cal. Rptr. 782, 679 P.2d 433 1984). Each jurisdiction, for example, is defined by county and/or census tract boundaries. The boundaries of the judicial districts for both municipal and superior courthouses in Los Angeles County are defined by census tracts, and each census tract has a known distance from each courthouse. The list for jury summonses on which impanelment is based also lists potential jurors' residences and their corresponding census tracts. In other states, when there is only one superior court per county, the geographic boundary of the judicial district is generally isomorphic with that of the county boundary (Van Dyke, 1977).

The gerrymandering of judicial districts and thus of minority representation in the jurisdiction has often been based on census tracts and the distance of each juror's residence from courthouses. Kairys (1972), for instance, illustrated the practicality of using census tracts to generate a statistical index (goodness-of-fit chi-square values) and to examine the jury representation of specific tracts and areas within a district. Because discrimination in jury representation is based on travel distance to the courthouse, in some states the distance to the courthouse marks geographic boundaries used to exclude particular neighborhoods or other adjacent communities from the judicial districts.

The Federal Jury Selection Act of 1968 authorizes each district court to

> fix the distance, either in miles or in travel time, from each place of holding court beyond which prospective jurors residing shall, on individual request therefore, be excused from jury service on the ground of undue hardship of traveling to the place where the court is held. [U.S. 1968, Section 1863(b)(7)]

The distance requirement often discriminates against those who live in rural areas. For instance, the superior court of San Bernardino County, California, oversees the largest jurisdictional area in the United States. The jurisdiction encompasses 20,117 square miles, and the SMSA (Standard Metropolitan Statistical Area) within which the superior court is located is geographically the largest in America. Because the superior court excuses any prospective juror who lives more than 25 miles from the county courthouse, which is located at the center of the city of San Bernardino, near the western edge of the county, residents in the large portion of the Mojave Desert and areas close to the state of Nevada—namely, Hispanics and native Americans—are automatically excluded from serving on juries.

Given the vast differences in geography from district to district, the mileage figures also range from 25 miles in the federal court for the Eastern District of New York to 250 miles for grand jurors in South Dakota. Of the federal districts, 30 do not set a maximum mileage despite the instruction in the statute (Van Dyke, 1977, pp. 124–125). Nevertheless, in the first stage of the jury selection process, the judicial district and the population are defined by the demographic characteristics of community members residing within the geographic boundaries of the district.

Stage 2: Source Lists

Once the population and the geographic boundaries have been defined, the second stage of jury selection is to determine what lists containing the names of potential jurors are to be used. The Jury Selection and Service Act of 1968 encourages the use of voter registration lists (ROV) (U.S., 1968, Section 1861). Congress was persuaded that voter rolls would meet the representativeness, or fair cross-section, test of random selection from the community, a requirement guaranteed by the Sixth Amendment to the U.S. Constitution. In the federal system, voter registration lists are used as a source list, whereas the ROV list may be supplemented by other sources of names secured by federal statute [28 U.S.C. section 1863(b)(2), 1982].[3] The states, however, are given considerable leeway in the application of fair cross-section principles (see *Taylor v. Louisiana*, 419 U.S. 522 538 1975).

The use of ROV lists alone, however, does not lead to a representative cross section of the community because of the different registration rates of economic and racial groups (see Tables 2–1 and 2–2). Another source of the inadequacy of ROV lists is the variation in the registration laws among the states. Arizona, for instance, has a 50-day residency requirement for registering to vote, whereas Arkansas, Hawaii, Indiana, and many other states do not impose any residency requirement (Fukurai, 1985; Van Dyke, 1977).

The residency criterion also imposes a restriction that affects the minority–majority composition of juries. As shown in Chapter 2, people with jobs in the less unstable secondary labor markets have high residential and geographic mobility and low residential ownership. Their high residential mobility makes it less likely that they will register to vote, particularly if there is a stringent residency requirement. Thus, the use of voter rolls neither standardizes the makeup of the jury pools required for fair representation nor leads to a jury representation of a cross section of the community.

Research estimates that voter lists automatically exclude approximately one third of the adult population, tipping prospective jury selection toward the elderly, the relatively affluent, and the self-employed and government workers, and away from minorities, including blacks, Hispanics, and women (Kairys, 1972, pp. 777–780).

Some observers of jury selection take the position that minority underrepresentation resulting from the exclusive use of the voter list is justified because it is the individual's responsibility to register to vote and because those persons uninterested in voting probably will not make good jurors. As a result, the voter list can be viewed as a screening mechanism to eliminate those who are deemed undesirable (U.S. 1968, Sections 1792, 1796). Irvin Kaufman, chairman of the committee that drafted the 1968 Jury Selection Act, stated that the voter list "supplies an important built-in screening element. It automatically eliminates those individuals not interested enough in their government to vote or indeed not qualified to do so" (U.S., 1967:253). This position clearly is contradictory to the representative guideline specified in the Federal Jury Selection Act of 1968, which disqualifies only noncitizens; those under age 18;

those who have not "resided for a period of one year within the judicial district"; those "unable to read, write, and understand the English language with a degree of proficiency sufficient to fill out satisfactorily the juror qualification form"; those "unable to speak the English language"; those with "mental or physical infirmity"; and those under indictment or convicted of an offense punishable by imprisonment of more than one year [U.S. 1968, Section 19859(b)]. Because there is no legally mandated criterion in the act, participation in the electoral process has become a *de facto* prerequisite to jury participation. This view has now taken on the status of *stare decisis,* the binding power of precedent.

The rationale of the jury system is to lend legitimacy to justice through verdicts reached by a cross section of the community. Excluding certain segments of the population from jury service because they failed to register to vote appears to contradict the democratic principle of the jury selection system itself. Further, some people purposely fail to register to vote because they try to avoid jury duty (U.S., 1975). Thus, the exclusive use of voter lists as the source of potential jurors not only fails to produce representative juries, but also discourages some people from voting and thus jeopardizes the democratic nature of both elections and jury trials ("Jury-duty fear discourages voter registration," 1990).

The American Bar Association (ABA, 1983, Section 3.7) provides the two standards for the overall source list: (1) inclusiveness and (2) representativeness. *Inclusiveness* refers to the proportion of the adult population on the source list; *representativeness* refers to the proportionate presence of cognizable groups on the list. The ABA guideline for establishing source lists also suggests that (1) the names of potential jurors be drawn from a source list compiled from one or more regularly maintained lists of persons residing in the court jurisdiction; (2) the jury list be representative and as inclusive of the adult population in the jurisdiction as is feasible; (3) the court periodically review the jury source list for its representativeness and inclusiveness of the adult population in the jurisdiction; and (4) the court determine if improvement is needed in the representativeness or inclusiveness of the source lists and if corrective action should be taken (ABA, 1983, Section 2). The ABA suggests that voter lists supplemented by lists of licensed drivers will provide reasonable inclusiveness and representativeness.

In some parts of the United States, local censuses are used as a source list. In Kansas City, Kansas, for instance, an annual census is combined with the voter list as a source of prospective jurors (see *Kansas v. Campbell,* 217 Kan. 756, 539 P.2d 329 1975). In California, a 1981 law mandates the use of both voter registration lists (ROV) and driver registration lists (Department of Motor Vehicles, DMV) in an attempt to rectify voter registration bias (CA, 1981, Section 16.204.7). In addition, as shown in Table 3–1, seven California counties used multiple source lists before 1981 (CA, 1975). The sources shown here are typical of the enlarged jury pools available to other courts through the use of multiple lists. The use of both ROV and DMV lists, for instance, yielded an increase in the number of potential jurors of approximately 70% over the use of ROV lists alone.

However, some areas find a greater advantage in using DMV lists because they cover a larger population than ROV lists. In the Eighth Judicial District of Nevada (serving Las Vegas and surrounding Clark County), drivers' lists have been the sole source of potential jurors since 1980 (Lowman, 1981). The exclusive use of the drivers' list, however, tends to discriminate against certain segments of the population, including the elderly, who generally drive less frequently than the young; the poor; racial minorities, particularly in urban settings; and women, who are less likely to hold drivers' licenses than men (Van Dyke, 1977). The percentage of males holding drivers' licenses nationally was 91% in 1981; the percentage of female drivers was 75%. Thus, the use of DMV lists would eliminate one fourth of female prospective jurors from jury selection ("Comparing voters' and drivers' lists," 1982). Besides DMV lists, other supplemental lists include those of utility company subscribers, welfare recipients, selective-service registrants, telephone subscribers, and those in city directories and on tax rolls.

Despite the obvious advantages of using multiple source lists, the majority of states, as well as virtually all federal courts, continue to use only the ROV list to identify potential jurors. The impact of narrowly defined source lists on minority representation is undoubtedly severe and becomes a larger problem in the latter stages of jury selection.

Stage 3: The Master File

The third stage of jury selection deals with the task of constructing the master file based on the names supplied from source lists. A master file, or wheel, of prospective jurors is compiled differently at the federal and the state levels. There are three areas of methodological concern in compiling the names of prospective jurors in a master file: (1) random selection from source lists; (2) the updating of names; and (3) the duplication of names on the lists.

The 1968 Jury Selection and Service Act established a detailed procedure for the compilation of the master file in order to ensure that it would be broadly representative of the population of each geographically bounded judicial district. Each district court was also directed to compile

TABLE 3-1
Seven California Counties Using Multiple Source Lists[a]

Courts	Names on ROV list	Names on DMV list	Names on master list	Increase over ROV (%)
Santa Cruz (superior & municipal)	87,000	100,144	117,297	35
San Luis Obispo (superior & municipal)	65,000	82,437	96,896	49
San Diego (superior & municipal)	628,217	925,497	1,038,576	65
San Francisco (superior)	345,954	395,000	575,306	66
Solano (municipal)	75,000	126,000	139,136	86
San Mateo (superior & municipal)	226,372	361,652	426,655	88
Monterey[b] (municipal)	80,000	140,000	191,300	139

[a]Judicial Council of California, "A Report to the Judicial Council on Ways to Improve Trial Jury Selection and Management," prepared by National Center for State Courts, Western Regional Office, San Francisco, April 28, 1978, p. 37.
[b]Also uses property tax lists, which contained 72,000 names.

a master file by taking names from the list at chosen intervals, thereby selecting what is called an "interval number." Once the master list was prepared, it was to remain unchanged and unsupplemented for four years [U.S. 1968, Section 1983(b)(4), as amended by Public Law No. 92-269, Section 3(c), April 6, 1972].[4] In some states, however, because factors such as residential mobility and persons reaching eligible age affect the population of potential jurors, a new master wheel is prepared at least once every 12 months [CA, 1981, Section 204.5(a)].

Because of the variation in residential mobility among racial and ethnic groups, the frequency of updating master files becomes important in ensuring a representative jury. The rate of geographic mobility for selected groups between 1986 and 1987 is indicated in Table 3–2. The geographic mobility rate of Hispanic-origin persons (22.6%) and blacks (19.6%) is higher than the rate for whites (17.8%). Minorities are also more likely than whites to make short-distance moves, that is, within a county rather than between counties (Long, 1988; McAllister *et al.*, 1971; Palen & London, 1984; Van Arsdol *et al.*, 1968). Similarly, 13.8% of blacks and 17.6% of Hispanics reported moving within the same county, compared with 11.2% of whites. New job locations or searches, unpaid or rising rents, and other costs are obvious reasons for such moves, which may remove people from source lists. Moreover, high geographic mobility among racial minorities—even short-distance moves—reduces the feeling of community involvement and commitment that is an essential ingredient of jury participation.

A frequent updating of the master file is clearly crucial to maintaining a representative master list. In all federal courts, the statute requires that the master list be updated only every four years [U.S. 1968, Section

TABLE 3-2

Geographic Mobility by Race and Hispanic Origin, 1986–1987 (Percentages)[a]

			Moved between counties			
Race	*Total*	*Moved within county*	*Total*	*Same state*	*Different state*	*Moved from Abroad*
White	17.8	11.2	6.6	3.8	2.9	0.4
Black	19.6	13.8	5.7	3.3	2.4	0.5
Hispanic origin[b]	22.6	17.6	5.0	3.1	1.9	1.7

[a]U.S. Bureau of the Census, *Current Population Reports,* Series P-20, No. 430, "Geographic Mobility: November 1986 to March 1987," U.S. Government Printing Office, Washington, DC, 1987.
[b]Persons of Hispanic origin may be of any race.

1983(b), as amended by Public Law No. 92-269, Section 3(c), April 6, 1972]. Such a lengthy period between updatings accentuates the weakness of using voter registration lists, which already underrepresents minority populations. If updating is done every four years, for example, those who were seventeen years old at the time of the last updating will not be included in the list until they are 21—a violation of federal, and sometimes state, laws on eligibility for jury service.

The potential number of people who are likely to be excluded depends on the time period during which the master lists are updated. Table 3–3, created from a 1986 California Survey, shows the extent to which the frequency of the source list update influences the inclusiveness of racial and ethnic groups in the source list. Two variables, residential and geographical mobility, are used to estimate the impact on racial representation. The analysis shows that, even if the master list is updated every year, some potential jurors less than 30 years of age will be systematically eliminated from jury service.

Empirical analyses further point out that, when the master list is

TABLE 3-3

Frequency of Source List Update and the Estimated Proportion of Potential Jurors Not Included

	Whites (%)			*Black/Hispanics (%)*			*Others (%)*		
Updating periods	*< 30*	*30–54*	*55+*	*< 30*	*30–54*	*55+*	*< 30*	*30–54*	*55+*
Every year[a]	26.5	9.8	3.2	17.7	7.9	0.0	35.0	5.0	14.3
Every two years	42.2	15.3	5.3	38.3	30.6	0.0	45.0	7.5	14.3
Every four years	63.8	30.6	13.1	70.6	43.4	0.0	65.0	35.0	14.3
Every ten years	80.0	66.5	35.6	88.3	74.2	10.0	95.0	77.5	42.9
N	185	451	374	34	39	20	20	40	7

[a]Based on a number of years at the current residence.

updated every four years—that is, every presidential election year—approximately two thirds of the potential minority jurors under age 30 are excluded until the next presidential election. That is, 70.6% of black and Hispanic prospective juror candidates under age 30 are excluded from jury selection. Similarly, 43.4% of black and Hispanic jurors between the ages of 30 and 54 are excluded for a four-year interval, whereas only 30.6% of white jurors are subject to such systematic elimination. Thus, the frequency of the master file update is crucial in maintaining representative jury lists.

Although the use of multiple source lists in the selection process results in a greater representativeness of the pool, it also means that duplicate names must be eliminated because a large number of registered voters are also on the motor vehicle rolls (Kadane & Lehoczky, 1976; Munsterman, 1978). The elimination of duplicate names, however, poses some serious programming problems (Lowman, 1981). For example, the Colorado Judicial Department estimated that about 10% of the names on its master lists were duplicates even after the computer's scanning efforts were completed (Van Dyke, 1977, p. 103), and *New Jersey v. Long* (1985) revealed that in Atlantic City County, New Jersey, the driver's license list and the voter registration list had often been merged incorrectly. The testimony revealed that approximately 180,000 names appeared on the merged list, whereas only 130,000 prospective jurors between the ages of 18 and 72 lived in the county. Thus, the Atlantic County jury panel had 40% overrepresentation of jurors, particularly with Jewish and Italian backgrounds. The testimony revealed that the selection method relied on constant numbers rather than random numbers in choosing jurors from the master list and that certain parts of the list were frequently used for selection and other sections were rarely used. For instance, when fifth-letter alphabetization was used to pick jurors, the panel would have the same fifth letter in their last names and so some panels had large numbers of Jewish names (e.g., Wise*m*an and Feld*m*an) or Italian names (e.g., Fera*r*do and Dina*r*do). As a result, the judge invalidated the jury selection system and required the Jury Commission to develop a new selection scheme (Hans & Vidmar, 1986, pp. 56–57).

Duplicate names also seem to have another serious effect on minority groups' chance to be included in the master file. A breakdown of juror availability based on source lists and a 1986 California survey is shown in Table 3–4. The figures are also broken down according to the year of master file updates, every four years or possibly longer. The large proportion of white jurors is identified on both ROV and DMV lists (70.5% and 87.8%). The analysis suggests that, regardless of the time interval between source list updates, a large number of white prospective jurors on both

TABLE 3-4
Estimated Percentage of Potential Jurors Identified by Multiple Source Lists: White, Black/Hispanics, Others

	White (%)		*Black/Hispanics (%)*		*Others (%)*	
Source lists	*< 4 Years*[a]	*4+ Years*	*< 4 Years*	*4+ Years*	*< 4 Years*	*4+ Years*
ROV[b]	3.7	4.9	0.0	1.7	0.0	0.0
DMV[c]	22.8	6.2	43.2	20.7	68.0	35.7
Both lists	70.5	87.8	51.4	72.4	24.0	59.5
Neither list	3.0	1.2	5.4	5.2	8.0	4.8
Total	100.0	100.1[d]	100.0	100.0	100.0	100.0

[a]Number of years lived at current residence.
[b]Registered voters' rolls.
[c]Drivers' motor vehicle registration lists.
[d]Due to rounding errors.

lists would still be included in the master file. By contrast, the majority of black and Hispanic jurors are identified only through DMV lists. In fact, almost no additional names would be contributed by ROV lists if a four-year interval were used for updating the master list. Similarly, other minority jurors would not be identified if the ROV were the sole source list. The finding also substantiates that minority jurors are mostly identified by DMV lists, not by ROV lists. Their names are more likely to come from DMV lists and are less likely to overlap the names on ROV lists. This analysis illustrates the importance of multiple source lists in maintaining racially representative jury lists. It also points out that, even when both DMV and ROV are used, minorities remain less well represented than whites because their names are more likely to be identified only once. Because of the difficulty of purging the master file of duplicate names, white prospective jurors are likely to appear in the file more than once; thus, their chances of being chosen in a random selection are enhanced.

Stage 4: Qualified-Juror Files

The fourth step in the jury selection procedure is to compile the names of qualified potential jurors, after the randomly selected jurors are screened by jury qualification questionnaires. Once the master file has been created, jury commissioners can take two discretionary steps in compiling the qualified-jurors file: (1) setting qualification standards and (2) designing the method for compiling the list of qualified jurors.

The 1968 Federal Jury Selection and Service Act specifies the qualifications for jury service in the federal courts: (1) being "a citizen of the United States eighteen years old who has resided for a period of one year within the judicial district"; (2) having an ability "to read, write, and understand the English language with a degree of proficiency sufficient to fill out satisfactorily the juror qualification form"; (3) having an ability "to speak the English language"; (4) not being unable, "by reason of mental or physical infirmity, to render satisfactory jury service"; and (5) not having "been convicted in a State or Federal court of record of a crime punishable by imprisonment for more than one year," unless the person's civil rights have been restored by pardon or amnesty [U.S. 1968, Section 1965(b), (5)].

At the state level, because of the variations in statutory qualifications, there are generally 12 different sets of mandatory statutory qualifications. These include the elements of (1) being mentally sound (38 states); (2) having had no criminal conviction (35 states); (3) being physically sound (33 states); (4) being of a certain age (30 states); (5) having the ability to read, write, and speak English (27 states); (6) not having served prior jury service within a particular time (27 states); (7) having "key-man" characteristics as described below (26 states); (8) being a resident or a citizen of the state (24 states); (9) being a resident or a qualified elector (23 states); (10) being a resident or a citizen of the county (22 states); (11) being a U.S. citizen (17 states); and (12) becoming a juror by solicitation (8 states) (Benokraitis, 1975, p. 37).

The important notion here is that some mandatory qualifications rely on *subjective criteria* (especially 1, 3, and 7) in determining the eligibility of potential jurors. There is no doubt that such subjective evaluations have played an important role in creating racially demarcated juries in the race-conscious court structure in the South. For example,

> of the eleven southern states, ten states require that a prospective juror be "mentally sound"; ten states require that there be no conviction for a felony or "immoral crime"; eight require physical soundness; and eight states stipulate that prospective jurors have "key-man" qualifications of "good character," "sound judgment" and "intelligence." (Benokraitis, 1975, p. 38)

These subjective criteria play an important role in determining jury representativeness in other states as well. For instance, in California, Assembly Bill No. 1454, passed in 1981, contains subjective discretionary powers by stating:

> The qualified jury list . . . shall include persons suitable and competent to serve as jurors. In making such selections there shall be taken only the names of persons . . . who are in the possession of their natural faculties, who are of fair character and approved integrity, and who are of sound judgment. [CA, 1981, Section 17.205(a)]

At the state level, court officials may decide whether potential jurors are qualified or exempt by using three methods: (1) personal knowledge;

(2) personal interviews; and (3) questionnaires. Because the first two selection criteria are subjective, minority representation can be influenced by jury commissioners and district clerks, as they have substantial discretion regarding both the *sources* and the *methods* of selection (Benokraitis, 1975, p. 40). Even in a judicial district where objective questionnaires are used as the primary means of selecting qualified jurors, adequate racial representation may still be lacking. The use of *written questionnaires* demanding thoughtful contemplation, for example, has resulted in the loss of from 15% to 30% of potential jurors (*People v. Murphy*, 35 Cal. App. 3 & 905, iii Cal. Rptr. 295, 302, 1973). While no figures have been given for racial and ethnic breakdowns, it is highly likely that the majority of excluded jurors have been members of racial minorities.

A number of screening questions are also used to identify potential jurors. These include questions in the following three areas: (1) qualifications; (2) exemptions; and (3) excuses. The 1986 California Survey reveals that screening questions contribute to racially imbalanced representation.

Similar to federal standards, the qualification criteria in California include requirements on age, citizenship status, residency, English proficiency, sound intelligence and good judgment, and no previous felony convictions. The citizenship criterion excludes approximately 20% of black and Hispanic females from jury service and disqualifies a large number of other minority jurors (31.25% and 37.50% of nonblack and Hispanic minorities, both male and female) (see Table 3–5). An English proficiency criterion also plays an important part in disqualifying a large proportion of black and Hispanic jurors (36.59% of males and 25.81% of females).

Language requirements set limits on minority participation. All federal and many state courts currently disqualify prospective jurors devoid of English-language competency. Consider a county such as Los Angeles with a Hispanic population in 1990 accounting for 37.8% of the community, almost 10% increase from 1980. A large portion of the population is made up of short-distance migrants from other adjacent counties, as well as from Mexico. The language requirement restricts many of those with Hispanic backgrounds from participating on juries.

The 1980 U.S. Census revealed that more than 1 million residents in Los Angeles County spoke Spanish at home (1,118,081) and that 21% of those over age 18 were Spanish speakers. Further, 39% of those who spoke Spanish at home said that they spoke English not well or not at all (439,976 out of 1,118,081). Thus, of the total of potential jurors in Los Angeles County, 8% did not speak English well or at all (439,976 out of 5,446,115). Although no figures were given for the racial and ethnic breakdown of noncitizens, it is highly likely that most noncitizens were

TABLE 3-5
Effect of Qualification, Exemption, and Excuses on Racial Representativeness

	White (%)		Black/Hispanics (%)		Others (%)	
Variable	*Male*	*Female*	*Male*	*Female*	*Male*	*Female*
Qualification						
Citizenship	8.09	5.88	14.63	20.97	31.25	37.50
Age (18+)	7.02	4.15	7.32	8.06	11.95	11.76
Residency	11.91	11.76	12.20	16.13	6.25	25.00
English proficiency	7.45	4.84	36.59	25.81	25.00	40.00
Natural faculties	8.30	5.36	9.76	9.68	3.13	15.00
Conviction	7.87	4.33	12.20	11.29	0.00	12.50
Member, grand jury	7.02	4.15	9.76	8.06	0.00	12.50
Exemption						
Peace officer	8.30	4.15	7.32	8.06	0.0	12.50
Excuse						
Mental incapacity	19.36	20.24	19.51	19.35	3.13	17.50
Personal obligations	11.06	20.42	17.50	24.19	6.25	27.50
Economic hardship	33.40	19.72	19.51	16.13	15.63	15.00
Transportation[a]	10.64	12.46	12.20	22.58	3.13	17.50
Served on jury	20.43	18.17	9.76	13.11	6.25	20.00
Other excuses	16.38	11.76	19.51	12.90	9.38	20.00
N	470	578	41	62	32	40

[a]Transportation and/or travel difficulties.

members of the large Mexican and Hispanic population. If it is assumed that, in fact, those who spoke Spanish at home were all Hispanics, the language proficiency criterion alone would have eliminated 39% of the entire eligible Hispanic population. Thus, the language qualification engenders a complicated political issue. If a significant percentage of defendants are Spanish-speaking Hispanics, the participation of Spanish-speaking peers is called for. On the other hand, bilingual trials are expensive and require added technical support systems.

Another important factor setting limits on minority participation is the lack of follow-up of qualification questionnaires sent to prospective jurors. As discussed in the previous chapter, highly mobile people have the least chance of receiving them. Though some receive the questionnaires, the reluctance to fill them out and return them is strong among racial and ethnic minorities (Fukurai, 1985; Fukurai *et al.*, 1991b). Many minorities see no reason to participate in an institution controlled by those who lord it over them. Their perceived images of social justice are so overwhelming that these images have also led to their widespread mistrust of government and those with legal authority (Van Dyke, 1977, p. 32). As a result, blacks and other ethnic and racial minorities have learned to mistrust the fairness in most racially dominated institutions of power, such as law enforcement agencies (Loh, 1982) and court decisions by racially demarcated juries (*Batson v. Kentucky*, 106 S.Ct. 1712 1986).

Besides the mistrust of the judicial institutions by minority groups, other legal variables, such as excuses from jury selection, provide additional opportunities for their voluntary self-elimination from selection processes. The 1986 California Survey indicates that, among those who asked to be excused from jury service, personal obligation was the most important item for black and Hispanic jurors (17.5% for males and 24.2% for females). Only 11.1% of male and 20.4% of female white jurors asked to be excused for personal reasons. A high proportion of white female jurors also asked to be excused because of mental and physical incapacities (20.2%). Approximately 21% of white male jurors requested to be excused from jury duty because they had previously served on juries; this figure is the highest among the male population. With respect to difficulties in traveling to the courthouse, both black and Hispanic jurors are more likely to request an excuse than their white counterparts. One notable and perhaps unexpected finding is the high proportion of white jurors requesting to be excused because of the economic hardship that jury duties entail (33.4% and 19.7% for white males and females, respectively).

Two factors may shed light on this unexpected finding. First, white jurors may be characterized by greater apprehension of serving on juries. They may feel that jury service is an undue hardship to be avoided by all means. Given the high incidence of economic excuses among white jurors, their apprehension may be stronger than that of racial minorities.

In order to rectify some of the selection biases, by 1983, 39 states had adopted the one-day–one-trial scheme (U.S., 1983, p. 67). Although the procedural operation varies, prospective jurors report for one day, and if they are not selected, they are excused. If they are chosen, that jury is the only one on which they are required to serve. Nevertheless, a great deal of the prospective jurors' time is still spent waiting. Most jury commissioners summon many more jurors than they need, requiring that prospective jurors make personal sacrifices to report for jury duty (Van Dyke, 1977). Because of the lengthy time commitment required by many jury trials, the perceived threat to economic well-being may be more strong among whites than among blacks.

Second, excuses are closely linked to both the age and the economic status of individual jurors (see Table 3–6). For instance, prospective jurors who have just entered into the labor market may face greater economic hardship because of jury duty, whereas employees with greater seniority

TABLE 3-6
Excuse Items and Racial Representation

	Whites (%)			Black/Hispanics (%)			Others (%)		
Excuses	< 30[a]	30–54	55+	< 30	30–54	55+	< 30	30–54	55+
Mental incapacity	6.99	10.70	36.95	2.86	15.38	50.00	0.00	14.63	28.57
Personal obligation	13.98	20.52	12.14	14.29	21.05	40.00	4.55	19.51	42.86
Economic hardship	29.03	33.19	16.02	20.00	15.38	20.00	9.09	17.07	28.57
Transportation/travel	9.68	8.73	16.02	17.14	12.82	35.00	9.09	9.76	28.57
Previously served on grand jury	13.98	23.80	16.80	8.57	10.53	20.00	13.64	9.76	42.86
Other excuses	21.51	12.66	12.14	20.00	10.26	20.00	13.64	12.20	42.86
N	185	451	374	34	39	20	20	40	7

[a]Age of the respondents.

are less likely to be burdened by the economic loss. The 1978 Jury System Improvement Act offered, in the federal court, the carrot of increased compensation and travel allowances and forbade employers from firing jurors or causing them to lose seniority as a result of their services (U.S., 1980, Section 1869). However, the highest percentage of economic excuses is still found in the prime earning years (30–54) and among prime earners (white males). For example, in 1986 approximately 33% of white jurors between the ages of 30 and 54 requested to be excused from jury duty, whereas 15% of black and Hispanic jurors and 17% of other minority populations asked for economic excuse. White potential jurors earn more, but they have more to lose in objective and monetary terms. The relationship drops at 55, the retirement age for large numbers of whites. It may be that the perception of jury duty varies according to the age group and is, indeed, more of an economic hardship to the middle-aged majority group.

The relationship among excuse items, sex, and age for white and minority jurors is examined in Table 3–7. It is apparent that, among white jurors, the older the juror, the less likely he or she is to request to be excused for economic reasons (.185). Similar patterns are also found for other excuse items. Thus, the economic excuse is closely related to racial background, employment status, and seniority in a company (or possibly retirement).

Stage 5: Jury Impanelment Lists

The fifth stage of the jury selection process is to compile a short list of prospective jurors to be summoned to each courthouse. There are two major methods for determining who will be summoned to serve. Both

TABLE 3-7
Correlation Coefficients among Excuse Items, Age, and Sex for White (above Main Diagonal) and Black/Hispanic Jurors (below Main Diagonal)[a]

	Excuse questions									
Variable[b]	*A*	*B*	*C*	*D*	*E*	*F*	*Age*	*Sex*[c]	*Mean*[d]	*SD*
A	—	.170***	.050	.423***	.110***	.216***	−.368***	−.010	.748	.367
B	.326***	—	.142***	.372***	.180***	.288***	.072*	−.126***	.925	.402
C	.350***	.352***	—	.240***	.044	.179***	.185***	.155***	.834	.372
D	.460***	.378***	.447***	—	.253***	.354***	−.154***	−.028	.845	.362
E	.445***	.412***	.433***	.457***	—	.218***	.019	.028	.873	.333
F	.374***	.339***	.405***	.386***	.457***	—	.075	.066	.845	.362
Age	−.390***	−.198***	−.063	−.173*	−.157*	−.038	—	.010	39.420	15.246
Sex	−.084	−.159***	.028	−.168*	−.113	−.008	.039	—	.576	.495
Mean	.801	.837	.741	.883	.808	.861	47.720	.551		
SD	.399	.368	.438	.320	.393	.345	16.930	.497		

*$p < .05$.
**$p < .01$.
***$p < .001$.
[a]Significance is based on Cochran's test (1954) for linear relationship.
[b]A = Physical or mental incapacities: (0) asked; (1) did not ask.
B = Personal obligations.
C = Serious economic hardship and burdens.
D = Difficulty in transportation and/or travel to the courthouse.
E = Served as a juror in the past 12 months.
F = Other excuses.
[c](0) male; (1) female.
[d]Black/Hispanic jurors.

involve drawing names from the qualified juror file: (1) a procedure in which drawing names is left to the discretion of court officials and (2) selection by key numbers or random selection (Benokraitis, 1975, pp. 39–40). The Jury Selection and Service Act of 1968 mandates the use of random selection. The federal act notes that "the jury commission or the clerk shall publicly draw at random from the qualified jury wheel such number of names of persons as may be required for assignment to grand and petit jury panels" [U.S., 1968, Section 1866(a)]. Thus, the jury impanelment list should consist of those who are randomly selected from the qualified-jurors file and, therefore, who are representative of a "cross section" of the community. Similar requirements have been mandated in many states, including California (CA, 1981, Section 219, 229.255).

Involved, however, is an extralegal dimension—particularly in large judicial districts in metropolitan areas, where court competition by district courts affects the minority composition of potential jurors at the impanelment stage. Some large metropolitan areas, such as Los Angeles, where 32 superior and municipal courts are crowded into a single county, have been given a legal definition of what constitutes a judicial district. The law provides that "in counties with more than one court location, the rules shall reasonably minimize the distance traveled by jurors. In addition, in the County of Los Angeles no juror shall be required to serve at a distance greater than 20 miles from his or her residence" (CA, 1981, Section 7.203). Yet, the practicalities in large judicial districts such as Los Angeles County require that its 32 courts obtain the necessary number of jurors every week. This requirement has put the various courts in competition for potential jurors in overlapping regions where jurors have multiple opportunities of serving in more than one courthouse. Because judicial districts overlap, people living in overlapping geographic regions have multiple chances of being called to serve in various courts (see, for example, Fukurai, 1985).

The effect of overlapping judicial districts on racial representation and the competition in securing a sufficient number of jurors are also found in other metropolitan counties where multiple courthouses are crowded into the same jurisdiction. In Los Angeles County, for example, overlapped regions are more likely to be found in the central portion of the county (see region A in Figure 3–2). Consequently, in some courts, persons in peripheral areas of the county tend to dominate the makeup of juries impaneled in particular courts (Butler & Fukurai, 1984). Region A in Figure 3–2, for example, shows one area in which different superior-court judicial districts overlap; the area is bounded by the 20-mile radius circle of four superior court districts: Pasadena, Long Beach, Norwalk, and Van Nuys.[5]

Although there are a number of other overlapping regions, Region A embodies two geopolitically important implications. First, Region A maximizes the participation of potential jurors living in the overlapping region, as people living in Region A can be called into a large number of different superior courts. Thus, the racial and ethnic composition in Region A becomes more important than in other overlapped regions because each resident has multiple chances of serving in any of the eight superior courts in Los Angeles County.

Second, because every census tract in Region A has a significant impact on the racial and ethnic jury composition in all jurisdictions, the systematic selection and/or deletion of the census tracts in Region A from each judicial district may lead to possible evidence of institutional control over racial jury participation.

When the racial and ethnic breakdown in Region A is compared with the overall composition in Los Angeles County, Region A is characterized by a high concentration of racial and ethnic minorities. For example,

FIGURE 3-2. Overlapped Superior Court Judicial Districts in Los Angeles County.

the racial breakdowns for whites, blacks, and Hispanics in Los Angeles County are 40.3%, 12.6%, and 27.6%, whereas they are 11.5%, 48.3%, and 36.3% in Region A. That is, according to the 1980 U.S. Census, approximately 85% of the residents living in Region A are members of racial and ethnic minorities.

Table 3–8 reveals that several Los Angeles superior court districts have excluded a substantial number of census tracts in the overlapped region, even though the law specifies a 20-mile radius from the respective courthouses for the impanelment of prospective jurors. Long Beach and Van Nuys judicial districts have excluded more than 50% of the tracts in the region (130 and 123, respectively). In five of eight superior court districts, the excluded tracts accounted for more than 20% of the total of tracts in Region A. Thus, 70.9% of black jurors have been left out of these outlying districts, and blacks make up only 48.3% of eligible jurors in Region A. That is, in the superior court districts where Region A's exclusion may have a more significant impact on the minority composition of juries, approximately 22% of black jurors have been systematically excluded from participating in juries in the outlying districts. Thus, there is a significant deficit of minorities serving in jurisdictions outside Region A.

Table 3–8 also suggests that the 20-mile rule has never been fully applied in constituting the judicial district. Systematic exclusion has been exercised in overlapped Region A, in which approximately 85% of the residents are minorities. Although there is no evidence to support such systematic exclusion in other overlapped areas, it is highly likely that the 20-mile superior court districts guarantee neither the inclusion of all areas within the 20-mile radius nor the exclusion of the tracts that fall outside the radius. In fact, such a violation has been reported in several jurisdictions including Torrance, Van Nuys, and North Valley (Butler, 1980a, b, 1981; Fukurai, 1985; Fukurai & Butler, 1991a, b; Fukurai *et al.*,1991a).

Table 3–9 indicates the expected racial composition of different jurisdictions if every census tract in Region A were included in the judicial districts as defined by the law. When Region A is completely excluded from the 20-mile-radius court jurisdiction, impaneled whites are disproportionately overrepresented and make up approximately 80% of potential jurors living outside Region A. On the other hand, if all the tracts in Region A are included in the defined boundaries of every jurisdiction, the expected racial compositions show that the representation of blacks and Hispanics would be increased by an average of approximately 11% and 2%. Thus, the inclusion of the entire overlapped region in the particular court jurisdiction would enhance the degree of minorities' participation at the impanelment stage of jury selection.

TABLE 3-8
Los Angeles County Census Tracts and Region A

Superior Court District	Race/ Ethnicity	Overlapped census tracts not included No.	Overlapped census tracts not included %	Included registered voters in Region A No.	Included registered voters in Region A %	Excluded registered voters in Region A No.	Excluded registered voters in Region A %
L.A. Central	Anglo	149	(23.1)[a]	36,759	20.3	10,724	12.3
	Black			93,241	51.4	72,184	82.4
	Hispanic			37,734	20.8	2,677	3.0
	Others			13,768	7.5	1,986	2.3
Santa Monica	Anglo	8	(3.8)	44,192	17.0	3,291	37.7
	Black			163,848	62.9	1,577	18.0
	Hispanic			37,278	14.3	3,133	35.8
	Others			15,029	5.8	752	8.6
Van Nuys	Anglo	123	(58.0)	34,782	31.1	12,701	8.5
	Black			53,552	47.9	111,873	74.8
	Hispanic			21,857	19.6	18,554	12.4
	Others			1,524	1.4	6,485	4.3
Pasadena	Anglo	88	(41.5)	11,886	10.0	35,597	23.7
	Black			63,934	53.7	101,491	67.7
	Hispanic			33,991	28.5	6,420	4.3
	Others			9,331	7.8	6,423	4.3
Norwalk	Anglo	46	(21.7)	32,699	16.8	14,784	19.9
	Black			114,355	58.7	51,070	68.8
	Hispanic			36,437	18.7	3,974	5.4
	Others			11,404	5.8	4,350	5.9
Torrance	Anglo	14	(6.6)	46,524	18.1	959	7.9
	Black			163,282	63.6	2,143	17.5
	Hispanic			32,890	12.8	7,521	61.6
	Others			14,166	5.5	1,588	13.0
Long Beach	Anglo	130	(61.3)	11,159	11.2	36,324	21.5
	Black			62,375	62.5	103,050	60.9
	Hispanic			21,574	21.6	18,837	11.1
	Others			4,757	4.7	10,997	6.5
Compton	Anglo	3	(1.4)	46,297	17.4	1,186	38.2
	Black			164,417	61.9	808	26.0
	Hispanic			39,913	15.0	498	16.0
	Others			15,136	5.7	618	19.8

[a]Divided by the total number of census tracts in overlapped regions, 212.

Courts' competition to obtain a sufficient number of prospective jurors may lead to greater structural racial discrimination in jury selection. Table 3–10 indicates the frequency of 1980 summons requests by different court locations in Los Angeles County. The Central District alone (approximately at the center of Figure 3–2) drew over one third (33.9%) of the total number of potential jurors in Los Angeles County. As it drew jurors first, the Central District Court pulled them

TABLE 3-9
Los Angeles County Registered Voters Living Inside and Outside Overlapped Region A

Superior Court District	Ethnicity	Registered voters outside overlapped region No.	%	Registered voters inside overlapped region No.	%	Difference %	Proportionate increase by inclusion of region %
L.A. Central	Anglo	850,991	83.3	898,474	69.6	−13.7	5.3
	Black	70,173	6.9	235,598	18.3	11.4	70.2
	Hispanic	60,121	5.9	100,532	7.8	1.9	40.2
	Others	40,460	3.9	56,214	4.3	0.4	28.0
Santa Monica	Anglo	693,359	85.1	740,842	68.3	−16.8	6.4
	Black	98,985	12.1	264,410	24.4	12.3	62.6
	Hispanic	15,533	1.9	55,944	5.2	3.3	72.2
	Others	7,107	0.9	22,861	2.1	1.2	68.9
Van Nuys	Anglo	1,068,398	87.7	1,116,881	75.1	−12.6	4.2
	Black	80,721	6.6	246,146	16.5	9.9	67.2
	Hispanic	37,804	3.1	78,215	5.3	2.2	51.7
	Others	30,920	2.6	46,674	3.1	0.5	33.8
Pasadena	Anglo	934,393	80.6	981,876	68.8	−11.8	4.8
	Black	78,420	6.8	243,845	17.1	10.3	67.8
	Hispanic	98,933	8.5	139,344	9.8	1.3	29.0
	Others	46,834	4.1	62,588	4.3	0.2	25.2
Norwalk	Anglo	781,442	75.2	828,925	63.4	−11.8	5.7
	Black	107,017	10.3	272,442	20.8	10.5	60.7
	Hispanic	104,419	10.0	144,830	11.1	1.1	27.9
	Others	46,311	4.5	62,065	4.7	0.2	25.4
Torrance	Anglo	853,091	79.4	900,475	67.0	−12.4	5.3
	Black	131,426	12.2	296,851	22.1	9.9	55.7
	Hispanic	54,887	5.1	95,298	7.1	2.0	42.4
	Others	34,768	3.3	50,522	3.8	0.5	31.2
Long Beach	Anglo	609,915	78.6	657,398	62.9	−15.7	7.2
	Black	78,630	10.1	244,055	23.4	13.3	67.8
	Hispanic	61,995	8.0	102,406	9.8	1.8	39.5
	Others	24,953	3.3	40,707	3.9	0.6	38.7
Compton	Anglo	1,038,007	77.3	1,085,490	67.4	−9.9	4.4
	Black	145,947	10.9	311,372	19.3	8.4	53.1
	Hispanic	108,314	8.1	148,725	9.2	1.1	27.2
	Others	49,968	3.7	65,722	4.1	0.4	24.0

from much of the central part of the county, leaving a smaller number of eligible and qualified jurors available for the outlying courts. Competition for a sufficient number of summoned jurors, particularly by the dominant superior courts such as the Central District, thus tended to undermine the representative nature of the jury selection process.

TABLE 3-10
Summonses Requested by Court Location[a]

Court district[b]	Number of panels requested	%	Total jurors summoned	%
Central S (Los Angeles)[c]	68	10.4	43,400	33.9
Northwest S (Van Nuys)	39	6.0	8,125	6.4
Antelope Valley M (Lancaster)	16	2.5	1,540	1.2
Newhall M	11	1.7	1,320	1.0
East Los Angeles M	27	4.1	4,744	3.7
Northeast S (Pasadena)	40	6.1	5,613	4.4
Alhambra M	18	2.8	2,525	2.0
East S (Pomona)	35	5.4	3,525	2.8
Citrus M (West Covina)	21	3.2	2,250	1.8
Rio Hondo M (El Monte)	22	3.4	2,075	1.6
Southeast S (Norwalk)	36	5.5	5,420	4.2
Los Cerritos M	5	0.8	660	0.5
Southgate M	19	2.9	3,400	2.7
Huntington Park M	17	2.6	3,250	2.5
Whittier M	27	4.1	3,125	2.4
Downey M	14	2.1	2,250	1.8
South S (Long Beach)	38	5.8	3,200	2.5
South Central S (Compton)	59	9.0	10,725	8.4
San Pedro branch of Los Angeles	22	3.4	2,243	1.8
Southwest S (Torrance)	8	1.2	950	0.7
Inglewood M	5	0.8	825	0.6
West S (Santa Monica)	27	4.1	5,500	4.3
Culver M (Culver City)	2	0.3	550	0.4
Beverly Hills M	15	2.3	2,350	1.8
Malibu M	4	0.6	725	0.6
West Los Angeles branch of Los Angeles M	24	3.7	3,240	2.5
North Central S (Glendale)	24	3.7	3,375	2.6
North Central S (Burbank)	10	1.5	950	0.7
Total	653	100.0	127,855	100.0

[a]Prepared by R.F. Arce, Director of the Los Angeles Juror Service Division, June 19, 1980.
[b]S = Superior; M = Municipal.
[c]City where the court is located.

Stage 6: Jury Panels

The sixth stage of jury selection takes place at the courthouses, when potential jurors are actually called in to serve on juries. Here two factors affect the racial composition of jury panels: (1) the method of summons and (2) the method of selection.

The Federal Jury Selection and Service Act of 1968 recommends the use of registered or certified mail or the personal delivery of summons by the clerk, the jury commission, or a marshal to the selected person at his or her usual residence or business address [U.S., 1968, Section 1866(b)]. As in the fourth stage of jury selection (sending qualification questionnaires to prospective jurors), residentially mobile groups of individuals are less likely to receive such summonses, and the federal act does not have statutory procedures requiring follow-up at this stage of the jury selection process.

Once they have been summoned, potential jurors may be eliminated by three methods: (1) excuses; (2) exemptions; and (3) disqualifications. These factors are identical to those at the qualification stage of jury selection (Stage 4). The basic assumption remains the same: Potential jurors who have not met the statutory requirements are to be identified and excluded from subsequent jury-selection procedures. This time, however, the screening process is performed at the courthouse, not through the mail.

About 60% of all people whose names have been pulled from the master wheel and who have received a questionnaire seeking to determine their qualifications for jury service return the document requesting to be excused (Bermant, 1982; Ginger, 1984; Van Dyke, 1977, p. 11). Only a few jury commissioners grant temporary excuses and then call the person again when the juror becomes available. It is much easier administratively to summon someone else from the list than to bother keeping track of those who have been excused for illness. It is unknown whether the permanent removal of these names results in less representative juries, although it is likely that a large number of sick people are older persons and that the proportion of the elderly is thus reduced.

Five factors affect the group of individuals likely to be excused from jury service at both the federal and the state levels: (1) economic hardship; (2) lack of child care; (3) age; (4) the distance traveled and transportation; and (5) illness. Although these excuse items are almost identical to those on the jury qualification questionnaire, excuses given by summoned jurors and sanctioned by the judges in the courthouse are likely to exert a more profound effect on the representative nature of the juries than at the previous stages of jury selection. Using a tilter of excuses, the jurors who are summoned and appear at the courthouse are more likely to represent particular segments of the community that are different from the larger, target population at the previous stage of jury selection. They are more likely to be (1) less geographically and residentially mobile; (2) white; (3) male; (4) white-collar workers or employees in a stable, primary labor market; (5) middle-aged; and (6) of higher income (Fukurai, 1985; Fukurai & Butler, 1991b).

Because the previous five selection procedures have already operated effectively to screen and exclude prospective jurors with characteristics opposite those mentioned immediately above, additional opportunities for the surviving candidates for voluntary self-elimination from jury service further refines the nonrepresentative nature of juries. As a result, socioeconomic and demographic factors such as race, sex, age, education, and income level become the basis for further discrimination at the jury impanelment stage. In addition, these excuse factors are likely to overlap one another to provide more complex pictures of the absence of racial and ethnic representation on jury panels.

Fukurai *et al.* (1987), for example, examined the relationship between the educational and racial backgrounds of impaneled jurors. The survey was conducted in 1986 and examined the jurors who appeared at the superior courthouse in Sacramento County, California. Over 4,000 potential jurors appeared on 57 jury panels between April 21 and September 7, 1986. Table 3.11 shows the cross-classification of race and educational background of the prospective jurors. The study suggests that, in all racial and ethnic groups, potential jurors with less than a high school education were significantly underrepresented. Further, the black and Hispanic jurors who appeared at the courthouse did not resemble the representative profiles of the minority population in the community. For instance, for the pool of 0.8% and 2.9% of potential black jurors with both grade school and high school education in the general community, impaneled black jurors constituted 0.1% and 1.9% of the jury panel, respectively. That is, 87.5% and 34.5% of the same groups were excluded from jury panels. By the same token, 95.5% and 32.8% of white jurors with similar educational levels were eliminated from jury panels, and 95.0% and 40.6% of Hispanic jurors were similarly eliminated before they were called into the courthouse. The unrepresentative nature of the jury panel with respect to cross-sectional community representation is further compounded by the various legal and extralegal factors that have previously played an important role in preselecting and screening the jurors before they reach the courthouse. Severe underrepresentation on jury panels of minority groups and those without a high school education has also been reported in many other jurisdictions in California, including Indio, Los Angeles, Sonoma, Riverside, San Bernardino, San Diego, and Orange counties (Butler, 1980a,b, 1981; Butler & Fukurai, 1984; Fukurai, 1985; Fukurai & Butler, 1991a; Fukurai *et al.*, 1991a,b).

Because the nature of the excuses given by summoned jurors is different from the previous screening processes, it is important to examine the specific types of excuses that are allowed by judges or other officials at the courthouse. For example, even though some potential jurors from a lower social class may successfully make it to the courthouse, because the courts are generally underfunded and the jurors are

TABLE 3-11
Eligible Population and Jury Panels: Race and Education[a]

Variables	*Population*	*Jury panel*	*Absolute disparity*	*Comparative disparity*	*Z scores*
EDUCATION					
White					
Grade school	6.7(8.2)[b]	0.5(0.3)	−6.4(− 7.9)	−95.5(−96.3)	−16.20(−16.44)
High school	39.0(47.6)	26.1(31.8)	−12.8(−15.8)	−32.8(−33.2)	−16.61(−16.92)
Some college	19.8(24.2)	28.0(34.2)	8.2(10.0)	41.4(41.3)	13.02(13.33)
College	16.4(20.0)	27.6(33.7)	11.2(13.7)	68.3(68.5)	19.14(10.85)
Black					
Grade school	0.8(12.6)	0.1(1.2)	−0.7(−11.4)	−87.5(−90.5)	−4.97(− 5.49)
High school	2.9(47.0)	1.9(29.0)	−1.0(−18.0)	−34.5(−38.3)	−3.77(− 5.76)
Some college	1.7(28.0)	3.0(46.3)	1.3(18.3)	76.5(65.4)	6.36(6.51)
College	0.8(12.4)	1.5(23.5)	0.7(11.1)	87.5(89.5)	4.97(5.38)
Hispanic					
Grade school	2.0(27.1)	0.1(1.6)	−1.9(−25.5)	−95.0(−94.1)	−8.59(− 7.97)
High school	3.2(43.7)	1.9(38.8)	−1.3(− 4.9)	−40.6(−11.2)	−4.68(− 1.37)
Some college	1.4(19.1)	1.8(37.3)	0.4(18.2)	28.6(95.3)	2.15(6.43)
College	0.7(10.1)	1.1(22.3)	0.4(12.2)	57.1(120.8)	3.04(5.62)
Others					
Grade school	1.2(24.8)	0.1(0.3)	−1.1(−23.6)	−91.7(−95.2)	−6.39(− 8.76)
High school	0.6(12.6)	1.2(19.1)	0.6(6.5)	100.0(51.6)	4.92(3.14)
Some college	1.5(32.9)	2.5(37.7)	1.0(4.8)	66.7(14.6)	5.21(5.12)
College	1.3(29.7)	2.7(42.0)	1.4(12.3)	107.7(41.4)	7.82(4.32)

[a]The survey was conducted in Sacramento Superior Court Judicial District in 1986. 4,000 potential jurors appeared on 57 jury panels between April 21 and September 7, 1986.
[b]Percentages in parentheses are *intraracial* percentage comparisons of educational levels; i.e., percentages computed with respect to column totals of respective racial groups.

almost always underpaid "most jury commissioners and judges will automatically excuse laborers and sole proprietors of a business who claim that jury service will cause them to lose their daily wage or to close up their business for a period of time" (Van Dyke, 1977, p. 119).

In many districts, some women are also automatically excused because the courts do not pay a daily fee high enough to cover child care for their youngsters; or the duration of jury duty may be reduced to a manageable limit.[6] Van Dyke (1977, pp. 121–124) reported that, between 1971 and 1974, approximately 83% of the federal courts surveyed showed a significant underrepresentation of women on jury panels. Van Dyke noted that, in the Northern District of California, for example, over half the qualified women between the ages 25 and 44 had been excused because they had children; such substantial numbers of excuses were also common in other jurisdictions. DiPerna (1984, p. 86) also reported that, in 15 states, women with children younger than 16 could secure automatic excuse, and that, in four of them, excuse could also be extended to men caring for young children.

Age is another important factor that affects jury representation. For instance, young prospective jurors may appear at the courthouse, but they may be excused from jury service if their school activities overlap with jury duties. Young and old jurors tend to be excused, although there are no statutes for excusing those at these eligible ages in order to reschedule them during school vacations or, in the case of the elderly, to allow for physical disabilities. Poor health is also a major cause of excuse. A large number of the sick are elderly, and jurors requiring medical care and unable to serve for the required period of a jury duty are automatically excused (Van Dyke, 1977).

Besides excuses granted by the judge, the court, and the statutes, exemptions also play an important role in perpetuating disproportionate jury representation. Three groups of individuals are exempted: (1) those performing vital functions for society, such as elected officials, clergy, doctors, police officers, and members of the military; (2) lawyers and police officers, who may exert an unusual amount of influence on the other jurors; and (3) those with an occupational prejudice on the question of guilt or innocence, such as clergy and, again, police officers. For example, retired police officers may be exempted from jury service if the trials involve officers of law enforcement as defendants. The judge or other court officials argue that their occupational background and work experience may influence their impartiality (Van Dyke, 1977, pp. 130–131).

The 1968 Jury Selection and Service Act provides exemptions for three occupations in the federal courts: (1) those on active duty in the military forces; (2) firefighters and police officers; and (3) "public officers" in the federal or any local government [U.S., 1968, Section 1863(b)]. At the state level, a significant number of people in many jurisdictions are also exempted from jury duty because of their occupations.

At the state level, jurisdictions vary in granting exemptions. Besides the above-listed occupations, New York exempts other public employees, including Staten Island Ferry operators in New York City, who are responsible for people reaching Staten Island. Virginia exempts tobacco pickers during harvests (DiPerna, 1984, pp. 85–86).

A close relationship exists between the exemption of certain occupational categories and minority representation. The 1986 California Survey indicated that a large number of minority women had requested to be exempted from jury service because they were peace officers. The figures of racial representation on exemptions are based on the jury impanelment stage of jury selection when jury summons are sent to prospective jurors; however, similar patterns are observed at jury panels when some of summoned jurors actually appear at the courthouse (see Table 3–5). Whereas about 8% of black and Hispanic female jurors asked for exemptions, only 4% of white women asked to be exempted. However, no significant racial and ethnic differences were found for male jurors.

In other jurisdictions, such as Michigan, Washington, and 18 other states, no occupational exemptions are allowed. The American Bar Association also recommends that all automatic exemptions be eliminated (ABA, 1983, Section 6 at 60). Further research is needed to examine the effect of occupational exemptions on minority representation.

Stage 7: Voir Dire

The seventh stage of jury selection is *voir dire,* a process in which prosecuting and defense attorneys become the legally active agents involved in the selection of final jurors. Depending on the jurisdiction and the complexity of the cases or in cases involving extensive pretrial publicity, the length of *voir dire* varies. For instance, the Hillside strangler trial in Los Angeles, which had had massive pretrial publicity, took 49 days of *voir dire* and jury selection (Brodie, 1982). Generally, *voir dire* may be as brief as 20 minutes or as long as 8 hours for an average trial (Hans & Vidmar, 1986). A federal court study revealed that judges require an average of 30 minutes for *voir dire* when they conduct *voir dire* alone (Bermant & Shapard, 1981). In New York, lawyer-conducted *voir dires* average 12.5 hours, and some of them last up to six weeks, being as long as the trial itself in 20% of cases (Kaufman, 1984).

In many states, *voir dire* is conducted by attorneys, and in others it is carried out by the judge.[7] The most immediate factor that determines whether a prospective juror will be retained in the jury box is the peremptory challenge, a process used by both sides to remove, without cause (or stating the cause and showing that it is other than racial exclusion), "objectionable" prospective jurors (*Batson v. Kentucky,* 106 S.Ct. 1712 1986). This challenge is usually followed by challenges for specific, demonstrable cause.[8]

By proving a juror's bias to the judge's satisfaction in *challenges for cause* and setting the number of peremptory challenges that attorneys may use and how they are exercised, these methods coalesce in a way that defines the balance of the impaneled jurors. In California, typical of most states, four statutory situations authorize a challenge of prospective jurors *for cause:* (1) if a juror is related to a party to the litigation; (2) if a juror has a unique interest in the subject matter; (3) if a juror has served in a related case; and (4) if the juror has a "state of mind" preventing her or him from acting impartially and without prejudice (Colson, 1986; Ginger, 1984).

Evidence shows that despite its explicit objective of exposing juror biases in order to identify and obtain impartial jurors, *voir dire* may elicit, accentuate, and enlarge the jury's bias. In criminal cases, the prosecution tends to look for prospective jurors with certain characteristics, such as being middle-aged, middle-class, and white. This type of juror is assumed to identify with the government rather than with the defendant, and to be more likely to convict. Defense attorneys tend to look for jurors who are without extreme views and who are least "offensive" to juror sensitivities and biases (Brady, 1983; Simon, 1980, p. 242; Van Dyke, 1977, pp. 152–160).

In civil cases, certain juror characteristics are sought by both sides. In the case of property and personal injury cases brought by those with lesser socioeconomic power against those with greater status and wealth, the jurors found to favor defendants tend to be clerks, business people, or professionals, and of Protestant, Scandinavian, German, and "old American ethnic" stock, several family generations having been born in the United States. Those found to favor the plaintiffs tend to be skilled laborers with foreign ethnic origins, such as Polish, Irish, African, Jewish, or Italian (Simon, 1980, p. 35).[9] Thus, contrary to the statutory requirement that the jury meets the test of representing a fair cross section of the community (U.S., 1968, Section 1861; CA, 1981, Section 197), *voir dire* becomes the attorneys' fight to enlarge the jury's bias toward their clients and thereby undermines jury representativeness (Alvarez, 1982; Saltzburg & Powers, 1982; Silas, 1983).

Minority representation is also severely affected by *voir dire*. The effects of peremptory challenges on participation by racial minorities (i.e., the discriminatory use of peremptory challenges to eliminate minority individuals from becoming jurors) have been documented in a number of prominent cases:

1. *The trial of Black Panther Huey P. Newton in 1968*. The prosecution used 3 of its 15 peremptory challenges against blacks, to eliminate all but one black from the resulting jury panel. When four alternates were picked, the prosecution used 5 of its 6 peremptory challenges against blacks to eliminate all black jurors on the *venire* that would potentially try the case (Blauner, 1972).

2. *The trial of Angela Davis in 1972*. The prosecution used a peremptory challenge to eliminate the only black on the *venire*. When alternates were picked, the prosecution challenged a native American, the only nonwhite to reach the jury box (Aptheker, 1975; Major, 1973; Simon, 1980).

3. *The trial of the Harrisburg Seven in 1972.* The prosecution challenged two blacks and four whites who expressed antiwar or other liberal viewpoints. The defense then used its 28 challenges to eliminate jurors with prosperous backgrounds and other well-established jurors characterized by conservative views (O'Rourke, 1972).

4. *The Joan Little trial in 1975.* The prosecution in the 1975 murder trial of Joan Little used eight of its nine peremptory challenges to eliminate black jurors from the jury (Reston, 1977).

The systematic exclusion of racial minorities is not restricted to political and prominent trials. For example, in 53 criminal trials between 1972 and 1973 in the U.S. District Court, Eastern District of Louisiana, the federal prosecution used 68.9% of its challenges against black jurors, although blacks constituted only about a quarter of the eligible jurors on the *venire*. Similarly, in the federal court of the Western Division of the Western District of Missouri, 70 black jurors appeared for service in 15 trials involving black defendants in 1974. Of these, 57 (81.4%) were peremptorily challenged by the prosecution. This happened even though trials were held in federal courts where voting registration lists were the sole source of the eligible population, so that blacks and other racial minorities were already underrepresented in the pool.

Of course, peremptory challenges are directed not only at racial minorities, but also at groups that are seen as being favorable to the opposing side. In the Mitchell–Stans conspiracy trial in 1974, for instance, the defense used its 20 peremptory challenges to eliminate all jurors with a college education from the jury (Arnold, 1974; Zeisel & Diamond, 1976). In the Spock trial in 1968, the prosecution used two peremptory challenges against women and one against a black man; the result was a jury of all white men. Women were obviously a target in this trial of a prominent doctor who had written influential books on how mothers should care for their young children (Mitford, 1969, pp. 96–100).

During most *voir dire* screenings, opposing attorneys use their subjective and intuitive senses to evaluate prospective jurors. Unless the case has political or racial notoriety, such as the Joan Little case, attorneys often rely on their intuitive judgment of the psychological and behavioral patterns of prospective jurors rather than scientific research. One of the most important observations is that prosecutors are more likely than defense attorneys to peremptorily challenge minorities to remove them from the jury. Because many defendants in criminal trials are in fact minorities, it is likely that prosecutors view prospective minority jurors as being sympathetic to the defendant; or some minority jurors may be seen by prosecutors as inherently criminal because of their race (Hans & Vidmar, 1986; The case for black juries, 1970). Whatever the reason, prosecutors often rely on their own intuitive and subjective evaluations in exercising peremptory challenges, and most potential minority jurors realize that they will be challenged. This realization undoubtedly has a demoralizing effect on jurors and discourages people from making the sacrifices required for jury duty. Thus, the exercise of peremptories gives attorneys vast power to shape the racial and class balance of the jury, which, as a result, seldom resembles a fair cross section of the community, especially when racial and ethnic minorities are systematically excluded.

On the federal grand juries, jurors are *rarely* a fair cross-section of the community.[10] Women, racial minorities, those with less education, younger persons, and those with low socioeconomic status are systematically underrepresented on grand juries (Carp, 1982; Diamond, 1980; Van Dyke, 1977).[11]

Stage 8: The Jury Box

Once *voir dire* is completed, the jurors finally enter the jury box, and their alternates are assembled for call in case of need. During its term in the box, the jury is put to work: (1) selecting a jury foreperson; (2) listening to evidence; (3) reviewing evidence and instructions; (4) identifying the jurors' verdict preferences; (5) checking whether a verdict-rendering quorum has been reached; (6) assessing progress toward consensus; and (7) requesting additional instructions if progress toward a verdict is impeded by disagreement or confusion concerning the law or the evidence in the case (Hastie *et al.*, 1983, pp. 24–26; Kraft, 1982).

The position of the foreperson in jury deliberations is foremost in influencing the outcomes of jury room deliberations. Becoming a jury foreperson is significantly associated with gender, race, and social class background (Deosaran, 1981, p. 311; Nemeth, 1976). Jury forepersons tend to be male and of higher social economic status. They also dominate the jury, using approximately one quarter of the total jury discussion time, far more than the average juror (Simon, 1967; Strodbeck, James, & Hawkins, 1957).

Nietzel and Dillehay (1986, pp. 55–57) examined the composition of juries in relation to forepersons, using criminal trial data in Fayette County Circuit Court (Kentucky) in 1973. Jurors who served once as forepersons were more likely to serve in that capacity again ($p < .001$); forepersons had generally had more experience in jury service than other jurors; and 89% of forepersons were men, whereas males comprised 56% of the jurors in the general pool. In addition, previous jury experience of the foreperson correlated significantly with the severity of the sentence recommended by the jury. A survey of 179 trials in San Diego also revealed that, although 50% of the jurors were male, 90% of the forepersons were male (Kerr & Bray, 1982).

Although, in principle, all jurors are assumed to be equal participants in the jury's decision-making process, this egalitarian ethic is seldom realized. Despite the forces designed to place all jurors on an equal footing and to neutralize individual differences, dominant hierarchies develop that reflect social status differences. The unequal distribution of resources among the 12 jurors in the jury box is also found and reflected in the selection of the jury forepersons. Forepersons then have the greater propensity to exert significant influence on the outcome of the trials.

Two cases offer typical examples of jury trials in which the verdicts were a product of significant influence exerted by the race and class of the jury forepersons: (1) the Mitchell–Stans trial and (2) one of the Huey P. Newton trials.

In United States v. Mitchell (Nos. 75-1381, 75-1382, 75-1384, 76-1441 [DC Cir 1976]), John Mitchell, former U.S. Attorney General, and Maurice Stans, former U.S. Secretary of Commerce, were put on trial in the Federal District Court for the Southern District of New York. The major charge against the defendants was conspiracy to impede a Securities and Exchange Commission investigation of Robert L. Vesco, a financier and a fugitive at the time of the trial, in return for a $200,000 cash contribution to President Nixon's campaign.

One hundred and ninety-six prospective jurors were examined before a jury of nine men and three women was finally chosen. During *voir dire,* the defense used its 20 peremptory challenges to eliminate all persons with a college education from the 12-person jury. Subsequently, when a vacancy appeared, one college-educated person who had been selected as an alternate joined the jury (Arnold, 1974). The jurors were a bank teller, a steel cutter, a telephone installer, a Western Union messenger, a mail room supervisor, a post office supervisor, a city highway-department employee, a shipping-clerk supervisor, a subway conductor, an insurance company clerk, and an elderly retired lady who became ill and was replaced by a vice president of the First National City Bank, Andrew Choa.

The role played by Choa, particularly during the deliberation, was so significant that it changed the outcome of the trial. Sequestration was almost unbearable for the 12 jurors, and Choa took his fellow jurors occasionally to the movies and to the St. Patrick's Day parade; he loaned them baseball bats for playing games and, in effect, became the jury's "social director." Although the members of the jury were divided eight to four on their first ballot, Choa, who was one of the four jurors voting for acquittal, persuaded the jury at several points to have the testimony as well as the judge's instructions reread. Both defendants were acquitted on all counts (Zeisel & Diamond, 1976, p. 162).

Another significant case involving the role of a jury foreperson was one of the Huey Newton trials. In *California v. Newton* (8 Cal. App. 3d 359, 87 Cal. Rptr. 394 1970), Huey Newton, a founder of the Black Panther Party in Oakland, California, was accused of shooting and killing a police officer. Two trials had resulted in hung juries, but a third trial produced a different result, primarily because of a black jury foreperson, David Harper, an upper-middle-class banker working for the Bank of America, a conservative financial institution in San Francisco.[12]

Before the selection of the jury, social scientists testified for two days, claiming that the jury selection system violated the 14th Amendment because the procedure systematically excluded low-income groups, young people, and, most important, blacks. The judge, however, ruled that a defendant could receive a fair trial under the prevailing system of jury selection. Attorneys then spent two weeks selecting jurors who would favor their clients. The prosecutor's peremptory challenges were directed toward excluding three groups: (1) blacks; (2) Berkeley residents—then known as extreme radicals; and (3) persons who opposed the death penalty (Blauner, 1972; Ginger, 1969). The prosecutor used 21 challenges in all, 15 in selecting the regular jury and 6 for alternates.[13] The defendant's challenges were directed toward excluding people from white suburban areas and middle-aged or elderly persons, because it was believed that young jurors would be more sympathetic to the black movement (Ginger, 1969).

In the jury selection stage, the defense accepted Harper, the only black juror to survive the *voir dire,* because "Harper was a strong personality and the defense was beginning to infer that he might be, or become, sympathetic to their case. In the informal camaraderie among prospective jurors the black banker was developing into a social leader" (Blauner, 1972, p. 246). Harper was also accepted by the prosecutor because the prosecutor saw him as being a highly assimilated "white" African-American who was solidly middle-class, lived in a primarily white section of Oakland, and worked for a conservative institution, the Bank of America. The prosecutor made an elementary mistake that one close observer pointed out: "He [the prosecutor] was evidently unaware that racial nationalism and political militancy are perhaps more likely to be the products of the ambiguous status and identity conflict of today's middle-class blacks than of the more oppressed condition of lower-class ghetto dwellers" (Blauner, 1972, p. 247).

The profile of the jury was 7 women and 5 men; 11 whites and 1 black; a laboratory technician, a housewife, an engineer, a secretary, a junior executive secretary, a bookkeeper, a bologna slicer, a drugstore clerk, a machinist, a bank lending official, a bank trust official, and a landlady. Harper, the black bank lending official, eventually became the jury foreperson.

David Harper then became the strong man of the jury and the leading influence. Although the prosecutors had been overconfident about the strength of the case, with the evidence against the defendant pointing to first-degree murder, the black foreperson was successful in influencing the other jurors toward a more favorable trial outcome (Blauner, 1972, p. 248). After four days of deliberating, the jury found Huey Newton guilty of voluntary manslaughter, not murder. They found him not guilty of assault with a deadly weapon. The judge sentenced Newton to 2–15 years. Then, on May 29, 1970, the California Appeals Court reversed the decision, and the government opted not to appeal (*California v. Newton*, 8 Cal. App. 3d 590 1970).

These two cases illustrate the powerful and intertwined relationship between the racial and socioeconomic backgrounds of jury forepersons and jury verdicts.

The outcome of jury trials may also be influenced by other legal and extralegal factors. Besides the background variable of jury forepersons, factors such as the sex of the defendant, the type of attorneys, and the existence of accomplices, for instance, influence prosecutors' decisions to try cases and the court tactics used. The sex of the offender and the race of the victim influence both juries and judges as well (Foley & Powell, 1982). Thus, jury composition becomes a crucial factor in trial outcome.

Jury research has found that the race, ethnicity, and socioeconomic background of the defendant significantly predispose certain jurors to a certain verdict (Feild & Bienan, 1980; Rokeach & McLellan, 1970, pp. 125–129). There is strong evidence that the racial and ethnic makeup of the jurors and of the offender is related to certain verdicts.[14]

Jury simulation analyses in the 1970s and 1980s also reflected the close and significant relationship between verdicts and jury composition. For example, the jury simulation research evoked extremely severe penalties for interracial rape. There is strong evidence that black men have historically received more severe sentences for rape than white men (Carter, 1979; Hagan, 1974). The U.S. Supreme Court finally declared the death penalty for rape unconstitutional in 1980. Between 1930 and 1979, however, 9 of every 10 men executed for rape were black (Inverarity, Lauderdale, & Feld, 1983). With respect to the association between the trial verdict and the racial composition of the jury, black jurors recommended comparable sentences regardless of the race of the defendant and the victim (Field, 1979). The strong negative reaction to black men accused of raping white women appeared to be limited to whites. When the victim was black, offenders were treated no differently. The unbalanced racial character of juries has therefore contributed to harsher penalties for black men who were found guilty of rape.

Other research has further pointed out:

1. Jurors treated black and white offenders no differently when a black woman was raped; however, when the victim was white, the black defendant was given a longer prison sentence.
2. If the rape victim was physically unattractive, her race had no influence on the sentencing of the black defendant. When the woman was attractive, the black attacker of the white woman was treated more severely than if he had attacked a black woman.
3. There were no racial differences in defendant sentencing for the sexually experienced victim regardless of her attractiveness. However, if the victim was sexually inexperienced and unattractive, the black rapist was given a longer sentence than the white one (Feild & Bienan, 1980, pp. 141–142).

This research has further pointed out that it is possible to predict juror decisions in rape trials by studying juror characteristics. Although rape trials are an isolated case, race undoubtedly is an extremely important extralegal factor affecting verdict patterns.

Another important factor related to the racial composition of a final jury is the authority given to the jurors in deciding the trial outcome. Thirteen states allow juries a significant role in sentencing in noncapital crimes as well as in death penalty sentencing (Neubauer, 1984).[15] Some states give sentencing authority to the jury in all serious criminal cases, whereas others restrict the authority to particular types of cases. In California, for instance, a defendant has the right to be sentenced by the jury. The degree of minority underrepresentation on juries, accompanied by the multiple effects of extralegal factors that restrict full-community participation, has potential repercussions in sentencing. As a result, it significantly influences the perception and evaluation of both the fairness of the judicial system and the legitimacy of jury trials.

Conclusions

The presence of both legal and extralegal factors forces us to question if the jury is one of our most democratic institutions. Jury decision making by ordinary citizens carries a strong notion of democratic legitimacy. But the benefits of democracy can be attained only if the assembled jury is representative of the community. Only by gathering together persons from all sectors of society can we be sure that all relevant perspectives will be considered and that the verdict will represent a unified judgment reflecting the community's collective sentiments and conscience. Both legal and extralegal factors, however, lead to nonrepresentative juries, which are abhorrent to the democratic ideals of a trial by jury. Many factors influence racial composition at every stage of jury selection and set limits on jury participation by minorities.

A number of important variables affecting the exclusion or inclusion of potential jurors are summarized in Figure 3–3. Those who have failed to register for elections and/or with the state motor-vehicle department are automatically excluded from the selection process. Further, the most recent entries on these lists are also likely to be excluded because source lists are updated infrequently (i.e., between every 12 months and every 4 years). Prospective jurors who do not respond to either jury qualification questionnaires or jury summonses are also systematically eliminated from subsequent jury-selection consideration because follow-up procedures are seldom carried out—even in those states where they are mandated by law. Court competition also influences the pool of potential jurors in some jurisdictions. And in the jury-panel stage, excuses provide additional opportunities for summoned jurors to exclude themselves voluntarily. The *voir dire* process then affects jury composition when the opposing attorneys eliminate certain categories of potential jurors, especially prosecutors systematically excluding racial minorities. The selection of jury forepersons is strongly influenced by the racial and class backgrounds of the final jurors and exerts a significant influence on the outcome of jury trials.

The factors outlined here are by no means exhaustive. At every stage at both the federal and the state levels, many elements determine and shape jury composition. The jury and its racial composition are also influenced by both statutory requirements (legal variables) and extralegal pressures, such as attitudinal prejudgments, socioeconomic attributes, demographic characteristics of the parties and the jurors, and other variables surrounding the case. Such extralegal factors often have a decisive influence on the jury's representativeness at every stage of the jury selection process.

How these explicit and implicit factors emerged and gained significance requires a deep historical and theoretical understanding of America's jury system. In the following chapter, we examine the contemporary contours and interpretation of the U.S. jury system from the

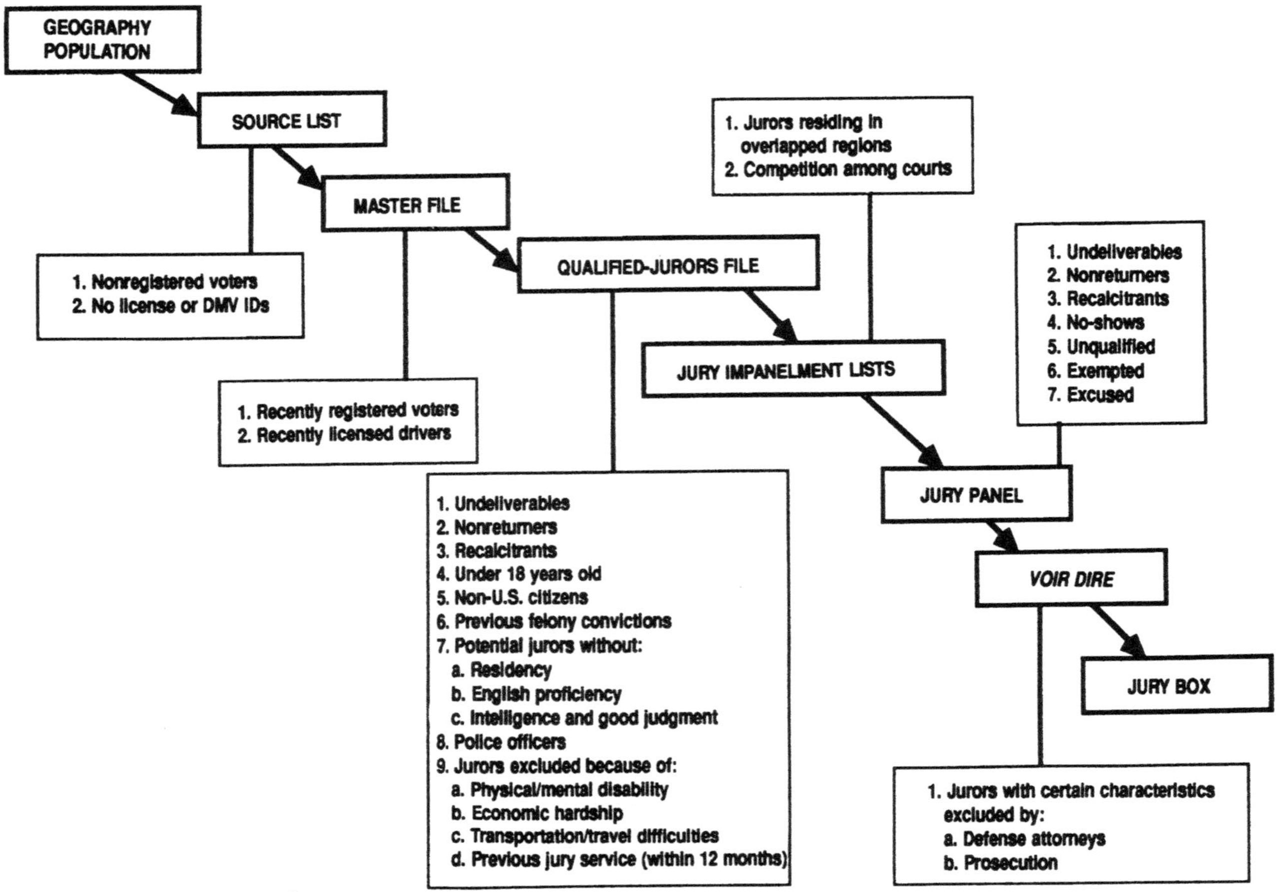

FIGURE 3-3. Potential jurors excluded at each stage of jury selection.

standpoint of the U.S. Supreme Court. Such analyses shed important light on the jury and its powerful influence. They also substantiate the enduring system of judicial control and the disenfranchisement of blacks and other minority groups.

Notes

1. In some counties, parts of the jury selection process have been consolidated. For example, in Riverside, San Bernardino, and Orange Counties in California, the actual qualification-screening process and summons takes place in a one-step process rather than the two-step process as described here.
2. Age is yet to be recognized as constituting a cognizable class. See, for example, *State v. Guirlando* (152 La. 570, 93 So. 796 1922); *International Longshoreman and Warehouseman's Union v. Ackerman* (82 F.Supp. 65, D. Hawaii 1943); *United States v. Fujimoto* (104 F.Supp. 727, D. Hawaii, cert. denied 344 U.SA. 852 1953); *Hernandez v. Texas* (347 U.S. 475, 478 1954); and *Taylor v. Louisiana* (419 U.S. 522 1975).
3. The U.S. Supreme Court does not impose on the states its conception of the proper source of jury lists, "so long as the source reasonably reflects a cross-section of the population suitable in character and intelligence for that civic duty" (*Carter v. Jury Comm.*, 396 U.S. 320, 333–334, 90 S.Ct. 518, 525, 24 L.Ed. 2d 549, 559 1970). Thus, the states are not obliged to use source lists and random selection methods as is the federal system. As a result, the states have retained systems that give authority to jury commissioners to exercise a wide range of choice in selecting jurors including the "key man" system that requires the evaluation of subjective juror qualifications such as "good character," "sound judgment," and "intelligence." (see *Castaneda v. Partida*, 430 U.S. 482, 97 S.Ct. 1272, 51 L.Ed. 2d 498 1977).
4. This act was drafted by the National Conference of Commissioners on Uniform State Laws and approved and recommended by it for enactment in all the states in 1970.
5. The analysis used the number of registered voters in the 1980 presidential election to examine racial representation. With respect to the analysis of the gerrymandered judicial districts, the following cases dealt specifically with the constitutionality of the relationship between the selection of potential jurors and the question of territoriality of judicial districts: *Sandoval v. Superior Court for Los Angeles County* (104 Cal. Rptr. 157, 27 C.A. 3d, 741 1972); *People v. Taylor* (120 Cal. Rptr. 762, 40 C.A. 3d. 513 1975); and *Bradley v. Judges of Superior Court for Los Angeles County* (531 F.2d. 413 1976).
6. To understand excuse criteria in jury selection is important in evaluating the nature of juror representation. For example, the jury selection plan used by the U.S. District Court for the Central District of California provides specific groups whose members may individually request excuse. Those groups are: (1) persons over 70 years of age, (2) actively engaged members of clergy, (3) persons who are not employed and have legal custody of a child under the age of 14 years, (4) actively practicing attorneys, physicians, dentists, and registered nurses, (5) persons who have served as grand or petit jurors prior to their current call in a state or federal court within the past two years, (6) teachers in public, parochial, or private school, (7) a sole proprietor of business, and (8) persons summoned for jury service with showing of undue hardship or extreme inconvenience (Ginger, 1984).
7. *Voir dire*, which figuratively means "to speak the truth," is a preliminary examination

of prospective jurors by attorneys to determine an individual's qualifications, reasons for disqualification, or bias that would eliminate her or him from a particular jury (Belmant, 1977, 1978).

8. There has been considerable debate over a possible reduction in the number of peremptory challenges at the state level. For example, because peremptory challenges are used by the prosecution to exclude blacks from a jury because of their race, Justice William G. Clark, of the Illinois Supreme Court, has called on the Illinois General Assembly to limit the use of peremptory challenges ("Justice proposes fewer challenges," 1984). Other research has also urged the need for an internal check on the misuse of peremptory challenges—see "Voir dire limitations as a means of protecting jurors' safety and privacy: United States v. Barnes," 1980; "Probing racial prejudice on voir dire: The Supreme Court provides illusionary justice for minority defendants," 1981; Nietzel, M.; & Dillehay, R., 1982; and "Sixth Amendment—trial by an impartial jury—the breadth of the basis for excluding veniremen under the Witherspoon doctrine," 1982.
9. Simon (1980, p. 35) also provided the following juror characteristics related to the verdicts: groups viewed to favor the prosecution include men; Republicans; upper-income groups; occupational groups such as bankers, engineers, and certified public accountants and others with positions of petty respectability; and those of Teutonic origin, such as Germans. Groups believed to favor the defendant include women, Democrats, middle and lower economic groups, social scientists, and racial and ethnic minority groups, particularly Latinos and Jews. Hastie *et al.* (1983, p. 122) suggested that attorneys in a criminal defense are advised never to drop an Irish person, because the Irish identify with defendants. When ethnicity is ranked on an emotional scale from high to low in evaluating the level of sympathy to defendants the ranking is Irish, Jewish, Italian, French, Spanish, and Slavic.
10. Grand jury composition is more unrepresentative and undemocratic than that of petit juries. They are chosen by the "key-man" system, that is, from among a list of names drawn up by state supreme court justices (Cole, 1973, pp. 209–210). Judges generally choose prominent businesspeople, lawyers, and others whom they consider influential citizens or respectable civic leaders (Frankel & Naftalis, 1975, pp. 33–35; see also *Castaneda v. Partida*, 430 U.S. 482 1977).
11. An exception is the three kinds of grand juries in the Southern District of New York: (1) a regular grand jury which passes on a great quantity and variety of criminal matters; (2) an additional grand jury, which deals with lengthy and complex investigations; and (3) a special grand jury created by the Organized Crime Control Act of 1970. Research indicates that despite these differences, the selection process for all three types varies very little; their members, however, are drawn from the same pool of citizens gathered to supply petit juries (Frankel & Naftalis, 1975; pp. 43–44).
12. A hung jury is a rare occurrence, largely because of the decisive role of a jury foreperson and the pressure of the dominant majority (Hastie *et al.*, 1983; Kalven & Zeisel, 1966, p. 488). The jury's social complexion is also crucial to the final outcome. Carp (1982; 256–257) noted that in evaluating the verdicts of federal grand juries over 95% of all juror votes were unanimous in keeping with the prosecutor's recommendation for the final outcome of the trial. Federal grand juries' close alliance with the prosecution stems from the fact that federal grand jurors are more likely to come from higher socioeconomic backgrounds and display a greater propensity to identify themselves with institutional ideologies of governmental agencies (Fukurai *et al.*, 1991b).
13. Huey Newton's Oakland trial was heard in a city with a 38% black population, but only 16 (8.8%) of the 180 people in the jury pool were minority members, and only 1 black ultimately sat in the jury box (Keating, 1970, pp. 131–133; Newton, 1968, pp. 202–204).

14. In introducing other demographic and socioeconomic factors, Hastie *et al.* (1983), however, did not find a statistically significant relationship between individual juror characteristics and jury verdicts. Hastie *et al.* recruited approximately 800 people from jury pools in Massachusetts and relied on sixty-nine 12-person mock juries. The "jurors" watched a three-hour videotape of a reenacted murder trial. It was found that, in a murder trial, no single characteristics correlated with the verdicts rendered, including the jurors' age, sex, race, educational attainment, occupation, income, marital status, or political affiliation.
15. See, for example, *McGartha v. California* (402 U.S. 183 1971); *Furman v. Georgia* (408 U.S. 238 1972); *Gregg v. Georgia* (428 U.S. 204 1976); and *Woodson v. North Carolina* (428 U.S. 280 1976).

4

The U.S. Supreme Court, the Constitutional Background of Jury Selection, and Racial Representation

Introduction

The "liberation" of slaves by President Lincoln's Emancipation Proclamation in the course of the Civil War laid a new foundation for the *legal rights* of blacks that then had to be vindicated by political, military, and legal steps. As Union troops advanced into the South, the Proclamation brought freedom to slaves in all conquered regions not specifically exempted from it (Trefousse, 1987). When the dust of war settled and southern blacks were once more being controlled by reestablished, majority-dominant legislatures and the narrow economic structures of sharecropping and company towns, the courts became the only avenue for securing the most nominal human or civil rights *case-by-case*.

Through recognition of slaves' rights to freedom and citizenship by the 13th, 14th, and 15th Amendments to the Constitution during the 1860s and 1870s, slavery was ended, and blacks finally acquired the right to participate in jury service. By passage of the Civil Rights Act of March 1, 1875, Congress made it a crime to exclude or fail to summon a qualified citizen for jury service for reasons of race. The 14th Amendment to the Constitution further guaranteed such equality and extended equal protection to all citizens in the selection of grand and petit juries without distinction of race, color, or previous condition of servitude. Now the law on such matters effectively stated that blacks were no longer the "other" without rights.

Yet, over the last 100 years, litigated cases have overwhelmingly revealed an implicit view of blacks as inferior, reaffirmed by the limitations imposed, or the tokenism used, to influence the jury selection process involving black jurors.

Over the last 135 years the U.S. Supreme Court has used its elevated place to legally define the black race as the explicit "other." "Negroes" were seen by the Court as "property" (*Scott v. Sanford,* 1857) or as an "emancipated" race (*Strauder v. West Virginia,* 1880). They have been called the "inferior race," as opposed to a "superior race" (*Strauder v. West Virginia,* 1880). Their "black color" has been seen as their distinctive mark of inhumanity (*Ex parte Virginia,* 1880; *Carter v. Texas,* 1900). They have been named "a citizen of African race" (*Neal v. Delaware,* 1881; *Bush v. Kentucky,* 1883) and of African "descent" (*Woody v. Brush,* 1891). They have been looked on as people apart, truly another race.

Equally, the U.S. Supreme Court has defined Mexican-Americans as "strangers"—"a separate *class,* distinct from whites" as a group, "those persons of Mexican descent," and "a person with a Mexican or Latin American name" (*Hernandez v. Texas,* 1954; *Casteneda v. Partida,* 1977).

The legal edicts offered by the Court have contended that race is the basis of *property* (owners v. slaves), of *power* (inferiority v. superiority), and of *ethnosocial attributes,* as when the place of origin of one's forbears or their surnames designate another "race." Race thereby becomes a way of casting black and Hispanics as outsiders—outside the bounds of rights to the nation's bounty (Barrera, 1979; Barth, 1969; Bonacich, 1972, 1973, 1980; Feagin, 1984).

Different tactics are used to control racial representation on juries. Some courts have set a quota or a proportional limit on the number of racial minorities permitted in a jury pool or on a panel. In *Akins v. Texas* (325 U.S. 398 1945), testimony revealed that all three jury commissioners in Dallas County *consciously sought* only one black grand juror. Also, in *Cassell v. Texas* (339 U.S. 282 1950), the Court found that jury commissioners had followed a procedure whereby "[they] have *consistently limited* Negroes selected for grand jury service to not more than one on each grand jury." Either by *conscious intent* or the *pattern of limitation,* then, discrimination has been implemented.

Although proportional limitation cases are unique because they typically do not involve a group that is necessarily significantly underrepresented, some courts, particularly in Texas, have considered proportional limitations a *benign* form of discrimination because there is no obviously "intentional" discrimination. In other words, using institutional mechanisms to limit the proportional representation of black jurors controls structurally the inclusion or exclusion of blacks in the jury selection process. Such a quota, or tokenist approach, has been exercised by the courts as an effective method of reenforcing racial discrimination.

Jury selection involving blacks has also been reviewed by the U.S. Supreme Court a number of times. Table 4–1 shows the substantive issues behind Supreme Court decisions involving jury participation between 1880 and 1980, and it shows that (1) the court has treated blacks and Hispanics differently with regard to their disproportionate underrepresentation, and (2) different states have had an unequal number of Supreme Court reviews.

The Supreme Court reviewed 41 cases involving the underrepresentation of blacks *vis-à-vis,* compared to 2 involving Hispanics. Both Hispanic cases were from the State of Texas. Also, the majority of litigated cases involving blacks' underrepresentation in jury service were from southern states such as Georgia (8), Texas (8), Alabama (6), Louisiana (3), and Mississippi (3). As shown in Figure 4–1, the timing and outcome of these cases were also inconsistent. Review patterns by the U.S. Supreme Court were being established by the stop–go sporadic rulings of the Court. Between 1880 and 1909, the Supreme Court reviewed 14 lower court decisions involving black jurors, but no comparable case was reviewed between 1909 and 1935. Though the absolute number of such cases later increased, decisions involving black jurors declined, especially during the 1970s, when the Supreme Court emphasized the aspects of jury selection related to (1) interpretation of the Sixth and Seventh Amendments; (2) the number of jurors to be included in the jury box; (3) the nature of unanimous decisions; and (4) the jury representativeness of women in proportion to their place in the population at large.

Substantive Guidelines

The U.S. Supreme Court has followed specific guidelines in evaluating a jury's representativeness. The Court has specified that three elements constitute an evidentiary basis for determining if jury selection procedures are discriminatory: (1) a showing of intentional discriminatory selection methods; (2) statistical evidence of the underrepresentation of cognizable groups; and (3) strong testimony by witnesses.

Discriminatory selection is based on three conditions: (1) a showing of biased, socio-psychological pressures that lead individual prospective jurors to "voluntarily" eliminate themselves from the jury selection process; (2) a showing of individual racism, such as by a jury commissioner and/or other personnel involved in jury selection in systematically and

TABLE 4-1
The U.S. Supreme Court Decisions Involving Jury Selection between 1880 and 1980, by States

	Underrepresentation of							
State	*Blacks*	*Hispanics*	*Women*	*Wage earners*	*No. of jurors*	*Unanimous decision*	*6th Amendment*[a]	*Others*
Alabama	6	0	0	0	0	0	0	0
California	0	0	1	0	0	0	0	0
Delaware	1	0	0	0	0	0	0	0
Florida	1	0	1	0	1	0	0	0
Georgia	8	0	0	1	1	0	0	0
Louisiana	3	0	1	0	3	0	1	0
Kentucky	2	0	0	0	0	0	0	0
Mississippi	3	0	0	0	0	0	0	0
Missouri	0	0	1	0	0	0	0	0
New York	1	0	0	2[b]	0	0	1	0
N. Carolina	2	0	0	0	0	0	0	0
Oklahoma	1	0	0	0	0	0	0	0
Oregon	0	0	0	0	0	1	0	0
Pennsylvania	0	0	0	0	0	0	0	1
S. Carolina	1	0	0	0	0	0	0	0
Tennessee	1[c]	0	0	0	0	0	0	0
Texas	8	2	0	0	1	0	0	0
Virginia	2	0	0	0	0	0	0	0
W. Virginia	1	0	0	0	0	0	0	0
Total	41	2	4	5	6	1	2	1

[a]The Sixth Amendment to the U.S. Constitution.
[b]Blue ribbon juries.
[c]Jury foreperson.

intentionally excluding members of racial and ethnic minorities from jury service; and (3) a showing of institutional racism, such as by an entire state judicial apparatus that uses structural discrimination to predesign a racially demarcated jury. Statistical evidence of racial and ethnic discrimination may include (1) current and "updated" census information; (2) a large absolute disparity; (3) a substantive comparative disparity; and/or (4) a statistical significance test such as Z scores.[1] The requirement of strong testimony means that a witness, or witnesses, must show a lack of jury service by blacks who have lived in the town or city from which the jurors have been selected (e.g., the testimony of the jury foreperson in *Rose v. Mitchell*, 443 U.S. 545 1979).[2]

In comparing representation in criminal cases and civil cases, the Court has used different criteria. Although a grand jury in criminal cases is supposed to be representative of the community (e.g., *Peters v. Kiff*, 1972, covers a case in which the appealing party belonged to a different

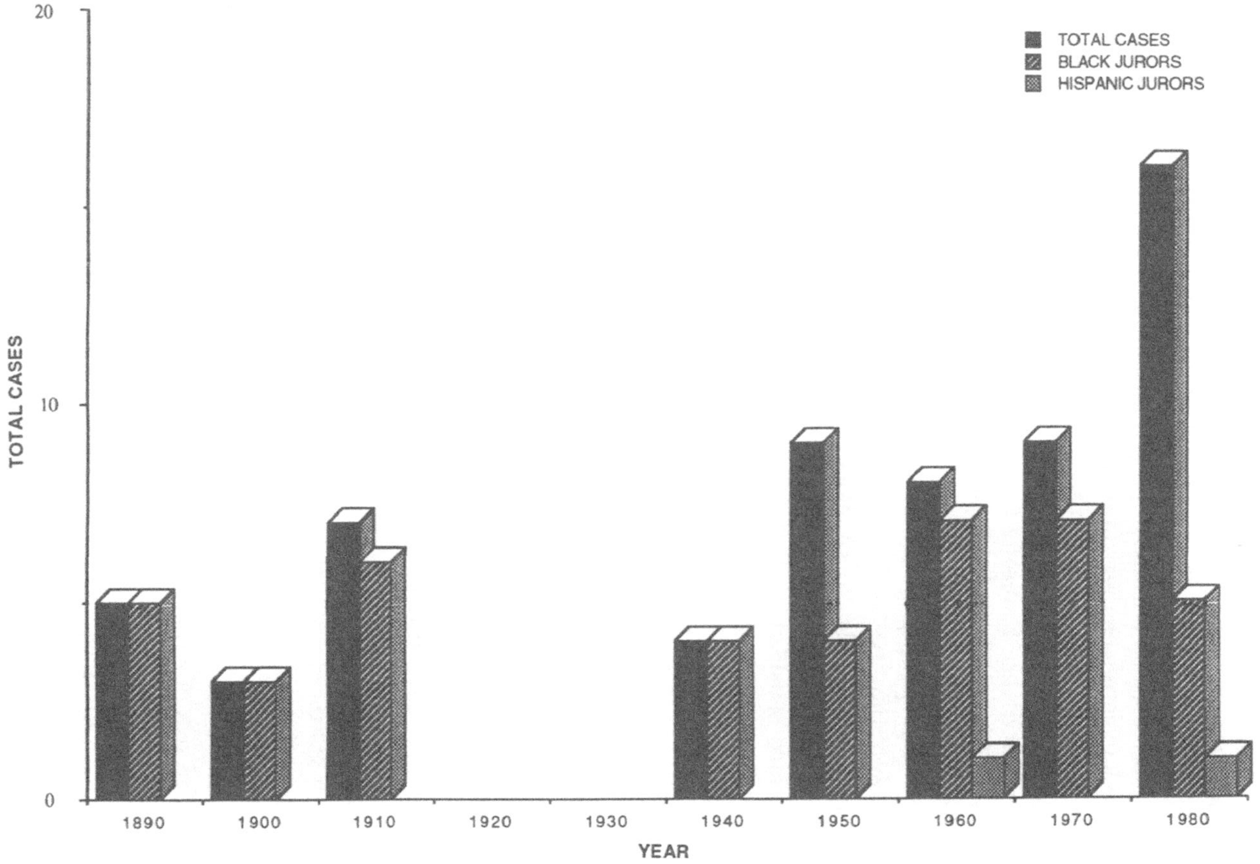

FIGURE 4-1. U.S. Supreme Court decisions involving jury selection between 1880 and 1980.

racial group from the jurors selected), the Supreme Court decided in *Fay v. New York* (1947) that an unrepresentative *blue ribbon jury* can rule against a defendant in civil cases.

The U.S. Supreme Court has been inconsistent in its view on racial representation. One reason for its inconsistency stems from periodic judicial and legislative changes at both state and federal levels. The overturning of the *Dred Scott* decision in the *Slaughter-House* cases, for instance, was due to the passage of the 14th Amendment to the Constitution. The recent reduction of Supreme Court decisions involving racial minorities in jury selection can similarly be attributed to the assumption that the 1968 Federal Selection Service Act, which was designed to standardize the various steps in jury selection procedures, has minimized the discretionary selection exercised by the various functionaries responsible for jury selection. Legislative changes have thus been assumed to limit the exercise of individual and institutional biases in the jury selection process.

Besides constitutional, legal, and statutory changes, socioeconomic and political gyrations have undoubtedly contributed to inconsistent Supreme Court decisions involving jury selection. The influences on jury selection, however, need deeper empirical and theoretical examination.

In this chapter, we examine the U.S. Supreme Court decisions in chronological order. The principal reason for analyzing court decisions sequentially is that the Court's decisions have often relied on previous rulings in similar cases. In addition, such historical analyses reveal the evolution of legal interpretations of democratic principles that underlie the Constitution.

We examine the Supreme Court's rulings between 1880 and 1980. The cases are further divided into six distinct periods: before 1880; 1880–1934; 1935–1948; 1949–1964; 1965–1967; and 1968–1980. Each time frame is characterized by a different social milieu, changes in the legal and statutory status of minorities, and the establishment of different criteria for evaluating racial representation in the jury system and jury selection. We also assess the Court's rulings on discrimination against other groups and examine the degree to which jury challenges involving black jurors have been extended to Hispanics, women, and the poor.

Blacks' Rights before 1880

Both the legal status and the historical background of blacks in America have influenced U.S. Supreme Court decisions. Two important Court decisions, *Dred Scott* (1857) and *Slaughter-House* (1873), greatly affected the status of blacks before 1880, when *Strauder v. West Virginia* was decided. Twelve years before the 14th Amendment added the equal protection clause to the Constitution, the Supreme Court held that because blacks were not United States citizens, they could not sue in U.S. courts and that the Constitution authorized their treatment as property.

Dred Scott, a black man living with his wife and children in St. Louis, complained that John F. A. Sanford, who resided in New York City, had "trespassed" on January 1853 in St. Louis. The Scotts argued that Sanford had assaulted them with force and arms, had imprisoned them for six hours, and had threatened to beat them and hold them in prison. The Scotts then raised the legal question of individual liberty and rights—the question of whether blacks could be regarded as free and protected as citizens of the United States. The Supreme Court not only held that blacks were not citizens but also affirmed that the Constitution authorized their being treated as property. The Court stated:

> The word "citizen" in the Constitution does not embrace one of the negro race—a negro cannot become a citizen—a slave is not made free by residence in a free state or territory—the Declaration of Independence does not include slaves as part of the people—the rights and privileges conferred by the Constitution upon citizens do not apply to the negro race—the constitution should have the meaning intended when it was adopted . . . the Constitution expressly affirms the right of property in slaves. (*Dred Scott v. John F. A. Sanford*, S.C. 19 How 393 1853)

The *Dred Scott* case clearly demonstrated the Supreme Court's interpretation of the Constitution, supporting slave ownership and the subordinate status of blacks in America.

In the *Slaughter-House* cases, five years after the 14th Amendment added the equal protection clause to the Constitution, the Court overturned the *Dred Scott* decision by ruling that blacks may be citizens both of the states where they reside and of the United States. The rights of citizenship were also extended to other racial and ethnic groups:

> While the 13th article of amendment was intended primarily to abolish African slavery, it equally forbids Mexican peonage, or the Chinese coolie trade when they amount to slavery or involuntary servitude; and the use of the word, "servitude" is intended to prohibit all forms of involuntary slavery, of whatever class or race. (*The Butchers' Benevolent Association of New Orleans v. The Crescent City Live-Stock Landing and Slaughter-House Company*, S.C. 16 Hall 36 1873)

The *Slaughter-House* cases demonstrated that the Supreme Court interpreted the 14th Amendment as proscribing *all states* of the union from discriminating against blacks. This 1873 ruling of the Supreme Court also marked the foundation for subsequent U.S. civil rights movements by blacks, including their right to participate on juries.

The Rights of Blacks between 1880 and 1934

Strauder v . West Virginia (1880) set the landmark for recognizing the right of blacks to serve as jurors. The U.S. Supreme Court declared unconstitutional a West Virginia statute explicitly limiting jury service to white males and thus discriminating against blacks and other racial minorities. Justice Strong delivered the following opinion of the Court:

> This is one of a series of constitutional provisions having a common purpose, namely: securing to a race recently emancipated, a race that through many generations had been held in slavery, all the civil rights that the superior race enjoy. The true spirit and meaning of the Amendments, as we said in the Slaughter-House cases, 16 Hall., 36, 21, L.ed., 394 cannot be understood without keeping in view the history of the times when they were adopted, and the general objects they plainly sought to accomplish. (*Strauder v. West Virginia,* 100 U.S. 306 1880)

This was the first black-exclusion case in which the Court took *official notice* of the results of the Civil War and its aftermath, following the adoption of the 14th Amendment, to rule that jury limitations based on race were unconstitutional. The case was a landmark for the civil rights of blacks because it granted partial participation in the administration of justice, and specifically the right to serve on juries.

Although the *Strauder* ruling (1880) demonstrated that systematic racial exclusion from jury service constituted a *prima facie* case of discrimination, this requirement was subsequently changed by (1) requiring proof of discriminatory intentions by jury commissioners to systematically exclude blacks or (2) requiring extensive statistical evidence of racial discrimination. Nevertheless, for the first time in American history, the Court recognized the right of blacks to participate in the judicial decision-making process.

During the 55 years following the *Strauder* decision, until *Norris v. Alabama* in 1935, the Court was reluctant to review jury challenges except in extreme situations. At the end of the Reconstruction era, this reluctance was clearly demonstrated, when *Plessy v. Ferguson* (163 U.S. 537 1896) proclaimed the justice of "separate but equal" facilities (Hurst, 1977). As the Court found that racially separate but equal facilities did not violate the 14th Amendment, segregation *per se* was not prohibited by the Constitution. After this decision, it is not surprising that the Court seemed less than eager to find opportunities to increase black representation on juries. Reluctance to recognize blacks' rights to be represented as peers of another black person was also reflected in the Supreme Court's review in *Thomas v. Texas* (1909). The Thomas case inhibited blacks from bringing suit because it laid down stringent requirements for raising discrimination issues. Despite the severe underrepresentation of blacks on juries, the Court affirmed a lower court decision that there was no unconstitutional discrimination in Texas (*Thomas v. State*, 49 Tex. Cr.R. 633, 95 S.W. 1069 1906). Chief Justice Fuller delivered the following opinion of the court:

> Indeed, there was a negro juror on the grand jury which indicted plaintiff in error, and there were negroes on the venire from which the jury which tried the case was drawn, although it happened that none of them were drawn out of the jury box.
>
> The [Texas] court said "It may be that the jury commissioners did not give the negro race a full *pro rata* with the White race in the selection of the grand and petit jurors in this case; still this would not be evidence of discrimination. If they fairly and honestly endeavored to discharge their duty, and did not in fact discriminate against the negro race in the selection of the jury lists, then the Constitution of the United States has not been violated." (*Thomas v. Texas* 212 U.S. 278 1909)

The case demonstrated that as long as even one black was involved at any stage of the jury selection process, the Court would rule that the actual jury had been put in the box in conformity with the constitutional requirement of a fair representation of the community. So significant was this decision that the Supreme Court did not hear another jury selection challenge until 1935.

The New Era of Jury Challenges: 1935 to 1948

Twenty years later, jury challenges entered a new era, when *Norris v. Alabama* (1935) demonstrated that, once the accused had established a *prima facie* case of discrimination, the burden of proof shifted to the prosecution to explain the *de facto* discrimination. Statements by jury commissioners that they had had no intent to discriminate were no longer considered sufficient to nullify a showing of apparent discrimination. The Supreme Court held that "action of state through legislative, courts, or executive or administrative officers in excluding all negroes, solely because of race or color, from serving as grand or petit jurors in criminal prosecutions against negroes, denies equal protection contrary to the 14th Amendment" (*Norris v. Alabama*, 294 U.S. 587 1935). The case also laid the ground for the use of testimony and census information in efforts to support the evidence of racial discrimination. Chief Justice Hughes, referring to the facts and evidence before him, delivered the following opinion of the Court:

> In 1930, the total population of Jackson County [Alabama], where the indictment was found, was 36,881, of whom 2,688 were negroes. The male population over twenty-one years of age numbered 8,801 and of them 666 were

> negroes . . . . It appeared that no negro had served on any grand or petit jury in that county within the memory of witnesses who had lived there all their lives. Testimony of that effect was given by men whose ages ran from fifty to seventy-six years. Their testimony was uncontradicted. It was supported by the testimony of officials. (*Norris v. Alabama,* 294 U.S. 591 1935)

The *Norris* case enumerated three important guidelines for evaluating jury challenges: (1) The state held the obligation and responsibility to explain underrepresentation once a *prima facie* case of discrimination was established; (2) the testimony of jury commissioners that they had no intent to discriminate was not in itself sufficient to overcome this presumption; and (3) census information could be used to support the evidence of racial exclusion.

Much of the litigation that followed *Norris v. Alabama* (1935) examined the question of what constitutes a *prima facie* case of discrimination and what the state must do to rebut such a case. Since 1935, the Supreme Court has ruled in favor of challenges in many instances, yet always requiring extensive proof of a uniform selection scheme that had resulted in a systematic and arbitrary exclusion of blacks. For example, the Supreme Court reversed the conviction of a defendant for rape on the grounds that the defendant had been denied equal protection of the law in violation of the 14th Amendment, where "negroes for *a long period* had been excluded from jury service in the county solely on account of their race or color" (*Hollins v. Oklahoma,* 295 U.S. 394 1935).

The Court has also examined both numerical underrepresentation and other factors in establishing a *prima facie* case of racial discrimination. In *Hale v. Kentucky* (1938), for instance, the Court reversed one conviction by stating that

> 8,000 of the county's population of 48,000 were negroes, that assessors' books contained names of about 700 negroes qualified for jury service, that jury commissioners filled the wheel for jury service for 1936 with between 500 and 600 names exclusively of white citizens, that no negroes had been summoned for grand or petit jury service from 1906 to 1936, and that for many years before 1936 no negroes had served on juries in federal court, showed a systematic or arbitrary exclusion of negroes from jury list solely because of their race or color. (*Hale v. Kentucky* 303 U.S. 613 1938)

The Supreme Court further held in *Pierre v. Louisiana* (306 U.S. 354 1939) that the petitioner's evidence, based on numerical figures and court officers' evidence about systematic exclusion of blacks, was sufficient to establish a *prima facie* case of discrimination. The Supreme Court found that "systematically, unlawfully and unconstitutionally [excluding] negroes from the Grand or Petit Jury . . . for at least twenty years" constituted a basis for establishing *prima facie* racial discrimination.

Since 1935, the Supreme Court has decided an average of one comparable case each year and has ruled in favor of the appellants. The Supreme Court decision in *Smith v. Texas* (1940) demonstrates the Court's approach to jury challenges in the years after the Depression and World War II. The facts of the case are almost identical to those in *Thomas v. Texas* in 1909. However, the decision was exactly opposite, this time favoring the defendant. Both cases took place in Harris County, Texas, and both cases challenged the racial composition of the grand jury that had indicted the defendant. Texas grand jurors were selected by the jury commissioners, who prepared a list of sixteen names. The opinion of the Court, delivered by Justice Black, stated that, when black grand jurors were listed, they almost invariably appeared as Number 16, and Number 16 was never called for service unless it proved impossible to obtain the required jurors from the first 15 names on the list. Between 1931 and 1938, the service of black grand jurors had been as follows: 1931, one; 1932, two; 1933, one; 1934, one; 1935, none; 1936, one; 1937, none; and 1938, none (*Smith v. Texas,* 311 U.S. 129 131 1940). In the same period, 379 whites served as grand jurors. Further, it was found that *the same individual had served in three separate instances.*[3]

Although the testimony of the jury commissioners indicated that they had had no intention of discriminating, the Court held that this lack of intention was insufficient to overcome the presumption of such discrimination. Justice Black, writing the opinion of the Court, expressed concern about the discretionary power given to the jury commissioner in jury selection:

> Here, the Texas statutory scheme is not in itself unfair; it is capable of being carried out with no racial discrimination whatsoever. But by reason of the wide discretion permissible in the various steps of the plan, it is equally capable of being applied in such a manner as practically to proscribe any group thought by the law's administrators to be undesirable. And from the record before us the conclusion is inescapable that it is the latter application that has prevailed in Harris County. (*Smith v. Texas,* 311 U.S. 130 131 1940)

This was the first Supreme Court decision expressly stating that the jury must be representative of the community. The Court held that "it is part of the established tradition in the use of juries as instruments of public justice that the jury be a body truly representative of the community" (*Smith v. Texas,* 311 U.S. 130 1940).

The Criterion of "A Fair Cross Section of the Community"

Inconsistent with both earlier and later Supreme Court decisions, *Atkins v. Texas* (1945) provided a unique halfway station of dissembling logic. L. C. Atkins, a black person, had been convicted of murder with malice by judgment of the Criminal District Court of Dallas County, Texas. The defense then presented substantive evidence that the grand jury was not a cross section of the community. The defense claimed racial discrimination, charging that whereas Dallas County was 15.5% black and an average of 1.9 blacks should have served on each 12-person grand jury panel, no more than 1 black had ever been selected, and only 1 black was on the indicting grand jury of 12. Testimony revealed that all three of the jury commissioners had consciously sought 1 black grand juror. Nevertheless, the Supreme Court affirmed the lower court's conviction.

Although Justice Murphy, Justice Black, and Chief Justice Stone dissented, Justice Reed's opinion for the majority concluded:

> About fifteen and one-half per cent of the population of Dallas County, Texas, is negro. A substantial percentage of them are qualified to serve as grand jurors. No exact comparison can be made between the White and negro citizens as to the percentage of each race which is eligible. On the strictly mathematical basis of population, a grand jury of twelve would have 1.8552 negro members on the average. Of course, the qualifications for grand jury service . . . would affect the proportion of eligibles from the two races. As one member of the negro race served upon the grand jury which indicted petitioner and one had appeared upon the other grand jury list which had been selected after the decision in *Hill v. Texas*, . . . we cannot say that the omission from each of the two lists of all but one of the members of a race which composed some fifteen per cent of the population alone proved racial discrimination. (*Atkins v. Texas*, 325 U.S. 405 1945)

Black defendants were left without rights concerning jury representation after the *Atkins* case. The case nevertheless provided two important criteria that the Court thereafter relied on in evaluating jury challenges: (1) A statistical figure showing underrepresentation of blacks by itself was no longer adequate to establish a *prima facie* case of racial discrimination, and (2) an explicit statement by the jury commissioners of their intention to limit black representativeness was also inadequate to establish a *prima facie* case. The *Atkins* case marked the beginning of an era in which the Court took an ambiguous stance toward racial discrimination.

Cross-Sectionality and Juror Representation

It seems impossible to reconcile statements in *Smith v. Texas* (1940) with the results in *Atkins v. Texas* (1945). A comparison of various Supreme Court opinions illustrates that *cross section* does not mean a cross section of the community, but only a cross section of whatever segment of the community is legally designated for jury duty. Thus, the phrase "a cross section of the community" is a legal obfuscation that places no real legal limit on restrictive selection procedures.

Continuing its pattern of ambiguity, the Supreme Court affirmed in *Patton v. Mississippi* (1947) that voter qualification is a reasonable requisite for jury service. Patton, a black, was indicted in the Circuit Court of Lauderdale County, Mississippi, by an all-white grand jury and was charged with the murder of a white man. He was convicted by an all-white petit jury and was sentenced to death by electrocution. The testimony revealed that out of the county's total adult population of 34,821 and an adult black population of 12,511, only about 25 blacks met the jury requirement of being a qualified elector. As a result, no black had served on a criminal-court grand or petit jury for 30 years; this, of course, was a strong showing of systematic exclusion of blacks from jury service (*Patton v. Mississippi,* 332 U.S. 463 1947). The Supreme Court reversed the conviction, and the case was remanded.

Three years later, in *Cassell v. Texas* (339 U.S. 282 1950), the Supreme Court found that systematic exclusion of black jurors had been exercised by the jury commissioners. The statement of the jury commissioners that they had chosen only those whom they knew for grand jury service, and that they knew no eligible blacks in a county where blacks made up approximately one seventh of the jury population, proved intentional exclusion, a *prima facie* case of discrimination.

Three Supreme Court decisions that followed the *Cassell* case dealt with discrimination against black jurors in Georgia. These cases focused on racially motivated procedural anomalies of jury selection and explicit means of establishing a demarcation between white and black jurors. In *Avery v. Georgia* (345 U.S. 559 1953), the Supreme Court held that any prejudice and racism on the part of state officials in jury selection constituted a *prima facie* case of discrimination. The defendant, a black, had been tried for rape in the superior court in Fulton County, Georgia, where approximately 60 names for the jury panel had been drawn from a jury box. The box contained the county tax returns, with the names of prospective white jurors printed on white tickets and the names of prospective black jurors printed on yellow tickets. As a result of the systematic selection of white jurors, not a single black had served on a jury. Justice Frankfurter, concurring with the Court opinion stated by Chief Justice Vinson, noted that "the mind of justice, not merely its eyes, would have to be blind to attribute such an occurrence to mere fortuity" (*Avery v. Georgia,* 345 U.S. 564 1953). The *Avery* case also evaluated the use of county tax returns as a source list for jury selection. The county tax returns eliminated approximately 44% of the eligible black jurors in Fulton County. Fulton County had a population of 691,797, and blacks comprised 25%, or 165,814. The tax receiver's digests, from which the jury list was selected, however, had 105,035 whites and 17,736 blacks, or 14%, that is, a 44% reduction in the number of eligible blacks. Then, the jury list for the year in question had had only 20,509 whites and 1,115 blacks, or 5%, a 64% reduction in the number of eligible blacks. Finally, the colored slips were used to differentiate between white and black, so there was no black representation on juries. The Supreme Court reversed the conviction, and the case was remanded.

Two years later, Aubry Williams, a black who had also been convicted in Fulton County, Georgia, of the murder of a white man and sentenced to death, argued a selection bias similar to that in *Avery v. Georgia* (1953). Although a judge of the Fulton County Superior court had condemned the practice of race-designated tickets in the *Avery* case, the *Williams* case revealed that the same county officials had continued to rely on race-designated tickets to select jurors even two years after the *Avery* decision. In addition, although four blacks had successfully entered the jury panel, they had all been eliminated during the *voir dire*. The defense argued that, in March 1953, a panel of 48 jurors had been selected from the 120 jurors who had originally been assigned to the *Williams* trial, but that 13 jurors, including 3 of the 4 selected blacks, had been excused for a cause. The state had peremptorily challenged the fourth black, so that no black had served on the jury of 12 to try Williams. The Supreme Court ordered the case to be remanded.

In the same year (1955), *Reece v. Georgia* provided the opportunity to examine tokenist approaches in setting proportional limits on black jury participation. Amos Reece, a black, had been convicted of the rape of a white woman in Cobb County, Georgia. The defense contended that Georgia's rule of requiring the defendant to challenge the composition of the grand jury before indictment violated the due process clause of the 14th Amendment (*Reece v. Georgia*, 350 U.S. 85 1955). Justice Black delivered the opinion of the Court:

> The 1950 census showed that the county had a White population of 55,606 and a Negro population of 6,224; the same census showed a population of 16,207 male White citizens over 21 years of age and 1,710 male Negro citizens over 21 years of age . . . . There were 534 names on the grand jury list and of this number only six were Negroes. Of the six Negroes, one did not reside in the county and the other five testified in this proceeding. Two were over 80 years of age; one was partially deaf and the other in poor health. The remaining three were 62 years of age. Each of the witnesses had lived in the county for at least 30 years. None had ever served on a grand jury nor heard of any other Negroes serving on the grand jury in the county . . . . This evidence, without more, is sufficient to make a strong showing of systematic exclusion. (*Reece v. Georgia*, 350 U.S. 87 88 1955)

The Court ruled that the mere inclusion of black names on the source list for the grand jury was insufficient to overcome the presumption of racial discrimination. A similar argument was made by the Supreme Court in *Eubanks v. Louisiana* (356 U.S. 584 1958). The Court held, in determining whether an accused black had been denied equal protection of the law by the exclusion of blacks from the indicting grand jury, that "chance and accident alone do not constitute adequate explanation for continuous omission of Negroes from grand juries over a long period of time." The Supreme Court reversed the convictions in both cases.

Jury Representation: 1965 to 1967

The Supreme Court continued its contradictory approach through the 1960s. The last of the ambiguous and controversial cases was *Swain v. Alabama* in 1965. The *Swain* case must be explained at a greater length, as it substantially influenced later lower court decisions.

During 1965–1967, three methods of jury selection were exercised in different states: (1) random selection based on voter registration lists or property tax rolls; (2) a "key-man" procedure whereby jury commissioners solicited and received names of prospective jurors from certain persons (e.g., business or political leaders); and (3) a mixed and somewhat arbitrary procedure, such as was in effect in Alabama at the time of the *Swain* trial. The source lists used included city directories, registration lists, club and church lists established by conversations with other persons in the community, and personal and business acquaintances (*Swain v. Alabama*, 380 U.S. 207 1965).

The *Swain* case involved a challenge of the jury selection procedure of Talladega County, Alabama, brought by a 19-year-old black male, Robert Swain, who had been convicted of raping a 17-year-old white female and sentenced to death. Testimony showed that blacks had made up 26% of the eligible population, and had constituted only 10–15% of grand and petit jury panels during the preceding 10 years. Even though 2 blacks had served on the 18-member grand jury for indictment, no black had served on a petit jury in Talladega County since 1950. Eight blacks had been on the panel that was called for Swain's trial, but no black served; two were excused and the other six peremptorily challenged by the prosecutor. Despite the evidence of systematic exclusion of blacks in the *voir dire*, the Supreme Court held that the defendant had not proved systematic and deliberate discrimination and affirmed Swain's death sentence. Justice White, in writing the opinion of the Court, stated that, as the defense counsel had also participated in the peremptory challenge process, a mere showing that blacks had not served during the specified period of time did not give rise to an inference of systematic discrimination.

One of the great inconsistencies in the *Swain* case resulted from the Supreme Court's interpretation of the concept "a cross section of the community"—the democratic notion reiterated in *Smith v. Texas* (311 U.S. 128 1940), *Glasser v. United States* (315 U.S. 60 1942), and *Thiel v. Southern Pacific Company* (328 U.S. 217 1946). Although Justice White's statement—that proportionate representation was not required on every jury—has been the consistent view of the Court, his acceptance of disproportionate representation contradicted the principles expressed in other cases, particularly *Smith v. Texas* (311 U.S. 128 1940) and *Glasser v. United States* (315 U.S. 60 1942). The Court opinion, delivered by Justice White, held that

> a defendant in a criminal case is not constitutionally entitled to demand a proportionate number of his race on the jury which tries him nor on the venire or jury roll from which petit jurors are drawn. . . . Neither the jury roll nor the venire need be a perfect mirror of the community or accurately reflect the proportionate strength of every identifiable group. . . . We cannot say that purposeful discrimination based on race alone is satisfactorily proved by showing that an identifiable group in a community is underrepresented by as much as 10%. . . . Undoubtedly the selection of prospective jurors was somewhat haphazard and little effort was made to ensure that all groups in the community were fully represented. But an imperfect system is not equivalent to purposeful discrimination based on race. We do not think that the burden of proof was carried by petitioner in this case. (*Swain v. Alabama*, 380 U.S. 208 209 1965)

According to the Court's interpretation of the Constitution, a jury representing a cross section of the community was no longer constitutionally required. Justice White called the disparity in the black population jury representation "small"—although it constituted "10%." Actually, blacks were underrepresented by almost 50%; that is, 50% fewer blacks were in the jury venire than would have been if the selection process had been truly random and fair.[4]

Another ruling by the Court in the *Swain* case gave permission for disproportionate racial composition via the *voir dire* process. The Court said that

> we cannot hold that the striking of Negroes in a particular case is a denial of equal protection of the laws. In the quest for an impartial and qualified jury, Negro and white, Protestant and Catholic, are alike subject to being challenged without cause . . . . In the light of the purpose of the peremptory system and the function it serves in a pluralistic society in connection with the institution of jury trial, we cannot hold that the Constitution requires an examination of the prosecutor's reasons for the exercise of his challenges in any given case. (*Swain v. Alabama*, 380 U.S. 221 222 1965)

This ruling allowed the *voir dire* process to disproportionately influence racial composition; thus, discrimination became justified as long as it was a result of the *voir dire* screening strategy. Also, the Court stated that the prosecutors are not required to provide reasons for exercising the peremptory challenges. This statement is ironic in that past Supreme Court cases had examined racial discrimination in jury selection perpetuated by jury commissioners, jury clerks, and some procedural anomalies such as the use of race-designated jury lottery slips. However, now the proof of racial discrimination was no longer applicable to prosecutors as long as such racism was exercised during the *voir dire* process. As shown in Chapter 3, prosecutors are more likely to peremptorily challenge minority jurors, particularly when the defendant is a member of a racial minority. Regardless of whether such exercises are racially motivated, the decision in the *Swain* case justified a racially disproportionate jury and had considerable impact on subsequent jury-challenge cases.

Institutional Racism

Supreme Court decisions from 1967 to 1980 both questioned and reaffirmed institutional discrimination against black jurors. According to some rulings, blacks could be kept in their place, with limited legal rights, so far as the reasoned opinions of the Court were concerned. At other times, the Court concluded that blacks were obviously being discriminated against in jury *venires*. Thus, it was still uncertain if there would be a return to the past system of control without legal recourse for blacks.

In 1967 the Court reviewed four cases that dealt with the underrepresentation of blacks on juries: one from Alabama and three from Georgia. All four cases resulted in conviction reversals. In *Whitus v. Georgia* (385 U.S. 545 1967), for example, the Supreme Court held that the state had used the same selection procedure in previously litigated cases—*Avery, Williams, Reece,* and many others—that had resulted in discrimination and had constituted a *prima facie* case of discrimination. The Supreme Court held that the State of Georgia had consistently selected the names of prospective jurors from books of the county tax receiver that were maintained on a racially segregated basis. The Court also reversed the conviction of a defendant and remanded the case (*Coleman v. Alabama,* 389 U.S. 22 1967) on the basis of the finding that "up to the times of petitioner's trial, no Negro had ever served on a grand jury panel and few, if any, Negroes had served on petit jury panels." Further, in *Jones v. Georgia* (389 U.S. 24 1967), the appellant provided a comparison of the salient facts in the *Whitus* and petitioner's cases. The comparative figures showed similar results. (Table 4–2 shows the factual comparison between *Jones v. Georgia,* 389 U.S. 24 1967, and *Whitus v. Georgia,* 385 U.S. 545 1967.)[5]

Comparisons of the *Whitus* and *Jones* cases revealed an intriguing fact that the Court recognized in the evaluation of racial representation. The race of the jury commissioners, who were all white, was one of the critical factors that ensured the underrepresentation of blacks in jury service. The composition of the judicial structure itself thus perpetuated the notion of racial supremacy, and such institutional racism was the core of the litigation brought to the highest court of the United States.[6]

In *Jones v. Georgia,* the Supreme Court held that the "presumption that jury commissioners discharged their sworn official duties and that jury commissioners eliminated prospective jurors on the basis of their competency to serve rather than because of racial discrimination did not satisfy the burden of the State to explain disparity between 20% Negro composition of tax digests and venires containing five percent Negroes" (*Jones v. Georgia,* 389 U.S. 24 1967). *Sims v. Georgia* (389 U.S. 404 1967) also attacked institutional requirements in creating disproportionate racial representation in Georgia. The testimony revealed that Georgia still required that both the grand and petit jury lists be drawn from county tax digests, which continued to list taxpayers by race. In both cases, the Court reversed the convictions, and the cases were remanded.

Carter v. Jury Commission of Greene County (1970) also specifically examined institutionalized racism and its operation, which allegedly involved the county jury commissioners, their clerk, the local circuit court judge, and even the governor of Alabama. This case is important because it became the first Supreme Court case that allowed a group of citizens

TABLE 4-2

Whitus *and* Jones *U.S. Supreme Court Decisions*[a]

Variables	Whitus	Jones
Eligible populations	42.6% Negro[b]	30.7% Negro
Jury commissioners	Whites	Whites
Source of juror names	Tax digests, which separated and identified on the basis of race	Three tax digests, which separated and identified on the basis of race
Taxpayers	27.1% Negro	19.7% Negro
Negro jurors	9.1% grand jury *venire* 7.8% jury *venire*	5.0% of jury list and box *venire* (1 Negro was on the grand jury that indicted the petitioner)

[a]From *Alexander David Jones v. Georgia,* 389 U.S. 24 1964.

to bring suit, claiming that they had been denied the right to serve on a jury. The majority of previous cases had dealt with either (1) a jury commissioner's racism in jury selection; (2) the use of segregated source lists; or (3) state jury qualifications. The *Carter* case went beyond the previous case by claiming that the *entire institutional state apparatus* was perpetuating racial inequality in jury selection.

The appellant sought to establish three principles in the case: (1) a declaration that qualified blacks were systematically excluded from grand and petit juries in Greene County, that the Alabama statutes were unconstitutional, and that the jury commissioner was operating a deliberately segregated governmental agency; (2) a permanent injunction forbidding the systematic exclusion of blacks from juries and requiring that all eligible blacks be placed on the jury roll; and (3) an order to vacate the appointment of jury commissioners and to compel the Alabama governor to select new commission members without racial discrimination (*Carter v. Jury Commission of Greene County,* 396 U.S. 332 1970).

The Supreme Court, however, affirmed the state's ruling and decreed that the state should "remain free to confine the selection [of jurors] to citizens, to persons meeting specified qualifications . . . and to those possessing good intelligence, sound judgment, and fair character" (*Carter v. Jury Commission of Greene County,* 396 U.S. 332 1970). Although jury qualification involves various subjective criteria, the Court nevertheless emphasized that, once a state uses discretionary criteria, it has an affirmative duty to seek out persons from all parts of the community who meet those standards. This was a weak solution at best, especially when court officials could set their own qualifications and then apply these standards to exclude prospective black jurors.

The decision in *Turner v. Fouche* (396 U.S. 346 1970), announced the same day as the *Carter* decision, also argued the notion that institutional racism in the judicial system of Taliaferro County, Georgia was closely tied to the requirement of school-board membership given only to freeholders. The petitioner's argument was important because the county board of education, which consisted of five freeholders, had been selected by the grand jury, which in turn had been drawn from a jury list selected by the six-member county jury commission. The commissioners had been appointed by the judge of the state superior court for the circuit in Taliaferro County. The argument here was that all board of education members were white, selected by all-white grand juries, which in turn had been selected by all-white jury commissioners. Because of racial discrimination against blacks, the petitioner alleged that "the board of education had deprived the negro school children of text books, facilities, and other advantages" (*Turner v. Fouche,* 396 U.S. 349 350 1970).

The petitioner sought to establish that the limitation of school-board membership to freeholders violated the Equal Protection Clause of the 14th Amendment. The Court affirmed that freeholder requirement in Georgia was in fact unconstitutional. Justice Steward delivered the following opinion of the court:

> It cannot be seriously urged that a citizen in all other respects qualified to sit on a school board must also own real property if he is to participate responsibly in educational decisions, without regard to whether he is a parent with children in the local schools, a lessee who effectively pays the property taxes of his lessor as part of his rent, or a state and federal taxpayer contributing to the approximately 85% of the Taliaferro County annual school budget derived from sources other than the board of education's own levy on real property. Whatever objectives Georgia seeks to obtain by its "freeholder" requirement must be secured, in this instance at least, by means more finely tailored to achieve the desired goal. We cannot say that the present freeholder requirement for membership on the county board of education amounts to anything more than invidious discrimination (*Turner v. Fouche,* 396 U.S. 364 365 1970).

The Court proceeded to point out two additional considerations that helped establish a *prima facie* case of discrimination: (1) 178 eligible jurors, of whom 171 were black, had been excused because of "their being unintelligent" or "not being upright citizens," and (2) 225 potential jurors, most of them black, had been eliminated from jury rolls because white jury commissioners could obtain no information about them. Taliaferro County was 60% black. However, only 11 blacks had found their way to the 130 member grand jury list. The Court argued that the jury commissioners offered no explanation for the overwhelming percentage of blacks disqualified as not "upright" or "intelligent," or for the failure to determine the eligibility of a substantial segment to the county's already registered voters and qualified jurors. The Supreme Court reversed the case.

Statistical Indices as Evidentiary Proof of Discrimination

The litigations reviewed so far relied on descriptive statistical information to show racial discrimination in jury selection. As the dimension of both the causes and the sources of discrimination involved not only the personal racism of the functionaries in charge of jury selection, but also the state institutional apparatus itself, the Supreme Court began to recognize an additional statistical index that would substantiate the presence of racial discrimination in jury selection.

The measure of disparity used most often in past Supreme Court cases had been *absolute disparity,* the mathematical difference between the racial composition of the population and that of the jury *venire.* This measure does not adequately show discrepancies when the population category being examined is small. Analyzing differences more effectively, *comparative disparity* measures the percentage by which the probability of serving on a jury is reduced for people in a particular category or cognizable group.

In the 1972 case of *Alexander v. Louisiana,* for the first time the Court considered *comparative disparity,* rather than "absolute" disparity as used in *Swain v. Alabama* (1967) and other litigated cases. The formula for computing comparative and absolute disparities is shown in Table 4–3 (Kairys, 1972).

Justice White, writing the Court's opinion in *Alexander,* stated that the drop-off of the black population was 7%—the absolute difference between 21% and 14%—but that this actually consisted of a reduction of 33%. There was also a subsequent reduction to 7% on the qualified juror list, which resulted in a further reduction of 50% (*Alexander v. Louisiana,* 405 U.S. 627 1972).

Table 4–4 shows the percentage of the eligible population, the jury *venires,* and the corresponding figures of both absolute and comparative disparities in six trials reviewed by the Supreme Court. In *Alexander,* the black population was underrepresented in the jury pool by 68%; that is, there were 68% fewer potential black jurors than there would have been if the jury had included a fair cross-section of the community.

Table 4–4 also shows Justice White's calculation mistake in the *Swain* case, when he concluded that blacks were underrepresented by only "10%" (*Swain v. Alabama,* 380 U.S. 209 1965). The actual absolute disparities range from 11% to 15%, and almost half of all eligible blacks had been excluded from the jury roll. Further, the comparative disparity in other trials indicates equally significant underrepresentation of eligible black jurors in jury *venires.* For example, 60%–82% of prospective black jurors were excluded from jury pools in the *Whitus, Jones,* and *Sims* cases. The Supreme Court reversed all of these lower court decisions in favor of the

TABLE 4-3
Absolute and Comparative Disparities

Disparity		*Computations*		
Absolute disparity	=	Proportion of the source that is in specified category	−	Proportion of the population in specified category
Comparative disparity	=	Absolute disparity	/	Proportion of the population in specified category

TABLE 4-4
Comparisons of the U.S. Supreme Court Decisions on Black Representation

Supreme Court decisions	*Black eligible population (%)*	*Jury venires (%)*	*Absolute disparity (%)*[a]	*Comparative disparity (%)*[a]
Swain v. Alabama, 1965	26.0	10–15 (over 10 years)	11–15	42.3–57.7
Whitus v. Georgia, 1967	27.1	9.1 (Grand)[b]	18.0	66.4
		7.8 (Petit)[c]	19.3	71.2
Jones v. Georgia, 1967	30.7	5.0 (general jury list)	25.7	83.7
Sims v. Georgia, 1967	24.4	4.7 (grand)	19.7	60.0
		9.8 (petit)	14.6	81.0
Turner v. Fouche, 1970	60.0	37.0	23.0	38.0
Alexander v. Louisiana, 1972	21.0	6.8 (grand)	14.3	67.9
		5.0 (petit)	16.0	76.1

[a]Underrepresentation of black jurors.
[b]Grand jury venires.
[c]Petit jury venires.

litigants because of systematic and arbitrary exclusion of blacks from jury service.

Another important consideration in *Alexander* was the reiteration of the litigant's significant role in establishing a *prima facie* case of discrimination. Once this case is established, the burden of proof shifts to the State to rebut the presumption of racial discrimination by showing that permissible, racially neutral selection criteria and procedures produced the discriminatory results (*Alexander v. Louisiana*, 405 U.S. 631 632 1972).

The *Alexander* case also established that the process of establishing a *prima facie* case is much easier if a litigant is attacking a discretionary selection scheme because the "opportunity to discriminate" is more obvious.[7] A basic problem in the Supreme Court's ruling in *Alexander*, however, is that it provided no guidance on what constitutes a sufficient State rebuttal once a *prima facie* case has been established. So uncertainty remained about the precise rights blacks had to proportional jury representation.

A White Defendant and Black Underrepresentation

All jury trials that the Supreme Court had reviewed so far had involved black petitioners who were attempting to establish that *their* "peers" had been excluded, claiming violation of the equal protection clause and/or the due process clause of the 14th Amendment. *Peters v. Kiff* (1972) became the first case in which a white petitioner alleged that his indictment and conviction could not stand because blacks had been systematically excluded from both grand and petit juries. The Supreme Court held that regardless of the racial background of the petitioners, the indictment and conviction of a white man could not stand if blacks had been arbitrarily excluded from jury service. Justice Marshall announced the judgment of the Court:

> The precise question in this case, then, is whether a State may subject a defendant to indictment and trial by grand and petit juries that are plainly illegal in their composition, and leave the defendant without recourse on the ground that he had in any event no right to a grand or petit jury at all. We conclude . . . that to do so denies the defendant due process of law. (*Peters v. Kiff*, 407 U.S. 502 1972)

The *Kiff* case thus demonstrated that, regardless of the racial background of the defendant, the violation of the requirement of a "cross section of community" denies constitutional rights guaranteed to the defendant. Thus, the rights of defendants transcend racial barriers.

Discrimination and Jury Forepersons

In 1972, an attack on discriminatory practices by jury forepersons began. In November 1972, James E. Mitchell, James Michols, Jr., and two other men were jointly indicted by the grand jury of Tipton County, Tennessee. The four were charged in two counts of first-degree murder. In the trial, the litigants alleged that both the grand jury array and the foreperson had been selected in a racially discriminatory fashion. The Supreme Court, however, ruled that the plaintiffs had failed to make a *prima facie* case of discrimination (*Rose v. Mitchell*, 433 U.S. 574 1979).

The defense relied on testimony given by persons including those who had served as jury forepersons. By comparing the decisions in *Rose v. Mitchell* (433 U.S. 574 1979) with *Norris v. Alabama* (294 U.S. 587 1935), which had witnesses confirming that no black had ever served as a grand juror in at least 50 to 76 years, the Supreme Court ruled that the evidence presented by the litigants was weak because

> all that we have here to establish the *prima facie* case is testimony from two former foremen and from a briefly-serving present foreman that they had no knowledge of a Negro's having served. There is no evidence that these foremen were knowledgeable about years other than the ones in which they themselves served. . . . It thus was error for the District Court to have concluded initially that respondents made out a *prima facie* case [of discrimination]. (*Rose v. Mitchell*, 433 U.S. 574 1979)

Because of the lack of evidence, the Supreme Court held that the respondents had failed to make a *prima facie* case of discrimination violating the equal protection clause of the 14th Amendment.

Justice White, in the dissenting opinion, however, pointed out the strength of the evidence provided by the respondents. He stated that

> any possible weakness in respondents' statistical presentation was more than overcome by the additional evidence. . . . First, the selection of a foreman is left to the complete discretion of a single person—the circuit judge. . . . Moreover, the particular judge who chose the foreman of respondents' grand jury had never chosen a black in any of his five counties for which he appointed foremen over a 6-year-period. . . . Finally, the judge himself admitted that he had never even considered appointing a black foreman. Although these facts are not necessarily inconsistent with an ultimate conclusion that respondents' foreman was not chosen on racial grounds, they raise, in conjunction with the previously described statistical presentation, a strong inference of intentional racial discrimination, shifting the burden to the State. (*Rose v. Mitchell*, 433 U.S. 592 593 1979)

The *Rose* case, nevertheless, became the first Supreme Court decision that examined the question of the possible discriminatory selection of grand jury forepersons, especially in relation to the underrepresentation of black foremen. As we demonstrated previously, there is little doubt that the race of the foreperson is of crucial importance in affecting the outcome of a jury trial (Deosaran, 1981; Simon, 1967; Strodtbeck *et al.*, 1957).

Discrimination against Hispanics

U.S. Supreme Court decisions involving jury selection have demonstrated the principle that blacks are a clearly identifiable group (or "cognizable class") and that they have suffered substantial discrimination in jury selection. However, other groups have had to prove that they have legally recognizable status and have suffered discrimination. The Court did not recognize Hispanics as a "cognizable group" until 1954, when it reviewed the case of *Hernandez v. Texas* (347 U.S. 475 1954) and reversed the conviction of a Hispanic who had been tried before a jury from which Hispanic persons had been systematically excluded. Chief Justice Earl Warren delivered the following opinion of the Court:

> The State of Texas would have us hold that there are only two classes—white and Negro—within the contemplation of the Fourteenth Amendment. The decisions of this Court do not support that view. . . . The Fourteenth Amendment is not directed solely against discrimination due to a "two-class theory" that is based upon differences between "white" and Negro. . . . Until very recent times, children of Mexican descent were required to attend a segregated school for the first four grades.[8] At least one restaurant in town prominently

> displayed a sign announcing "No Mexicans Served." On the courthouse grounds at the time of the hearing, there were two men's toilets, one unmarked, and the other marked "Colored Men" and "Hombres Aqui" ("Men Here"). No substantial evidence was offered to rebut the logical inference to be drawn from these facts, and it must be concluded that petitioner succeeded in his proof (of discrimination against Hispanics). (*Hernandez v. Texas*, 347 U.S. 478 479 480 481 1954)

A careful reading of the case reveals three types of logical requirements to identify a "cognizable group": It must be (1) a recognized group in the community; (2) a class subject to some community prejudice; and thus (3) a class with a demonstrable need to seek group-based protection. The *Hernandez* decision is thus seen as possibly having extended protected status to other groups in subsequent jury selection cases, such as women, the young and the old, and those with lower incomes and inadequate education (Daughtery, 1975, p. 62).

Castaneda v. Partida (1977) became the second case reviewed by the Supreme Court with respect to Hispanic participation on juries. Though the *Castaneda* case attacked discrimination in the grand jury selection process, three of the five jury commissioners who were charged with racial discrimination belonged to the same Hispanic ethnic group as the litigants.

This case was nonetheless important because the Supreme Court specified (1) three steps for litigating jury challenges for racial discrimination and (2) the question of the "governing majority," that is, whether litigants can claim violation of the equal protection clause of the 14th Amendment in a community in which the elected officials in charge of the selection process are of the same racial group as the litigants.

The Supreme Court specified *three steps* in a challenge of discrimination in the jury selection process: (1) the showing of "statistical disparity" (i.e., absolute and/or comparative disparities, the statistical indices recognized by the Supreme Court in *Alexander v. Louisiana*, 1972); (2) the showing of a discriminatory "method of selection," such as a selection process subject to a discretionary method (key-man or any subjective selection criteria); and (3) the showing of "any other relevant testimony" about how the selection process was implemented (*Castaneda v. Partida*, 430 U.S. 501 502 1977). Once the tripartite showing by the litigants establishes a *prima facie* case of discrimination, the burden of proof shifts to the State to dispel the inference of intentional discrimination.

The question of the "governing majority" in jury selection provides a vital theoretical underpinning of the Court's definition of race relations: In governing-majority relations, it is assumed that "human beings would not discriminate against their own kind" (*Castaneda v. Partida*, 430 U.S.

500 1977). Sociologically speaking, the Court appears to support internal colonial perspectives on racial minorities and cultural pluralism assumptions. That is, different racial or ethnic groups are limited within their independent *subautonomous* and homogeneous political and economic subsystems.[9]

The cultural pluralist position has been argued as an important theoretical model of racial and ethnic relations in the United States (Barth, 1969; Geschwender, 1978; Glazer and Moynihan, 1975; Murguia, 1975). The model suggests that racial and ethnic minorities retain their own cultural and social heritage even though a substantial amount of dominant assimilation in the direction of a culturally homogeneous society is inevitable. The internal colonial model also emphasizes the significant role played by the differences in racial and ethnic identities. Compared with the cultural pluralist position, the internal colonial perspective focuses more on the historical subordination of racial groups and examines the intrasocietal colonial situations imposed by the majority, that is, whites (Blauner, 1972; Casanova, 1965; Cox, 1976; McKay, 1982; Miles, 1980). The Court's definition of the governing majority therefore provides a legitimization of racial discrimination as each racial or ethnic group is held accountable for judicial discrimination because of its different cultural underpinning and interpretation of both legal and judicial structures, which are fundamentally and inherently different from those of the racial majority (Barrera, 1979).

The Supreme Court, however, ruled that the governing-majority and pluralistic view did not apply in the present case because of evidentiary deficiencies, which were "the lack of any indication of how long Mexican-Americans have enjoyed the 'governing majority' status, the absence of information about the relative power inherent in the elective offices held by Mexican-Americans, and the uncertain relevance of the general political power to the specific issue in this case" (*Castaneda v. Partida,* 430 U.S. 501 1977). Thus, the Supreme Court affirmed the court of appeals holding of a denial of equal protection of the law in the grand jury selection process in the respondent's case.

Castaneda v. Partida is also significant because the Supreme Court took judicial notice of the use of statistical significance tests based on probabilities to examine the inference of racial discrimination (*Castaneda v. Partida,* 430 U.S. at 496 n.17 1977). The statistical index modeled by binomial distribution (Z scores) was referred to by the Court in showing the statistically significant underrepresentation of Mexican-Americans on juries. Although statistical significance tests have been cited and used by the Supreme Court and many lower courts, they have never been the sole evidence used in making a decision. Two courts have even rejected them:

Test v. United States, 550 F.2d 577 (10th Cir. 1976) and *United States v. Maskeny,* 609 F.2d 183 (5th Cir. 1980). Although statistical significance tests are not as intuitively comprehensible as the absolute or comparative disparity standards, the Supreme Court indicated that the statistical significance test can be referred to in substantiating the underrepresentation of cognizable groups.

Discrimination against Women

Besides blacks and Hispanics, women have struggled for their right to participate in the court process. From the first Supreme Court decision concerning the composition of the jury in *Strauder v. West Virginia* to the decision in 1979 in *Duren v. Missouri,* the Supreme Court gradually expanded and redefined women's constitutional right to a trial by jury. The exclusion of women from jury trials was inherited from the English common law system, in which women were systematically excluded until 1919. In the United States, after 1920, however, women's organizations such as the League of Women Voters and the National Women's Rights Party took up the jury issue and attempted to improve women's jury participation (see, for instance, *Glasser v. United States,* 1942). By 1975, women were eligible for jury duty in all federal and state courts.

Glasser v. United States (315 U.S. 60 1942) became the important jury challenge case reviewed by the Supreme Court, examining the jury representation of women. The notion of the jury's being representative of the community was reiterated in the Court's decision in the *Glasser* case. The decision in 1942 also provided guidelines for evaluating the cross-sectionality of community representation, a criterion that was later applied to jury challenge cases involving black and Hispanic jurors.

In *Glasser,* the defendant charged that all the women in a particular jury *venire* were members of the League of Women Voters who had received lectures by the prosecutors; thus, potential jurors might share views with the prosecution. The Court held that the recruitment of federal jurors from lists supplied by public service organizations prevented the creation of a representative jury list. The Court further condemned "the deliberated selection of jurors from the membership of particular private organizations," as this would make the jury an "organ of a special class."

Another significant contribution of *Glasser v. United States* was the reiteration of the concept "a cross section of the community" as a standard for jury selection. The majority opinion of the Court by Justice Murphy noted that the officials charged with choosing federal jurors

> must not allow the desire for competent jurors to lead them into selections which do not comport with the concept of the jury as a cross-section of the community.... The deliberate selection of jurors from the membership of particular private organizations definitely does not conform to the traditional requirements of jury trial.... The jury selected from the membership of such an organization is then not only the organ of a special class, but, in addition, it is also openly partisan. (*Glasser v. United States*, 315 U.S. 86 1942)

Justice Murphy noted that a jury selected from the membership of a special class acquired "bias in favor of the prosecution." The *Glasser* case thus described two concise issues that would preserve a representative jury: (1) The jury as a body truly representative of the community needs to reflect a cross-section of the community, and (2) the deliberate selection of jurors from the membership of particular groups or classes violates the notion of a representative jury, preventing full community participation in the judicial decision-making process. These criteria set the standard for jury selection until the *Swain* case in 1965.

The Supreme Court's view of women has evolved over the years. In *Hoyt v. Florida* (368 U.S. 57 1961), a woman was convicted of killing her husband with a baseball bat. She was driven to the murder of her husband by her husband's adultery and his rejection of her. As a defense, she pleaded temporary insanity. However, an all-male jury convicted her of second-degree murder. She challenged the affirmative registration practice in Florida, which required women who wanted to serve on juries to go to the courthouse and formally register, whereas men were automatically registered and eligible for jury service. Because of this discriminatory practice, she complained that she had been denied her constitutional right to the due process of law. The affirmative registration certainly limited women's judicial participation. For instance, in Hillsborough County, where the crime was committed, of the 114,000 registered voters, approximately 46,000 were female. However, only 220 women had volunteered for jury duty through affirmative registration (*Hoyt v. Florida*, 368 U.S. 64 1961). The defense argued that a true representation of women on the jury might have been crucial, as women may have been more sympathetic to the defendant's case. However, the Supreme Court denied her claim and stated, through Justice Harlan, that jury selection in Florida

> has given women an absolute exemption from jury duty based solely on their sex, no similar exemption obtaining as to men.[10] ... Despite the enlightened emancipation of women from the restrictions and protections of bygone years, and their entry into many parts of community life formerly considered to be reserved to men, woman is still regarded as the center of *home and family life*. (*Hoyt v. Florida*, 368 U.S. 64 1961)

The Court's view on women's role as "the center of home and family life" was finally rejected in *Taylor v. Louisiana* (419 U.S. 522 1975). This time it was a man who argued against burdens placed on women under affirmative registration in Louisiana. His arguments were similar to those in *Hoyt*. But this time, the Supreme Court agreed with his argument. The *Taylor* decision, however, did not end the problem of women's underrepresentation on juries because the Court rejected exclusion of all women but upheld the principle of excuses for hardship. Thus, the *Taylor* case suggested that the statute that allowed an automatic excuse to women with children potentially led to the underrepresentation of women on juries. Justice White, in the Court's opinion, stated:

> The States are free to grant exemptions from jury service to individuals in case of special hardship or incapacity and to those engaged in particular occupations the uninterrupted performance of which is critical to the community's welfare. (*Taylor v. Louisiana*, 416 534 1975)

The *Taylor* case still did not provide a solution to women's equal representation on juries because, although the Court supported the law that protected women from discrimination in jury selection, the Court also allowed the state to exercise its discretion in exempting and excusing women.

Nevertheless, the *Taylor* case was reviewed by the Court when a number of significant social changes were taking place, including changes in the perception of the domestic role of women, an increase in female labor force participation, and the Court's expressed desirability for more egalitarian jury representation. These factors contributed to a rejection of the Court's domestic view of women as expressed in the *Hoyt* case and to a reversal of earlier decisions permitting a special treatment of women.

The last significant Court decision affecting the automatic exemption of women from jury duty was *Duren v. Missouri* (439 U.S. 355 1979). After the *Taylor* case, only Missouri and Tennessee provided an automatic exemption for women requesting not to serve. Duren was indicted for first-degree murder and first-degree robbery in Jackson County, Missouri. He challenged that an automatic exemption from jury service had resulted in an unconstitutional underrepresentation of women on his jury and violated the defendant's constitutional right to a jury constituting a fair cross section of the community. The Court's decision relied on the following three criteria to establish a *prima facie* violation of the "fair cross- section" requirement: The defendant must show that (1) like blacks and Hispanics, women were a "distinctive" group in the community; (2) the representation of women in the *venires* from which juries were selected was not fair and reasonable in relation to the number of women in the community; and (3) female underrepresentation was due to systematic exclusion from the jury selection process.

The Court examined the three criteria described above. Justice White, delivering the Court's opinion, stated that, with respect to the distinctive nature of women, they "are sufficiently numerous and distinct from men" and the first requirement to establish a *prima facie* case of discrimination was satisfied. With respect to women's representation, the second criterion, only 15% of impaneled jurors were women; thus, women were not fairly represented in the jury *venire*, and the second requirement was satisfied. The underrepresentation of women was also observed in the earlier stages of jury selection, including a jury wheel, a summons, and finally a *venire*. Thus, women were systematically underrepresented, and the third criterion was satisfied. Those three findings satisfied the requirement to establish a *prima facie* case of discrimination against women. The Supreme Court reversed the conviction and remanded the case.

In a dissenting opinion, Justice Rehnquist insisted that the only winners in the Court decision were those in the same category as Duren, "freed of his conviction of first-degree murder" (*Duren v. Missouri*, 439 U.S. 377 1979). He saw the automatic exemption as an effective method of minimizing the inconvenience of serving on juries and believed that the genders should be clearly demarcated in their chances to serve on juries. He stated, "If the Court ultimately concludes that men and women must be treated exactly alike for purposes of jury service, it will have imposed substantial burdens upon many women" (*Duren v. Missouri*, 439 U.S. 375 1979). Although his view may have rested on a belief that women were still the center of home and family life, future reviews of cases on women's representation in *venires* need to consider the ever-changing roles of women in society. The Court also needs to take such social changes into the consideration in evaluating the criteria for establishing a *prima facie* case of discrimination against women.

Economic Discrimination

Besides discriminating against racial and ethnic groups and women, the Supreme Court also recognized discrimination based on social class position. The first jury challenge case based on economic discrimination that the Supreme Court reviewed was *Thiel v. Southern Pacific Company* (1946). The *Thiel* case also became the first to apply *Glasser*'s cross-sectional standard, examining the jury representation of women. Yet, although the *Thiel* case did not specifically address racial questions, it set the standard for defining evaluative schemata that the Supreme Court later applied to black jury challenges.

The *Thiel* case held another dimensional impact, too. Here the appellant had charged that the policy of the clerk in the federal court of the Northern District of California was intentionally to exclude all daily wage earners from jury rolls. Justice Murphy delivered the Court opinion:

> After demanding a jury trial, petitioner moved to strike out the entire jury panel, alleging *inter alia* that "most business executives or those having the employer's viewpoint are purposely selected on said panel, thus giving a majority representation to one class or occupation and discriminating against other occupations and classes, particularly the employees and those in the poorer class who constitute, by far, the great majority of citizens eligible for jury service." ... Recognition must be given to the fact that those eligible for jury service are to be found in every stratum of society. Jury competence is an individual rather than a group or class matter. The fact lies at the very heart of the jury system. To disregard it is to open the door to class distinctions and discriminations which are abhorrent to the democratic ideals of [a] trial by jury. (*Thiel v. Southern Pacific Company*, 328 U.S. 219 220 1946)

The *Thiel* case added several criteria to those used by the Supreme Court in evaluating jury challenge cases: (1) The notion of "class" used as a cognizable category for elucidating the evidence of discrimination was seen as the same definition applied to racial groups; (2) a voluntaristic view of an individual's competency to serve as a juror was derived; and, therefore, (3) tacit Supreme Court approval was given to the practice of excusing persons for individual hardship. In rendering the Court opinion, Justice Murphy further stated:

> It is clear that a federal judge would be justified in excusing a daily wage earner for whom jury service would entail an undue financial hardship. (*Thiel v. Southern Pacific Company*, 328 U.S. 224 1946)[11]

Although the underrepresentation of a particular class or group is clearly in violation of the equal protection clause of the 14th Amendment, the underrepresentation of individuals who make up the class was seen as constitutional. Here emerged the notion of self-caused disenfranchisement, for which the Court could justify the underrepresentation of a certain class or group through voluntary self-elimination from participation in jury selection. In line with this logic, blacks, as a "group" that falls within one of the 14th Amendment categories for special protection, may be underrepresented because blacks are left with the option to eliminate themselves from consideration for jury service.

A second case involving the underrepresentation of poor persons was *Fay v. New York* (1947), which gave constitutional sanction to the blue ribbon jury. The Supreme Court demonstrated that a cross-sectional standard of the community representation does not apply to a "blue ribbon" jury, which is selected almost exclusively from among the wealthy.

The case set up the Supreme Court's criteria for evaluating jury representation, which it later also applied to black jury-challenge cases. Whereas the Court had reversed the lower court decision in *Thiel v. Southern Pacific Company* (1946), it changed course to affirm the conviction in the *Fay* case. The defendants, Fay and Bove, both vice presidents of labor unions in New York, argued that the blue ribbon jury was unconstitutional for the following three reasons: (1) "laborers, operatives, craftsmen, foremen and service employees were systematically, intentionally and deliberately excluded from the panel"; (2) "women were in the same way excluded"; and (3) "the special panel is so composed as to be more prone to convict than the general panel" (*Fay v. New York,* 332 U.S. 273 1947).

A survey of 2,911 special jurors on the 1945 panel for New York County, Manhattan, was conducted, and the result was presented as evidence of the systematic exclusion of certain persons. There was substantial disparity between the percentage of jurors in each occupation on the jury list of 1945 and the occupational distribution of employed persons or experienced persons seeking employment in Manhattan in 1940. Of 2,644 classifiable occupations, 18.8% of those on the jury list were professionals, compared with 12.1% in the Manhattan work force; 43% on the list were proprietors, managers, and officials, compared with 9.3% in the labor force; 38% were clerical, sales, and kindred workers, compared with 21.3% in the work force; 0.2% were craftsmen, foremen, and kindred workers, compared with 7.7% in the labor force; and most important, no person was included on a jury list from operatives and kindred workers, service workers, laborers, farmers, farm managers, and farm laborers, whereas they made up 49.6% of the Manhattan labor force.

Further, a 1933–1935 study also indicated that the blue ribbon jury convicted at a rate of 83.5% in certain homicide cases, whereas ordinary juries in comparable cases convicted at the rate of only 40%. This was compelling evidence of both disproportionate representation on the blue ribbon jury and a high conviction rate by the special jury. Yet the U.S. Supreme Court majority, speaking through Justice Jackson, rejected the challenge. For occupational and class representation, Jackson noted, "Apart from the discrepancy of five years in the dates of the data and the differences in classification of occupations, the two tables do not afford statistical proof that the jury percentages are the result of discrimination." As to the exclusion of women, Jackson said that "the law of New York gives to women the privilege to serve but does not impose service as a duty. . . . Hence, only those who volunteer or are suggested as willing to serve by other women . . . are subpoenaed for examination." The survey showed, for example, that, between 1933 and 1935, only 30 women had served on the grand jury. Further, the Court said, because the defendants were convicted March 14, 1945, "when the statistics offered here as to relative propensity of the two juries to convict were more than ten years old . . . the conditions which later may have produced the discrepancy in ratio of conviction had long since been corrected" (*Fay v. New York*, 332 U.S. 276 1947).

The Court's nullification of the jury challenge can be characterized by two factors that both the Supreme Court and the lower courts frequently used in rejecting potential jury challenges: (1) the rejection of "outdated" survey or census information comparing the composition of jury *venires* with that of the community and (2) the legitimization of self-selection and self-censorship or voluntary nonparticipation by potential jurors. Thus, those unwilling to serve could be justifiably eliminated from jury service.

Conclusions and Unresolved Questions

In examining U.S. Supreme Court decisions, a cautionary note is in order. The Supreme Court deals only with contested cases, and few jury challenges are subject to Supreme Court review.[12] An examination of Supreme Court decisions provides the significant cases involving jury selection. Yet, such reviews are only the tip of the iceberg of such cases.

The Supreme Court has touched on various theoretical underpinnings of jury selection. Supreme Court decisions in the 1970s, for example, involved multidimensional challenges to jury selection. Included were questions of

1. Interpretation of the Sixth Amendment extending to the state (*Baldwin v. New York*, 399 U.S. 66 1970).
2. Interpretation of the Seventh Amendment, that is, rights of action and procedure in civil cases (*Atlas Roofing Co. v. Occupational Safety and Health Review Commission*, 430 U.S. 442 1977).
3. The size of the jury (*Ballew v. Georgia*, 435 U.S. 223 1978; *Brown v. Louisiana*, 447 U.S. 323 1980; *Burch v. Louisiana* 441 U.S. 130 1979; *Colgrove v. Battin*, 413 U.S. 149 1973; *Johnson v. Louisiana*, 406 U.S. 356 1972; *Williams v. Florida*, 399 U.S. 78 1970).
4. The question of unanimous verdicts (*Apodaca v. Oregon*, 406 U.S. 404 1972; *Brown v. Louisiana*, 447 U.S. 323 1980; *Burch v. Louisiana*, 441 U.S. 130 1979).
5. No right to jury trial for juveniles (*McKiever v. Pennsylvania*, 403 U.S. 528 1971).
6. The representativeness of jury forepersons (*Rose v. Mitchell*, 443 U.S. 545 1979).

Clearly, democracy in the jury system was beginning to emerge.

A review of Supreme Court cases between 1880 and 1980 revealed that the Court often used the terms *class* and *race* interchangeably. The Court has defined *class* mainly on the basis of an unequal distribution of income, status, and occupation. Race relations have often been subsumed under the class definition, however, with an emphasis on racial differences as distinct from socioeconomic categories or ideological considerations. Although the Supreme Court has acknowledged the existence of two levels of racism—(1) individual prejudice (e.g., by jury commissioners) and (2) institutional racism (i.e., by the entire State apparatus)—the approach to problems of racially disproportionate representation is based on the elimination of racism by legal changes (the 1968 Federal Selection and Service Act) or the Court's interpretation of statutory "representativeness." This method is thus based on the assumption that the elimination of ideological prejudice and discrimination at both the individual and the structural levels constitutes the basis for a more racially representative jury.

What is lacking in this analysis of Supreme Court decisions? The answer to this question is to ask what social, moral, economic, and/or political pressures have influenced the Court to include various cognizable classes within constitutional protection over the last two centuries. True, the legislative enactment of amendments and the execution of statutory requirements have taken place at both state and federal levels. But is the promise of a limited or expansive democracy the only ideological criterion propelling the Supreme Court to deny or guarantee the cross-sectionality of a jury for fair trials? And most important, what institutional apparatus, in which economic and political climate, with what types of exterior pressures, define the theoretical underpinning of fair trials, democracy, and the detailed processes of jury selection? Although the Supreme Court has intermittently seemed to operate under the assumption that the elimination of ideological prejudice at both individual and structural levels constitutes the basis for more racially representative juries, are there other theoretical foundations for the approach taken by the federal and state courts?

These aspects of the jury system and jury selection need deeper theoretical and empirical elaboration. It is particularly important to examine empirically the ideological assumptions of the jury system and the structural causes of the ever-enduring system of racially discriminatory juries. In Part II, we examine empirical aspects of jury participation in different stages of the jury selection procedure, the function these procedures serve in a pluralistic society, and the proportional strength of minority participation in jury trials.

Notes

1. Several Supreme Court decisions have cited the statistical significance of racial underrepresentation. However, judicial notice was taken on the basis of probability only, rather than statistical indices (Z scores from a bimodal distribution) as in *Castaneda v. Partida*. See *Alexander v. Louisiana*, 405 U.S. 1972 at 630 n.9 (probability 1 in 20,000) and *Whitus v. Georgia*, 385 U.S. 1967 at 552 n.2 (probability 6 in 1,000,000).
2. For a detailed discussion of expert testimony on jury decisions, see Tandon (1979), Hosch (1980), Hosch, Beck and McIntyre (1980), Morse (1982), and Poythress (1982).
3. Rowland (1979, p. 324) suggested that the nonrepresentation biases in the selection of grand juries and in discriminatory performance in Harris County, Texas, continued to persist between 1972 and 1975. The research points out that, 30 years after *Smith v. Texas*, Harris County grand juries were still typified by the pattern of homogeneous racial composition and rubber-stamp performance (also see Carp, 1974).
4. In reality, the black population was underrepresented in the jury pool by 42%–50%; that is, by using a statistical index called comparative disparities (see Table 4.3) there were approximately 50% fewer potential black jurors than if the jury had included a full cross-section of the community. The underrepresentation of black jurors in the *Swain* case will be reiterated in a later section (see Table 4–4).
5. The table figures are based on the statements from the Supreme Court Recorder, not from the actual case transcript from the lower court.
6. It is not surprising that, in 1967, the same year all four of these causes were decided, Carmichael and Hamilton coined the term "institutional racism" in their book *Black Power: The Politics of Liberation in America* (1967).
7. For example, in *Castaneda v. Partida* (430 U.S. 482 1977), the Supreme Court ruled that, once a *prima facie* case has been established, it is the State's responsibility to rebut the presumption of discrimination by answering such questions as: How many Mexican-Americans listed in the census figures were not citizens of the State? How many were migrant workers and not residents? How many were illiterate? How many were not of sound mind and good moral character? And how many had been convicted of a felony or were under indictment for or legal accusation of theft or a felony? Traditionally, however, litigants emphasized *representation* more than they have attacked a *discretionary selection scheme*.
8. The footnote from the *Supreme Court Reporter* noted: "The reason given by the school superintendent for this segregation was that these children needed special help in learning English. In this special school, however, each teacher taught two grades, while in the regular school each taught only one in most instances. Most of the children of Mexican descent left school by the fifth or sixth grade" (*Hernandez v. Texas*, 347 U.S. 479 1954).
9. These two models appear to support the Court's position, as the Court draws a clear racial demarcation for the function of discrimination.
10. The footnote says that men in Florida could have requested an exemption because of the following limitations: age, bodily infirmity, or being engaged in certain occupations (*Hoyt v. Florida*, 368 U.S. 62 1961). Underscores are added to highlight the Court's view on women's domestic role.
11. In the footnote, Justice Murphy stated, "See statement of Judge John C. Knox in Hearings before the House Committee on the Judiciary, 79 Cong., 1st Sess., on H.R.3379, H.R.3380, H.R.3381, Serial No. 3, June 12 and 13, 1945, p. 4. 'When jurors' compensation is limited to $4 per day, and when their periods of service are often protracted, thou-

sands upon thousands of persons simply cannot afford to serve. To require them to do so is nothing less than the imposition upon them of extreme hardship.' Id., P. 8."

12. Of significance, of course, is how cases are selected for U.S. Supreme Court review. Despite our search of the research literature, our courtroom experience, and historical and contemporary court cases involving the underrepresentation of racial and ethnic minorities on juries, we still have not been able to ascertain, either historically or currently, why some cases are reviewed and others with virtually identical underrepresentation of minorities do not receive any recognition beyond the local superior court level.

II

Analyses of Racial Inequality on Juries

Empirical Issues

5

Anatomy of Economic Excuses

Organizational Resources and Company Support for an Egalitarian Jury System

Introduction

The jury, speaking for the community, is viewed as an essential element of a democratic government that derives its power from the people. Further, the democratic principle of fair and equal participation in the judicial decision-making process underlies the assumption of a trial by one's peers. Although jury service is supposed to be a right and privilege of citizenship, it is often considered a nuisance, and many people do not believe in the necessity of democratic participation in jury service.

There are a number of reasons for the widespread negative perception of jury service. First, jury service frequently represents a financial hardship. In some jurisdictions, for instance, jurors may be sequestered and required to serve for several months continuously. For example, in 1988, 96 federal criminal trials lasted a month or longer, up from 35 in 1975 (Why some trials go on and on and on, 1989). Federal judges held 5,222 civil jury trials in 1986, 335 of which lasted more than two weeks (Tell, 1987). Because of lengthy jury trials, prospective jurors with heavy work responsibilities may fear loss of income. Blue-collar workers in insecure job positions may also face job loss. In fact, many definitely lose income because the daily fee paid to jurors remains minimal, thanks to the underfunding of the court system.

Second, travel to the courthouse every day may pose a problem of distance, time, and costs. For example, parents must find someone to care for children during their jury duty. For others, including the elderly, students, and the sick, appearance at a courthouse on an assigned date may be difficult because of transportation difficulties or conflicts with classes or other scheduled activities. Although jury commissioners may be able to reschedule appearance dates, they seldom do, and jury panels therefore systematically exclude some important sectors and elements of the community.

Third, when summoned jurors appear at the courthouse, a great deal of their time is spent waiting. Of the prospective jurors who appear, a few will serve, and many never sit on a jury. For example, of the 205 jurors called for the 1987 McMartin child-molestation trial in Los Angeles, 12 jurors and 6 alternatives were selected, and only after several months of lengthy *voir dire* screening (Butler *et al.*, 1992). As most jury commissioners summon more jurors than they need, the lack of efficiency and the slowness of the selection process discourage many prospective jurors from making the necessary sacrifices to report for jury duty (Duncan, 1987).

In an effort to protect a certain class of individuals who may face undue hardship if they serve as jurors, many types of excuses from jury duty are written into the law and granted by the courts. Recognized categories of excuses generally include economic hardship, physical and mental disabilities, personal obligations, travel and transportation difficulties, and other jury service within the previous 12 months.

Several stages of jury selection offer potential jurors the opportunity to ask for excuses. Specifically, an excuse may be granted at three different points in the jury selection process: (1) when the persons selected from the master file are sent a qualification questionnaire; (2) when they are sent a summons for jury duty; and (3) when they actually come into the courthouse on the day for which they have been called. Besides *voir dire*, where attorneys on both sides exercise discretionary power in influencing the composition of the jury, the economic excuse is the most important influence on jury composition (Fukurai, 1985; Fukurai & Butler, 1991a; Van Dyke, 1977). Because of the lengthy time commitment required of many juries, excuses for economic hardship represent the single most significant form of voluntary self-exclusion from jury selection.

Consider the following example. Few persons making a minimum wage can afford a sudden and involuntary pay cut for a period of weeks or more. For many prospective jurors, the question of whether their salaries will be continued during jury duty is of paramount importance. Consequently, prospective jurors with guaranteed salaries are more likely to serve on juries and those without financial compensation are more likely to request economic excuses and are thus weeded out of jury selection. Because economic excuses are generally granted in most state and federal courts, a systematic bias in juror pools is introduced if these excuses are not randomly distributed in the population (Fukurai *et al.*, 1991a; Van Dyke, 1977).

The impact of the nonrandom nature of excuses for economic hardship has been observed in many state and federal courts. For example, between 1983 and 1984, almost 1 million affidavits (963,836) were mailed to potential jurors in Los Angeles County (see Figure 5.1). Approximately 37% (360,047) of the prospective jurors requested to be excused and were subsequently screened out of jury selection. Of those who requested excuses, almost three quarters (73%, or 261,537 jurors) stated that they could not serve because of hardship, including economic difficulties. Consequently, jury panels in Los Angeles County did not reflect a cross section of the community (Butler *et al.*, 1992; Fukurai, 1985; Fukurai *et al.*, 1991a).

Besides *voir dire*, where attorneys on both sides and sometimes a judge exercise discretionary power in influencing the composition of the jury, the economic excuse, thus, becomes the most important determining influence on the ultimate jury composition (Fukurai, 1985; Fukurai *et al.*, 1991b; Van Dyke, 1977). Although economic excuses are routinely granted in most state and federal courts, the factors that lead to the economic excuse and its effect on the makeup of juries have not been systematically examined. This chapter, then, examines the array of causes of economic excuses and explores the relation among economic excuses, jury participation, racial representation, and consequent jury verdicts under the current court system and jury selection procedure.

Anatomy of Economic Excuses: Structural Determinants of Inequality In Jury Representation

In order to examine the determinants of economic excuses, we have chosen to focus on three *structural factors* that determine the economic position of potential jurors in society and that thus influence their chance of serving on a jury: *organizations*, which differ in work policies, including jury compensation and other work-related benefits, as well as size and extent of job security (Baron, 1984; Doeringer & Piore, 1968; Rosenfeld & Kalleberg, 1990; Weakliem, 1990); *labor markets*, that is, types of jobs and work responsibilities, as well as differences in skills (Feagin, 1984); and *authority positions* or, in the view of some neo-Marxist writers, "class," which reflects one's economic resources and thus one's ability to take time off for jury duty. The class position also reflects one's location in the firm's structure of power and ownership (Wright, 1979, 1980, 1985). These three factors are considered the important structural determinants of income, generating inequality among individuals and influencing economic excuses from jury service.

Organizational policies and institutional resources can affect one's

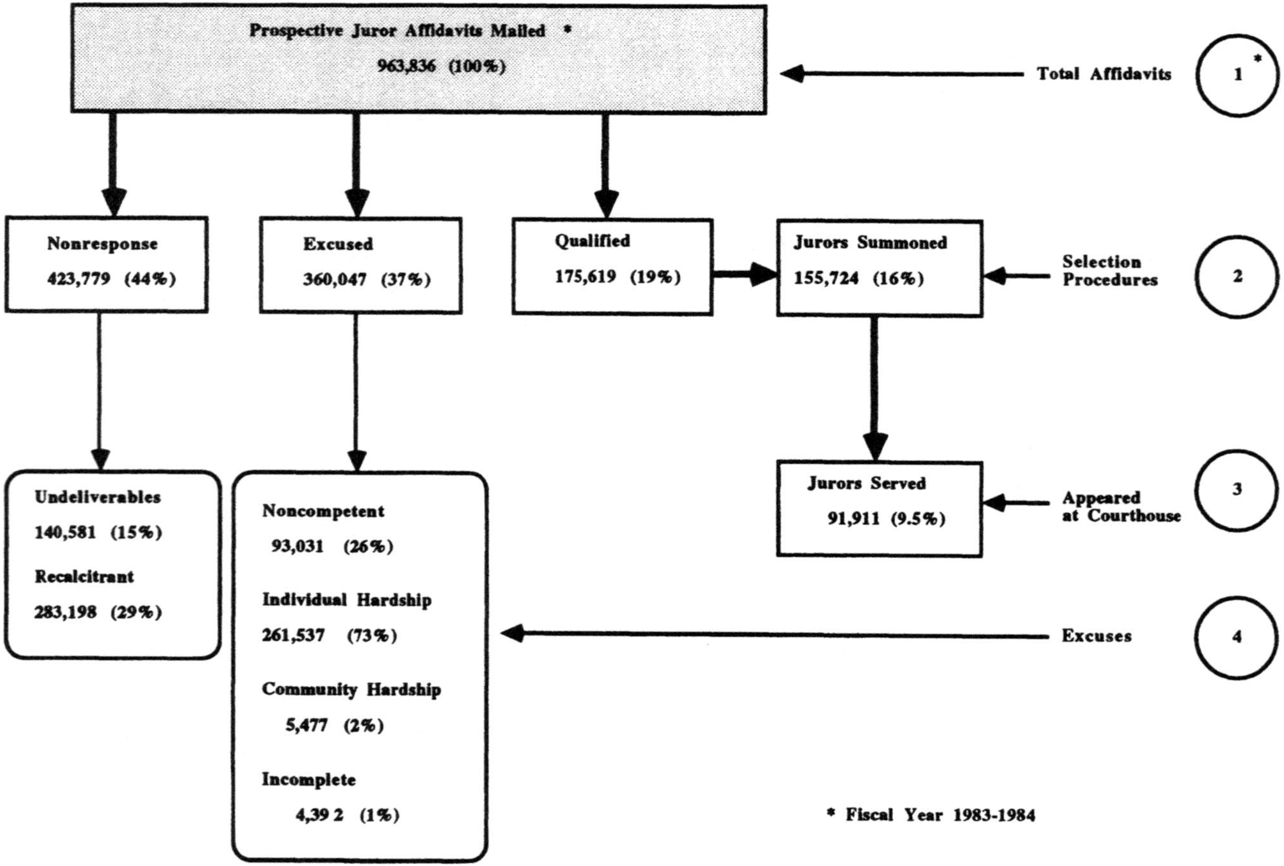

FIGURE 5-1. Los Angeles jury selection system.

availability for jury duty. For instance, major enterprises usually continue the salaries of their employees while they are on jury service. As the fee for jury duty remains minimal, this policy supplements the deficit of the underfunded court and jury system. Consequently, employees from large firms are more likely than the self-employed and those from smaller firms to serve on juries and to participate in the judicial decision-making process. Further, work positions and job classifications also determine economic reward structures and other work benefits, including leave of absence and reimbursement policies, and therefore define an employee's chance of doing jury service.[1] For instance, a survey of jurors who served during September and October 1972 in Memphis, Tennessee, revealed that 133 (27.7%) of the 480 persons who qualified for jury duty worked for the seven largest organizations in the study area. During the same period, International Harvester supplied 8.8% of the jurors, although it employed fewer than 0.5% of the county's population (Cole, 1972).

Another important determinant of the economic excuse is the potential juror's authority position in the work place. Jurors employed in managerial positions and those who share firm ownership have entrepreneurial assets and greater economic and financial freedom, both of which increase their chances of serving on a jury. Their "class" position is directly tied to their income and thus influences their decision to sacrifice their work and carry out their civic duties by serving on juries. Nonmanagerial workers, placed differently in the labor hierarchy, are more likely to exclude themselves from jury service.

Judicial Inequality

Another set of factors also influences one's chances to serve on a jury. A person may not be eligible for jury duty even though he or she may not ask for economic excuse.

Before being considered as a prospective juror, each person has to fulfill basic *qualifications*, such as U.S. citizenship, being 18 years old, a residency requirement, English proficiency, sound intelligence and good judgment, and no previous felony convictions. *Exemptions* are also granted to certain potential jurors, such as police and other law enforcement officers, because their occupations and identification with the state may keep them from being impartial in a jury trial. Prospective jurors are also allowed *excuses* other than economic hardship, including physical or mental disability, personal obligations, travel and transportation difficulties, and jury service within the last 12 months (Butler *et al.*, 1992; Fukurai *et al.*, 1991). These judicial requirements and excuses show an intertwined relationship of economic excuses, jurors' class positions, organizational resources, and labor market characteristics.

Hypotheses

Our general discussion of economic excuses and differences in the structure of jury systems suggests a number of testable propositions. First, in view of the different structural forces impacting on jury service, we expect superior organizational resources, including reimbursement, leave of absence, and other fringe benefits, to have a significant effect on who asks for an economic excuse. Jurors with greater organizational resources are more likely to participate in the judicial decision-making process than employees with less organizational benefits. Specifically, the economic excuse should be closely related to the firm's economic and organizational resources (Lichter, 1989; Portes & Sassen-Koob, 1987; Smith & Welch, 1986).

Second, on the basis of our discussion of the relation of job positions in labor force and authority–class structures to jury participation, we expect the attributes of labor force and authority positions (complexity, control) to have a significant effect on economic excuses. Specifically, employees with job security and benefits are less likely to request economic excuses than their counterparts without such benefits and thus are more likely to serve on juries. These employees include full-time workers, supervisors, and employees with job seniority.

Finally, we introduce additional factors that influence jury representation, such as qualification, exemption, various noneconomic excuses, and the demographic characteristics of prospective jurors, including race. The addition of those extraneous variables into statistical analyses is important and routinely performed in empirical testings in order to examine the causal relationship among the determinants of the dependent variable. In our analyses, the dependent variable is the pattern of economic excuses. For example, jurors' racial and ethnic background shows the significant relationship to the economic selectivity and other structural and legal determinants of jury participation. Previous research has shown that racial minorities are more likely to be in the secondary labor market, and this economic disadvantage may cause them to request excuses for economic hardship more frequently than those in the majority (Fukurai, 1985; Fukurai *et al.*, 1991a, b).

A summary of the structural approach to analyzing economic excuses is shown in Figure 5–2. There are three basic components of economic excuses: structural determinants, human capital factors, and legal constraints. The structural determinants of economic excuses include or-

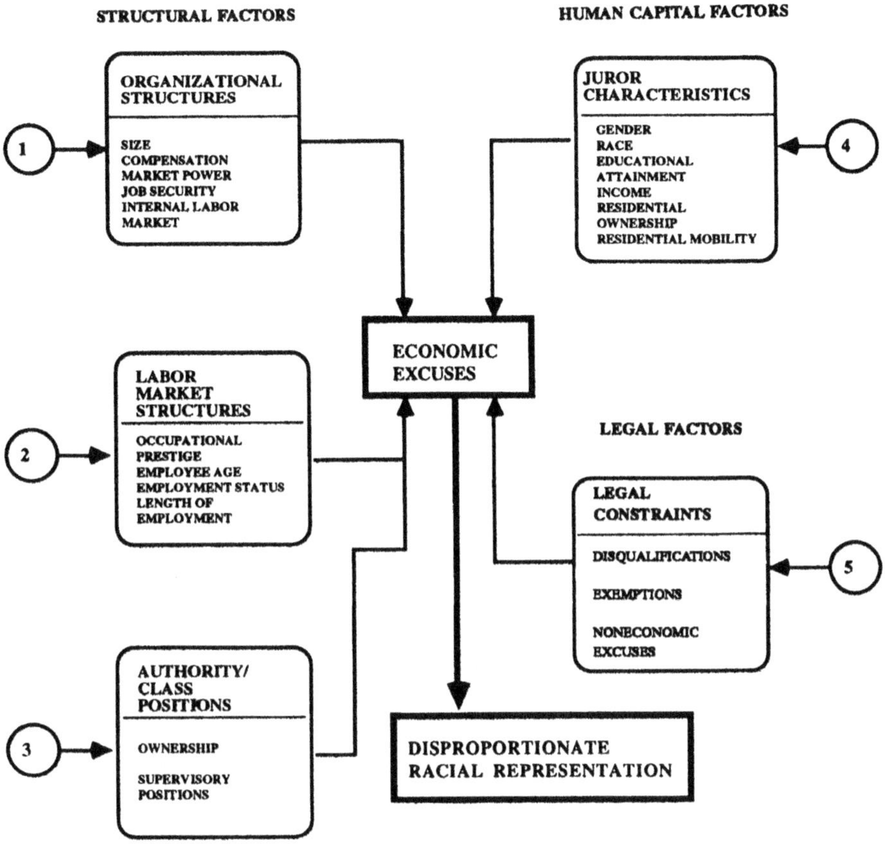

FIGURE 5-2. Structural determinants of economic excuses.

ganizational structures, labor force, and the authority–class positions of prospective jurors. Human capital and legal variables are also included in our statistical model in order to control for their effects on the determination of economic excuses. We contend that these five structural positions of individual jurors significantly influence economic excuses and lead to disproportionate jury representation.

Research Design

The Sample

A 1986 community research survey was used to examine jury representation. In 1986, survey questionnaires were sent to potential jurors who were randomly selected from a California County master key list during a three-month period in 1985. The data identify the socioeconomic and demographic profiles of those who were on the master list. More than 1,000 potential jurors were contacted for information on their eligibility to serve on juries. Their step-by-step progress through the jury selection procedure was carefully monitored, computerized, and analyzed.

Methods

A logit regression was used to explore the statistical relationship of the determinants of asking for an economic excuse. The logit regression treats a dichotomous categorical indicator as a dependent variable and a set of both dichotomous and continuous variables as predictors. The economic excuse was measured in a dichotomous fashion: requested economic excuse (excuse = 0) and did not request economic excuse (excuse = 1). This dichotomous endogenous variable was then regressed against a set of independent variables that were believed to determine the pattern of behaviors leading to requesting an economic excuse. In our model, the exogenous variables were organizational resources and benefits, labor market characteristics, and authority–class measures. Various legal and extralegal variables were also included in our empirical model to control for extraneous effects in explaining the determinants of requesting an economic excuse.

Measurement

ORGANIZATIONAL STRUCTURES. We measured the attributes of organizational structures and economic segmentation by using the size of the firm: the absolute number of persons employed at the time of the survey. This variable is represented in the natural log transformation, as the variable is highly skewed toward the large organizational size. An organization's size is closely related to its financial resources and the work benefits made available to workers to take time off and serve on juries.

Another important feature of organizational resources is the firm's ability to continue to pay their workers' salaries while they are on jury duty. Our comparisons of the firm's influence on jury compositions was facilitated by examining whether the firms paid salaries while their employees are on jury duty (pay = 0). Although the size of the corporation itself reflects the overall organizational resources and employee work benefits, the specific company policy on jury compensation also contributed to determining the likelihood of requesting an economic excuse or deciding to serve on a jury.

LABOR MARKET STRUCTURES. The measurement of labor market characteristics includes the following: job seniority (months employed by the company), employee age (in years), employment status (full time or otherwise), and occupational status and prestige. A Duncan socioeconomic index (Duncan SEI) is a continuous variable and included in our analysis to measure the level of prestige associated with various occupational categories. The SEI index ranges from 1 designating the least prestigious occupations to 96 as the most prestigious job categories. The use of month as a unit of analysis in measuring seniority provided detailed information on the extent to which young prospective jurors were affected by the labor force and labor market. This was especially important as young workers are more likely than older workers to be affected by economic hardship and thus to be restricted from jury participation.

We also measured labor market segmentation by employment status to indicate whether potential jurors have access to economic resources in work places (full time = 0). Although labor market segmentation is closely related to various work place variables, such as job security, employment stability, company benefits, and other attributes related to occupational reward structures, our data are limited in their ability to capture those dimensions of labor markets. However, as employment status is closely linked to labor market resources, employment status was used as a proxy to measure various employment benefits that influence the decision to request an economic excuse. That is, full-time workers are more likely than part-time employees to have access to jury compensation and other work-related benefits.

Length of employment was also used as a proxy to indicate employment conditions and employee benefits. It was measured in total months and represented in the natural log transformation. A socioeconomic status index (Duncan SEI) was used to capture occupational prestige and job status to indicate differences in job security and working conditions. The latter variables were added to further extend our knowledge of the job benefits that differentiate labor markets and influence jurors' chances for jury participation.

AUTHORITY–CLASS MEASURES. Two dummy variables were used to measure the class position of employed prospective jurors. First, we asked if respondents owned their own business (own = 0). Second, although a managerial position is more closely related to having authority status, the respondents' supervisory responsibility was used to indicate the extent of management control within a firm and job-related responsibility in the work place (supervisor = 0).

JUROR CHARACTERISTICS. We included several extralegal measurements as control variables that influenced a prospective juror's decision to ask for an economic excuse. A central hypothesis concerning the economic determination of jury participation was that employees are rewarded on the basis of ascriptive and social criteria such as sex, race, and marital status (see, for example, Fukurai, 1985; Fukurai *et al.*, 1991a). In order to examine their impact on judicial participation, we examined whether these personal attributes were more strongly related to the degree of jury participation. Sex was shown to be an important dimension of jury participation. For instance, besides economic reasons, women were likely to be excused because of child care responsibilities. Although some states, such as North Carolina, prohibit an automatic excuse for such reasons, most states still do not prohibit this excuse (male = 0) (Van Dyke, 1977). Race is also a strong predictor of jury participation. Minority groups have shown strong skepticism about participating in a majority-dominated legal and judicial institution that has historically oppressed them (race = 0) (Fukurai, 1985; Fukurai *et al.*, 1991a).[2] Educational attainment (in years) was included to measure the extent of human capital in affecting income inequality.

Other important variables were believed to play a role in jury participation. Residential status, for instance, reflects the ability of potential jurors to respond to jury calls. As most correspondence between the court and prospective jurors is done through the mail, jurors with high residential mobility tend to become "undeliverables" and are excluded from jury selection processes (Fukurai *et al.*, 1991a). Residential mobility was measured in years at the current residence, and residential ownership was represented by a dichotomous variable (own = 0). Annual family income reflects the economic well-being of potential jurors and further determines their chances to be on juries.[3] We included these extralegal variables to control for the other extraneous factors affecting the degree of judicial participation.

LEGAL VARIABLES. A variety of legal factors influence economic selectivity in jury participation: qualification measures (U.S. citizen, residency, age requirement, English proficiency, physical and natural faculty, felony conviction, previous grand jury experience), exemptions (police officer or judge), and other excuses (physical or mental disability, special personal obligation, travel and transportation difficulties, and prior jury service). These factors were measured by a set of dummy variables to control for other extraneous and legal variables that affect economic excuses; they were coded as 0 if prospective jurors asked to be excused and 1 if they did not. The descriptive statistics of all the structural variables in our model are shown in Table 5–1.

Results

Logit regression was used to examine the relationship of the structural determinants of economic excuses. Table 5–2 presents the results of our analysis. The first three columns in the table show the impact of both structural and legal variables on economic excuses. There, we report estimates of the direct effects of structural and control variables on economic excuses (a dichotomous variable). The fourth through ninth columns indicate the impact of the structural variables on the basis of company compensation and estimate the effect on the group-based work benefits: paid or unpaid while serving on juries. The different analyses for two organizational groups explore the relationship between jurors' economic position in the organizational structure and the impact of this position on economic excuses.

Organizational Structure and Labor Market Characteristics

We have clear and consistent evidence that the company policy on jury compensation is the single most important determinant of requesting an economic excuse: Potential jurors secure with specific compensation policies are less likely to request an economic excuse than those without jury compensation. For example, a juror's awareness of jury compensation had the greatest effect on the economic excuse ($t = 7.586$). However, the size of the organization did not show a significant effect on the decision to request an economic excuse. Moreover, prospective jurors lacking company support were more likely to request an excuse for economic hardship.[4]

Previous work by Kairys (1972), Fukurai (1985), and others has only speculated that company compensation has a significant effect on jury participation. Our empirical results provide strong evidence that whether one works for a large or a small firm is considerably less important than whether the firm pays while its employees are serving on juries.

Labor Market Structures

Our analysis shows mixed results on labor market structures. For instance, there is strong evidence that employee age influences jury participation. Our finding suggests that younger workers are more likely to ask for excuses than older workers. The same effect of age on economic excuses was

TABLE 5-1

Measures of Variables and Descriptive Statistics: Means

Variable	Asked economic excuse: Company with				Did not ask for excuse: Company with			
	Policy	(n = 53)	No policy	(n = 182)	Policy	(n = 330)	No policy	(n = 198)
Age	42.51	(12.20)[a]	38.80	(11.84)	42.97	(12.73)	39.47	(13.20)
English proficiency (1 = speak very well; 2 = speak well; 3 = speak not well)	.17	(.43)	.14	(.43)	.19	(.48)	.23	(.54)
Education (years)	15.25	(2.72)	13.98	(2.54)	14.52	(2.85)	13.65	(.20)
Annual family income (1 = < $5,000; 10 = $75,000 or more)	7.68	(2.06)	6.37	(2.37)	7.40	(2.09)	5.91	(2.82)
Occupational prestige (Duncan Socioeconomic Index)	55.86	(20.87)	49.46	(21.14)	56.27	(19.67)	43.50	(22.44)
Length of employment (in months)[b]	4.20	(1.47)	3.65	(1.38)	4.24	(1.31)	3.40	(1.49)
Firm size (number of employees)[b]	5.79	(2.44)	2.69	(1.93)	5.67	(2.62)	2.72	(1.82)
Sex (0 = male; 1 = female)	.32	(.47)	.45	(.49)	.57	(.50)	.58	(.49)
Marital status (0 = married; 1 = not married)	.67	(.47)	.65	(.47)	.68	(.46)	.60	(.48)
Race or ethnicity (0 =white; 1 = black/Hispanic)	.07	(.26)	.07	(.26)	.17	(.37)	.17	(.38)
Language spoken at home (0 = English; 1 = non-English)	.01	(.13)	.02	(.14)	.05	(.23)	.08	(.27)
Business ownership (0 = own business; 1 = do not own business)	.90	(.29)	.73	(.44)	.92	(.25)	.87	(.32)

Employment status (0 = full-time; 1 = non-full-time)	.03	(.19)	.11	(.31)	.11	(.32)	.52	(.50)
Supervisor (0 = yes; 1 = no)	.50	(.50)	.47	(.50)	.49	(.50)	.62	(.48)
Residential ownership (0 = rent; 1 = own)	.76	(.42)	.66	(.47)	.76	(.42)	.63	(.48)
Qualification (0 = disqualified; 1 = qualified)								
Citizen	.45	(.50)	.90	(.29)	.96	(.18)	.95	(.20)
18 years old	.45	(.50)	.91	(.28)	1.00	(.00)	1.00	(.00)
Residence	.41	(.49)	.89	(.31)	.93	(.23)	.88	(.31)
English language	.43	(.50)	.89	(.30)	.97	(.16)	.95	(.20)
Natural faculty	.45	(.50)	.91	(.28)	1.00	(.00)	.98	(.12)
Felony conviction	.45	(.50)	.90	(.29)	.99	(.05)	.99	(.07)
Previously served on grand jury	.45	(.50)	.91	(.28)	.99	(.05)	1.00	(.00)
Exemption (0 = exempted; 1 = not exempted)								
Peace officer	.45	(.50)	.91	(.28)	.99	(.09)	.99	(.07)
Excuses (0 = asked to be excused; 1 = did not ask to be excused)								
Physically handicapped	.45	(.50)	.89	(.30)	.94	(.22)	.89	(.30)
Personal obligations	.45	(.50)	.85	(.35)	.94	(.22)	.81	(.39)
Travel and transportation difficulties	.41	(.49)	.86	(.33)	.98	(.12)	.92	(.26)
Previous jury service (past 12 months)	.45	(.50)	.89	(.30)	.69	(.46)	.90	(.29)
Other excuses	.43	(.50)	.87	(.32)	.91	(.27)	.82	(.37)

[a]Standard deviation.
[b]A variable was transformed into natural logarithm

TABLE 5-2
Log-Linear Coefficients Obtained from Logit Regression on Economic Excuses

	Overall model			*Company compensation*			*No company compensation*		
Variables	*Coefficients*	*Standard error*	*Critical ratio*	*Coefficients*	*Standard error*	*Critical ratio*	*Coefficients*	*Standard error*	*Critical ratio*
Structural variables									
Age	.028	.012	2.227**	.033	.016	2.004**	.032	.024	1.353
English proficiency	.498	.269	1.847*	.223	.514	.434	−.239	.640	−.373
Education	−.218	.325	−.670	.057	.080	.711	−.196	.083	−2.348***
Annual family income	.847	.441	.192	−.031	.093	−.343	−.055	.156	−.355
Occupational prestige	.197	.125	1.584	−.004	.008	−.455	.024	.013	1.859*
Length of employment	−.040	.395	−.103	−.164	.143	−1.145	.043	.205	.213
Firm size	−.049	.059	−.870	.042	.101	.417	.015	.093	.169
Sex	−.022	.078	−.286	.545	.335	1.625	.792	.503	1.574
Marital status	.703	.390	1.800*	−.169	.428	−.396	.026	.561	.047
Race or ethnicity	.005	.007	.711	.500	.539	.927	.193	.112	1.717*
Language spoken at home	−.095	.115	−.826	.180	.141	1.281	.562	.324	1.737*
Business ownership	.215	.045	4.750***	.730	.485	1.506	.790	.773	1.023
Employment status	.037	.065	.571	.228	.052	4.327***	.482	.848	.568
Supervisor	−.492	.289	−1.704*	−.474	.384	−1.237	−.790	.491	−1.608
Employer compensation	−.235	.031	−7.586***	NA	NA	NA	NA	NA	NA

Residential ownership	-.325	.362	-.897	-.432	.449	-.964	-.762	.682	-1.116
Constant[a]	-1.522	2.042	-.745	-7.119	2.298	-3.095***	-5.686	—[b]	—[b]
Control variables									
Qualification									
Citizen	-.146	.080	-1.824*	-.044	2.427	-.018	-.124	.093	-1.332
Residence	-.141	.055	-2.535***	-.014	1.067	-.013	-.218	.067	-3.212***
English language	.271	.799	.339	.031	1.924	.016	-.675	.990	-.681
Natural faculty	.049	1.425	.034	NA	NA	NA	NA	NA	NA
Felony conviction	.323	1.421	.227	-.100	.690	-.146	-.900	1.430	-.630
Previously served on grand jury	-.009	1.214	-.008	-.000	.547	-.000	NA	NA	NA
Exemption									
Peace officer	-.013	.700	-.019	-.015	3.141	-.004	.603	.260	2.317**
Excuses									
Physically handicapped	-.196	.075	-2.600***	-.015	1.654	-.009	-.236	.080	-2.939***
Personal obligations	-.947	.447	-2.115**	.094	1.106	.085	-.192	.051	-3.729***
Travel and transportation difficulties	-.186	.691	-.269	.210	.144	1.454	-.104	.084	-1.236
Previous jury service	-.398	.101	-3.933***	-.015	.640	-.023	-.286	.108	-2.632***
Other excuses	-.208	.061	-3.381***	-.788	1.072	-.735	-.290	.077	-3.729***
Constant[c]	-.287	5.175	-.055	-.036	2.908	-.012	-.025	.520	-.049

*$p < .10$.
**$p < .05$.
***$p < .01$.
[a]Constant when structural variables are included as a set of predictors in the equation.
[b]The term did not pass the tolerance test with the tolerance limit of 10*E-25 in the inversion of the cross-product of partial derivative matrix. We believe that the limit is sufficiently small as a criterion for a reasonably realistic empirical model.
[c]Constant when control variables are included in the equation.

also found among potential jurors with company compensation ($t = 2.004$).

Employment status did not show a significant effect on jury participation. In firms with jury compensation, however, full-time workers were more likely to request economic excuses than part-time workers ($t = 4.327$). It is also important to note that only 3% of potential jurors who requested economic excuses were aware of the company's jury compensation policy (see Table 5–1). Another important finding is that the majority of part-time workers (52%) knew that their firms would not pay but decided not to ask for an economic excuse.

Our analyses point out that jurors' marital status also affected jury participation: Married jurors were more likely to request economic excuses than nonmarried jurors ($t = 1.800$, $p < .05$ one-tailed). Our last indicator concerning labor market structure was the length of employment. The coefficients associated with this variable were not consistent with a labor market interpretation, although they were quite interesting and again underscored greater inequality between jurors with and without company support. That is, for prospective jurors employed in companies with guaranteed jury compensation, a greater length of employment was associated with a higher incidence of economic excuses, whereas the reverse relationship was found for employees without jury compensation. Although the relationship was not found to be statistically significant, the difference shows that more elaborate analyses are needed of the structure of economic excuses and their impact on jury participation.

Authority and Class Measures

Our results for business ownership paralleled the excuse pattern connected with employees' supervisory position. That is, owners were more likely to request economic hardship excuses than workers. The relationship was statistically significant.

This finding is contrary to our previous hypothesis: Owners are more likely to be economically secure and thus less likely to request excuses for economic hardship. But this presupposition did not hold. A feasible explanation is that the majority of the owners in our sample owned small firms and still lacked economic security. For instance, 27.8% of the self-identified owners said that they had no employees other than their immediate family members. Moreover, the median for the number of employees was 3.

Our results on the effect of authority positions in the work place suggest that prospective jurors with supervisory responsibilities are less likely to request economic excuses than those without supervisory responsibility. And the pattern was found to be consistent regardless of company compensation, suggesting that those lacking authority in the work place are more likely to request an economic excuse and to be weeded out of jury selection procedures.

Extralegal Variables

In our sample, there was little consistency in jury participation across the different firms. The ascriptive characteristics of prospective jurors did not show a significant impact on economic excuses, although there were interesting relationships, and further investigation may provide plausible interpretations for some of the unexpected results. For example, white jurors were more likely to ask for economic excuses than minority jurors. This finding was consistent regardless of firm compensation. Also, prospective jurors with good English language abilities were more likely to ask to be excused than those with less English fluency. By the same token, jurors who spoke English at home were more likely to request economic excuses than jurors who did not speak English at home. This finding was consistent for jurors regardless of company compensation. It may have been that non-English-speakers were less familiar with the jury system and may have felt more obligated to participate in jury service. Nevertheless, further research is needed to assess this relationship. Another interesting finding was that, although the results were not statistically significant, renters of their current residence were less likely to request an economic excuse than prospective jurors who owned their residence. This finding was also consistent for jurors with and without company compensation.

The socioeconomic variables also provided mixed results. For jurors lacking company compensation, higher educational attainment was associated with a higher incidence of economic excuse. This relationship was found to be statistically significant ($t = 2.348$). Annual income was associated with economic excuses in the same way; that is, a higher income was associated with a higher incidence of economic excuses regardless of whether the company paid for jury duty. Occupational prestige showed a mixed result: whereas higher prestige was associated with a higher incidence of economic excuses in firms with compensation, the relationship was reversed in firms without compensation.

Legal Variables

The final explanatory variables in our model were the legal variables: jury qualification requirements and the use of noneconomic excuses. The unexpected finding was that qualifications other than the residence requirement did not lead to any significant explanation of economic excuses. However, the noneconomic excuse criteria played a major role in explaining voluntary self-exclusion based on the lack of economic resources leading to personal hardship. For example, other than travel and transportation difficulties, noneconomic excuse criteria such as physical/mental disabilities, personal obligation, and prior jury service were statistically significant in predicting the pattern of self-exclusion due to economic excuses, but only for those jurors with guaranteed company compensation. These results also showed that general excuses were more important dimensions of jury participation for those without company compensation. For potential jurors with company compensation, none of these variables appeared to be statistically significant in predicting the pattern of self-exclusion based on economic excuses.

Discussion

Our analysis substantiates that company compensation has a significant effect on jury participation: Jurors with compensation were less likely to ask to be excused than those without compensation ($p < .001$). Our analysis also indicates that whether a prospective juror worked for a large or a small firm was considerably less important than whether the firm compensated their employees for serving on juries ($p < .05$). The analysis also points out the different pattern of economic excuses based on organizational compensation and indicates that both one's organizational resources and labor market characteristics significantly influence jury participation.

There is strong evidence that employment status is an important factor in firms offering compensation while performing jury service. A higher incidence of the economic excuse was found among full-time workers than among part-time workers. Supervisory positions of potential jurors had a significant impact on the economic excuse in that employees with supervisory responsibility were less likely to request an excuse than those without this responsibility.

The personal attributes of potential jurors also indicated a strong relationship between the economic excuse and labor market characteristics. Although the relationship was not statistically significant ($p < .05$), employers are more likely to request an economic excuse than employees. Senior employees also asked for a higher proportion of economic excuses than workers with less experience. It could be that senior and more experienced workers see jury duty as a nuisance and do not share the junior workers' views on participation in jury service.

Although the married were more likely to be exempted from jury duty because of children, married jurors were also found to be more likely to request an economic hardship excuse, perhaps because they had greater economic responsibilities than the nonmarried. Although the sex of the potential jurors did not show a statistically significant relationship, female jurors had a higher incidence of economic excuses than male jurors. In many districts, women are automatically excused for economic reasons because the courts do not reduce the length of jury duty to a manageable limit or pay a daily fee high enough to cover child care (Mahoney & Sipes, 1988). Van Dyke (1977, pp. 121–124) reported that approximately 83% of the federal courts surveyed showed a significant underrepresentation of women on juries because of voluntary self-exclusion based on excuses including economic hardship. Our findings coincide with his analysis.

For employees without the benefit of company compensation, human capital variables are more significant predictors of economic excuses than labor market and class–authority indicators. Educational attainment and occupational prestige influence jury participation in that a higher education is associated with a higher incidence of economic excuses. At the same time, lower occupational prestige is related to a greater frequency of economic excuses than higher prestige; this finding coincides with our research hypothesis.

An unexpected finding is that, after we controlled for organizational and labor market characteristics, white and English-speaking jurors had a higher incidence of requests for an economic excuse than minority and non-English-speaking jurors. The relationship was statistically significant among prospective jurors without company compensation ($p < .01$). However, the same was not found for those employed in firms that provided compensation for jury service. This mixed result is contradictory to previous research findings (Fukurai, 1985; Van Dyke, 1977). Past research indicated that minority jurors are more likely to be underrepresented on jury panels than white workers because of greater economic hardship. In fact, many non-English-speakers in California are Hispanic jurors (Butler & Fukurai, 1984; Fukurai, 1985). In addition, widespread mistrust of the white-dominated judicial and court system leads to a higher incidence of minorities' voluntary self-exclusion from the jury selection process by requesting excuses.

Our finding, however, suggests that economic excuses are more often asked for by white prospective jurors than by minority prospective jurors. As excuses based on economic hardship significantly depend on one's organization's resources, it is of crucial importance to examine the relationship of a prospective juror's economic resources to the firm's influence on jury compositions. Our contradictory finding suggests that white jurors rely more on economic excuses to abandon their opportunity to serve on juries than do minorities. Further, this relationship is statistically significant (at $p < .05$ one-tailed) in companies without compensation.

One possible explanation is that the fear of losing an economic payoff because of a minimal daily fee is felt more strongly among white jurors than among minority groups. The negative perception of jury trials often helps generate widespread apprehension of jury service and jury selection. For example, white jurors may be more sensitive than minority jurors to the potential economic loss due to lengthy jury trials. The perception of potential threats to their economic well-being is greater in white jurors employed in companies in the secondary economic sector and without company compensation than in minority jurors. Even when potential jurors are aware of a company's reimbursement policy for jury duty, a large number of white jurors still use an economic excuse to avoid jury service.

Analyses of perceptions of jury service may give an important clue to the anatomy of economic excuses in different racial groups; however, we were not able to establish the causal link between the perception of economic loss and the decision to ask for an economic excuse. Although apprehension of jury service is shared by many potential jurors and is perhaps inevitable, the finding of racial discrepancies in jury participation needs further theoretical elaboration, and future research should examine potential jurors' perceptions of what jury service entails, as well as their economic status.

With respect to the impact of legal variables on jury participation, juror qualifications, exemptions, and other noneconomic excuses had a greater impact in predicting the excuse pattern for those without company compensation than for potential jurors with company compensation. All the excuse criteria except travel and transportation difficulties showed statistically significant relations with jury participation. They also showed that general excuses are used more by those *without* company support. For potential jurors with company compensation, none of these variables were statistically significant in predicting the pattern of economic excuses.

Conclusions

The anatomy of economic excuses was examined in terms of structural explanations. To psychological writers such as Hastie *et al.* (1983),

Hans and Vidmar (1986), Nietzel and Dillehay (1986), and Wrightsman (1987), the microstructure of economic excuses and jury participation are exotic vestiges of a human capital and psychological order that influence how jury composition is influenced. Our analyses partially supported their claims that human capital and individual characteristics influence the pattern of economic excuses. However, our data also provided a different look at jury participation. For example, company compensation plays a key role in determining the pattern of economic excuses and influences the resulting jury composition.

In the past, attempts have been made to equalize the economic burden of jury duty by securing mandatory company compensations. For instance, Hawaii, in 1966 and 1970 passed a statute requiring employers to continue an employee's salary during jury service. This law required every employer with more than 25 workers to continue the salary of any employee who served on a jury or participated on any public board. However, the law was later declared unconstitutional by the Hawaii Supreme Court as a violation of the equal protection clause and the taking clause of both the U.S. and the Hawaiian Constitutions (see, for instance, *Hasegawa v. Maui Pineapple Co.*, 52 Haw. 327, 475 P.2d 679 1970). The statute that required company participation in jury service simply made mandatory a practice already common among large businesses and organizations. But it also left out many potential jurors such as the hourly-wage and daily-wage earners, the underemployed, and the unemployed (Bowles, 1980). Prospective jurors whose livelihood depends on commissions were also inadequately compensated by mere salary-continuation plans. Whereas the statute must be combined with a higher daily compensation, today's court systems still remain underfunded and the compensation is not high enough to neutralize the burden of service to prospective jurors. For example, in 1991, although jury fees vary among counties, jurors were awarded $5 a day in most state and federal courts in California.

Our analysis also suggests that prospective jurors' employment conditions and structural location in the labor market are important in explaining the pattern of economic excuses for workers without company compensation. The labor market measures, such as employment status and employee age, are also important predictors of economic excuses for jurors with company compensation. Legal variables, such as non-economic excuses, are also important in explaining jury participation. Their impact is especially significant for jurors with no company compensation.

Individual characteristics also play an important role in predicting economic excuse. White and English-speaking jurors who work in the less stable secondary economic sectors and without company compensation are more likely to request an economic excuse than racial and ethnic minorities and non-English-speakers.

Our analysis also shed light on potential jurors' perceptions of jury service. Although apprehension of jury service is perhaps inevitable, it is important that future research examines potential jurors' psychological perceptions of what jury service entails, as well as their economic status.

Our empirical results suggest that, although some attempts in the past have failed, it is important to establish or implement laws or regulations encouraging corporate participation through medical reimbursement policy and/or guaranteeing an adequate economic reward from the court. Otherwise, the fair cross-sectional requirement of the law may not be met by the current jury selection procedure.

Notes

1. Organization differences, labor market segmentation, and intrafirm authority positions help create and maintain judicial inequality. Organizational characteristics often overlap with labor market segmentation. See, for example, Baron (1984) for detailed analyses of the interrelationship of dual economic sectors and dual labor markets in the United States.
2. Mistrust in the jury system may be fueled by prejudice toward jury duty. For example, the underrepresentation of minorities from lower economic strata has a profound effect on the strength and quality of the jury and criminal justice system. Discrimination and prejudice contribute to a widespread mistrust by minorities of most white-dominated institutions of power, such as law enforcement agencies (Fukurai *et al.*, 1991a,b: 32; Loh, 1982; Van Dyke, 1977). Besides racial minorities, youth and economically impoverished people are less likely to vote in elections and to participate in jury service because they have less confidence in political processes (Kairys, 1972).
3. The breakdown of income was (1) less than $5,000; (2) $5,000–9,999; (3) $10,000–14,999; (4) $15,000–19,999; (5) $20,000–24,999; (6) $25,000–29,999; (7) $30,000–39,999; (8) $40,000–49,999; (9) $50,000–74,999; and (10) $75,000 or more.
4. Almost a third (30.8%) of the prospective jurors said that their firms would pay while they served on juries; 69.2% of them said their companies would not pay.

6

Scientific Jury Selection in Voir Dire

The Hidden Structure of Jury Selection

Introduction

The purpose of *voir dire* is to find a fair and impartial jury. In reality, however, jury selection often becomes a battleground on which both prosecution and defense search out jurors who are likely to favor their side. With experience, counsel can develop a "critical eye," using insightful observation to identify favorably inclined jurors. Both the defense and the prosecution can dismiss, without cause, a limited number of potential jurors based on their subjective judgments alone. Such factors as race, physical stature, gender, age, religion, general appearance, presentation, and expressed beliefs may be seen as indicators that a potential juror will favor one side or the other. More recently, this intuitive approach has been expanded by the use of computers and sophisticated statistical techniques. Technology has elevated human judgments to a new and higher state in the systematic selection of prospective jurors during *voir dire.*

At first glance, the idea of "scientific" jury selection is antithetical to the juridical practice of picking an impartial body of citizens to judge a case involving a member of the same community. The practice of carefully selecting a jury favorable to the case seems calculated, not to render the justice that a court system is supposed to award, but to provide counsel with a kind of leverage that has little or nothing to do with the guilt or innocence of the defendant. We will return to this important issue at the end of the chapter.

By What and Whose Standard?

The tradition of trial by jury derives from a time when a jury of peers was a body composed of residents of the geographic community where the defendant resided or where the alleged crime was committed (Adams, 1934; Moore, 1972; Younger, 1963). Their similar moral and social standards were assumed to be the criteria that they would bring to bear in judging the defendant. In English courts, at least in theory, the man on the streets of London became the prototypical juror, that is, an honest fellow who was thoughtful in his considerations and most decidedly unbiased (Blackstone, 1884). In the United States, he was the yeoman, the craftsman, the gentleman of commerce and finance. There was no effort to include members of various racial and ethnic groups or socioeconomic classes, and women were considered incapable of fulfilling the duties of citizenship.[1] However, the concept of a jury of one's peers has changed. The impartial jury called for in the Sixth Amendment to the U.S. Constitution is now interpreted as a jury that reflects the racial, ethnic, class, and gender composition of the community.

Today, defense and prosecution have also come to focus on different aspects of the historical tradition. Defense counsels have increasingly focused on a jury of *peers*. They seek to limit the jury to the defendant's gender, race, religion, social class, and general mental frame of reference.[2] Although they look for jurors who will intelligently reflect on the evidence, they also want jurors who are in emotional sympathy with the defendant's life condition. Jurors who share the life experience and biases of the defendant are assumed to be more willing to impute to the defendant a weak intent, a lack of intent, or a condition blocking intent to commit the act in question. Thus, the defense wants to exclude jurors from wider geographic and socioeconomic boundaries who do not necessarily share the standards of life and morals that may have been underlying factors in the alleged crime.

On the other side, it can be argued that prosecutors emphasize the impartial jury referred to in the Bill of Rights. They seek out jurors with different experiences and biases and strive to extend the boundaries of the jury beyond the defendant's gender, race, class, and life condition.[3] In practice, however, they also want a highly emotive jury box, one that is either biased against the defendant's social or racial heritage or hypercritical of the accused's way of life. They seek jurors who will impute strong intent to the defendant's act, who will view this act as dastardly, and, most important, who will convict.

These are the real dynamics of *voir dire*. For judging the defendant, it is not only the act of the accused but the supposed intent behind the act that becomes the focus of the active search for a partial and favorable jury by both prosecution and defense. Sophisticated statistical techniques and computer technology make the search of each more accurate and complete. As the following case study shows, the process of seeking out jurors with so-called "high"- and "low"-risk potential is actually an analysis of the psychological dimensions of the defendant's intent and the jurors' likely interpretation of the defendant's act.[4]

Scientific Defense Voir Dire *Jury Selection*

In an effort to impanel a favorable jury, the accused's assumed state of mind becomes a critical factor in jury selection. In the dynamics of *voir dire,* a prosecution or defense counsel would be remiss in giving no consideration to the defendant's conscious intent or voluntary willingness to perform the act in question and the emotive or mindful purposes that prospective jurors are familiar with.[5]

This brings us to a major point in contemporary jury selection, illustrated here by an example. Suppose that a black man is put on trial for felony murder. He views society as racially dominated and has experienced discrimination and other racially motivated harm. His attorney successfully selects black men for the jury box who have a background similar to that of the defendant because they are more likely to understand the defendant's milieu and to have experienced similar social tensions. As black men, they may not be able to disregard proof of the defendant's having acted with deadly violence, but they may intuit that his intent is understandable, given their own knowledge of racial prejudices, social practices, and the circumstances that surround situations comparable to the one the defendant faced.

Even if they find the defendant guilty of murder at the time of sentencing, these same jurors may find that the act and assumed intent of killing, in the social frame of a racially defined society, was so predictable and so "normal" that it was not an absolute evil in itself demanding a death sentence, but a relative one requiring a more lenient sentence. Therefore, they may find that the defendant is a mirror image of the very society that helped make him a killer, that made him "guilty" of the crime, and that therefore cannot punish him with death, but only with a life of atonement in prison.

This chapter examines the use of systematic analysis for *voir dire* in the jury selection process to determine whether jurors' attitudinal, behavioral, and social characteristics have a significant impact on the sentence rendered in a capital case and how jurors interpret the accused's motives in light of his racial and social class background. An in-depth examination was undertaken of the *voir dire* process in the 1979 trial and subsequent 1985 retrial of *People of California v. Lee Edward Harris* (36 Cal. 3d 36 1984). A set of psychological attributes, socioeconomic backgrounds, and demographic characteristics and some systematic behavioral observations of prospective jurors were collected and systematically analyzed. A profile of each juror in relation to his or her final potential verdict (i.e., "risk factors") was derived to allow us to assess the potential outcome of the trial and to select potential candidates during the *voir dire* screening session. This case is unique as the defendant was black and the trial took place in Long Beach Superior Court, Los Angeles County, California, where 16.4% and 20.9% of the eligible jurors in the jurisdiction were black and Hispanic. The purpose of this discussion is: (1) to assess the adequacy of an empirical model in evaluating the causal relationship between the behavioral and social background of the selected jurors and their potential verdict and (2) to examine the feasibility of using scientific defense *voir dire* to obtain a final jury whose composition reflects a cross section of the community in race, ethnicity, gender, and social class.

Trial Background of People v. Harris

For a deeper understanding of the impact of using the *voir dire* process in a capital case, a brief synopsis of *People v. Harris* is important. This case involved a young black male charged with the felony murder of a white couple who managed an apartment complex in Long Beach, California. Included in the evidence were allegations that the defendant had participated in a crime spree from California to Colorado to Kansas. The original trial jury was composed of 12 white jurors. In the guilt phase of its decision, the jurors found the defendant guilty of first-degree murder with special circumstances (robbery). In the penalty phase, the jurors sentenced the defendant to death, but the California Supreme Court reversed and remanded the case on the legal grounds that there was a significant underrepresentation of blacks on the petit jury.

The defense attorney who tried both the original case and the retrial evaluated his first trial in 1979 and determined that there had been three major problems in the original trial strategy: (1) the lack of black jurors on the trial jury; (2) the defendant's misbehavior in court and his refusal to wear civilian clothes; and (3) the jury's mistrust of the defense attorney. In the penalty phase, the jury had been presented evidence about an out-of-state execution murder in which the defendant had allegedly participated. In postverdict interviews, the jurors revealed that, after having heard during the guilt phase of the trial that the defendant was not the type of individual to kill another, and then in the penalty phase having the prosecutor disclose the defendant's prior murder conviction in Kansas, they felt lied to, and they had turned against the defendant and, even more, against his attorney.

At retrial in July 1985, the jury was composed of seven whites, three blacks, one Hispanic, and one Asian. This jury again found the defendant guilty of first-degree murder with special circumstances. However, in the penalty phase, the jury sentenced the defendant to life imprisonment without possibility of parole.

A note of explanation is required here, for capital trials in California are bifurcated. In the first phase of the trial (the guilt phase), the jury decides on the guilt or innocence of the defendant. When the individual is found guilty, the jury hears evidence in the penalty phase of the trial about factors that aggravate and mitigate the defendant's guilt. The jury is instructed that, if it finds that factors in aggravation outweigh factors in mitigation, it may vote for the death penalty. The converse also occurs: If the jury finds that mitigation factors outweigh aggravation factors, it may vote for life imprisonment without possibility of parole.

Defense Voir Dire *Jury-Selection Strategies*

As discussed in previous chapters, there is an intertwined relationship between jurors' socioeconomic and psychobehavioral characteristics and their potential verdict. Thus, in the scientific jury selection strategy in the retrial of *People v. Harris*, a number of important factors had to be considered. The immediate task was to examine the potential link between jurors' social and psychological characteristics and their opinion on the final outcome of the trial. That is, the retrial strategies had to weigh the specific issues pertinent to the case and formulate specific goals of *voir dire*. Therefore, the defense team's strategy for retrial included: (1) use of a written questionnaire to elicit extensive information in advance of actual questioning of prospective jurors; (2) disclosure to prospective jurors of the prior murder conviction during sequestered *voir dire;* (3) making the defendant appear more amenable by dressing more appropriately; (4) developing good attorney rapport with jurors through self-disclosure; (5) attempting to empanel as many black jurors as possible; and (6) determining that the defense efforts should be directed toward the penalty phase of the trial, as conviction was assured.

Systematic jury selection had not been used in the original trial, and therefore, little information about the jurors was available, except that the

12 jurors had all been white. So the question became: How could the most "sympathetic" retrial jury be selected? First, it was necessary to survey the jury selection procedure currently used in Los Angeles County, the site of the original *Harris* trial and also of the retrial. There were eight stages of jury selection, and focus was placed on the final six stages and particularly the last three: (6) jury panel; (7) *voir dire;* and (8) jury box (see Figure 3–1 for the entire jury selection procedure).[6]

For purposes of jury evaluation, data were collected both by in-court participant observation and from prescreening questionnaires administered by the court to prospective jurors in the retrial, identifying specific demographic and attitudinal characteristics.

Between May 29 and July 17, 1985, a large number of potential jurors were asked to appear at Long Beach Superior Court in Los Angeles County. Those groups of prospective jurors were sent from the jury assembly room to the courtroom and were instructed by the judge about the charges in the *Harris* case. These people were referred to as *empaneled jurors.* Thereafter, the judge and attorneys questioned each juror about any hardship they might have in serving on the case. The hardships usually encompassed obligations and excuses relating to medical, financial, family, and travel necessities. After the prospective jurors with hardships were eliminated, the court administrators distributed a previously approved written questionnaire to all prospective jurors. A total of 120 prospective jurors were instructed to complete the *voir dire* screening questionnaires and return them to the court after completion (usually several hours were allotted to fill out the questionnaire).

Both prosecution and defense attorneys then questioned each prospective juror, away from the presence of the other potential jurors, on her or his views about the death penalty. It is important to note that information elicited from the prospective juror may result in a challenge for cause, by which a prospective juror will be eliminated if he or she would always vote for life without possibility of parole or if he or she would always vote for death (*Witherspoon v. Illinois,* 391 U.S. 510 1968). In addition, a prospective juror may be excused by stipulation of both attorneys if it is determined that the juror has a medical or financial hardship that was not originally disclosed. In this case, after the sequestered screening session, the general *voir dire* began, with questioning about each prospective juror's general attitude, and culminated in the exercise of peremptory challenges by both the prosecuting and the defense attorneys. As required in a capital case in California, each side had 26 peremptory challenges. Finally, 12 jurors and their alternates were selected to try the defendant. The jurors were then sworn by the clerk of the court and were ready to hear the opening argument of the case.

Jury Profile in Harris *Retrial*

The central question in jury selection was: Could a scientific method be designed for the selection of a specific number of jurors for a particular type of criminal offense? By means of a variety of statistical techniques, both socioeconomic and ideological profiles of the 120 potential jurors were critically examined. The codified and computerized *voir dire* questionnaires provided a statistical data base that identified risk profiles, that is, jurors who were more likely to vote for death (high risk) or who were more likely to vote for life imprisonment without possibility of parole (low risk). Seven questions were found to be statistically significant in predicting the potential verdicts of the selected jurors (see Table 6–1). The jurors were then reclassified into two distinct groups on the basis of their potential verdicts: (1) high-risk jurors, who are more likely to sentence the defendant to death, and (2) low-risk jurors, who are more likely to vote for life imprisonment without possibility of parole. Greater emphasis was placed on jurors' potential verdicts in the penalty phase than on their potential verdicts in the guilt phase because the defense team assumed that a guilty verdict was assured.

Statistical analyses revealed that the profile characteristics of the low-risk jurors were (1) being male; (2) previous assignment on the grand jury; (3) a strong ideological stance against the death penalty; (4) high leadership quality; (5) belief that Harris's childhood experience was a main cause of his crime; (6) belief that those with an economically impoverished background were more susceptible to the death penalty; and

TABLE 6-1
High- and Low-Risk Juror Profiles:
Voir Dire *Questionnaires and In-Court Observation of Prospective Jurors*

Variables	*Order of importance*[a]	*F values*	*Probability*[b]
Juror characteristics			
Sex	4	4.94	.02
Death penalty	3	3.38	.06
Leadership	6	1.12	.29
Prior jury service[c]	1	5.30	.02
Ideological questions			
Legal systems	2	4.45	.03
Causes of crime	7	1.08	.29
Racial prejudice	5	3.39	.06

[a]The order of importance was obtained from stepwise discriminant analysis; e.g., race was the second most important variable that separated "high"- from "low"-risk jurors.
[b]The probability was based on a two-tailed test.
[c]Grand jury, not petit jury.

(7) belief that racial prejudice was still prevalent in our society. The question on the causes of a crime was phrased: "Do you think the cause of crime is a function of education, class, race, or some other factor(s)?" The juror's belief about the accused's economic background related to the death penalty was elicited in the following way: "Do you think a poor person is more likely to receive the death penalty than a wealthy person?" The question on racial prejudice was phrased: "Do you think that prejudice against black people by white people is a thing of the past?" A yes response was coded 0 and no was coded 1 for all of these questions. High-risk jurors were then identified by the opposite profile characteristics by means of the same questions.

Table 6–2 identifies the four sociodemographic characteristics that separated the high- and low-risk jurors, namely: (1) age; (2) race; (3) gender; and (4) education. For instance, prospective high-risk jurors were characterized by (1) old age; (2) being white; (3) being female; and (4) having less than a high school education. Obviously, the defense strategy was to include jurors with low-risk profile characteristics and to peremptorily challenge high-risk jurors.

Scientific Defense Voir Dire

During the *voir dire* screening session, the potential jurors were either challenged for cause, peremptorily challenged, or excused by stipulation of the attorneys. Table 6–3 provides the final breakdown of socioeconomic and demographic characteristics of both expaneled and impaneled jurors. Among the original 120 prospective jurors who had been examined during the *voir dire* process, 22 persons were challenged for cause by the prosecution or defense attorneys and 29 jurors were excused by stipulation. The exercise of the defense's peremptory challenges eliminated 9 prospective jurors characterized as (1) whites (88.9%); (2) males

TABLE 6-2
Correlation Coefficients of Risk Factors[a] with Ascriptive/Achieved Status of Prospective Jurors

Variables	*Correlation Coefficients*	*Probability*
Age	.09	.13
Race[b]	–.13	.08
Education	–.09	.13
Sex[c]	.16	.06

[a]Risk factors were coded as 0 for low-risk and 1 for high-risk jurors.
[b]Race was coded as 1 for white and 2 for minority (nonwhite) jurors.
[c]Sex was coded as 1 for male and 2 for female jurors.

TABLE 6-3

Jury Compositions at Voir Dire *and Jury Box Selection Processes*[a]

Variable	Long Beach district (%)	Impaneled jury panel[b]	Peremptorily challenged by defense	Peremptorily challenged by prosecution	Challenged for cause	Excused by stipulation	Selected jurors: Jurors in jury box	Selected jurors: Alternates
Race								
Anglo	59.5	76 (73.8)	8 (88.9)	3 (50.0)	16 (72.2)	8[c] (66.7)	7 (58.4)	4 (100.0)
Black	16.4	12 (11.7)	0 (0.0)	2 (33.3)	4 (18.2)	0 (0.0)	3 (25.0)	0 (0.0)
Hispanic	20.9	10 (9.7)	0 (0.0)	1 (16.7)	0 (0.0)	4 (33.3)	1 (8.3)	0 (0.0)
Others	3.2	5 (4.8)	1 (11.1)	0 (0.0)	2 (9.1)	0 (0.0)	1 (8.3)	0 (0.0)
Gender								
Male	48.0	60 (50.0)	6 (66.7)	1 (16.7)	12 (54.4)	9 (31.0)	9 (75.0)	2 (50.0)
Female	52.0	60 (50.0)	3 (33.3)	5 (83.3)	10 (45.6)	20 (69.0)	3 (25.0)	2 (50.0)
Age								
18–20	8.1	0 (0.0)	0 (0.0)	0 (0.0)	0 (0.0)	0 (0.0)	0 (0.0)	0 (0.0)
21–30	26.9	19 (15.8)	0 (0.0)	2 (33.3)	3 (13.6)	4 (13.8)	2 (16.7)	2 (50.0)
31–40	19.0	21 (17.5)	1 (11.1)	1 (16.7)	4 (18.2)	3 (10.3)	4 (33.3)	1 (25.0)
41–50	15.2	22 (18.3)	2 (22.2)	0 (0.0)	4 (18.2)	6 (20.7)	0 (0.0)	0 (0.0)
51–60	14.2	31 (25.9)	2 (22.2)	2 (33.3)	2 (9.1)	11 (37.9)	4 (33.3)	0 (0.0)
61–70	9.0	22 (18.3)	4 (44.5)	0 (0.0)	6 (27.3)	4 (13.8)	2 (16.7)	1 (25.0)
70 & over	7.6	5 (4.2)	0 (0.0)	1 (16.7)	3 (13.6)	1 (3.5)	0 (0.0)	0 (0.0)
Education								
Grade school	32.2	6 (5.0)	0 (0.0)	1 (16.7)	1 (4.5)	1 (3.4)	0 (0.0)	0 (0.0)
High school	34.0	52 (43.4)	4 (44.4)	1 (16.7)	11 (50.0)	11 (37.9)	5 (41.7)	2 (50.0)
Some college	21.3	40 (33.3)	4 (44.4)	4 (66.6)	4 (18.2)	14 (48.4)	4 (33.3)	0 (0.0)
College[d]	12.5	22 (18.3)	1 (11.1)	0 (0.0)	6 (27.3)	3 (10.3)	3 (25.0)	2 (50.0)
Total (*N*)		120 (100.0)	9 (100.0)	6 (100.0)	22 (100.0)	29 (100.0)	12 (100.0)	4 (100.0)

[a]Figures in parentheses are percentages.
[b]May 29, 1985, through July 17, 1985.
[c]Seventeen people did not report their race/ethnicity.
[d]Figures are based on those who graduated from college.

(66.7%); (3) middle-aged or older (11.1%–44.5% for ages 31–70); and (4) those with some college or high school education (88.9%). The prosecution had its own strategy, eliminating by the peremptory challenges 6 prospective jurors who were (1) racial or ethnic minorities (50%); (2) female (83.3%); (3) relatively younger (50% between 21 and 40); and (4) relatively uneducated.

As had been true in previous trials of this type, the defense team was trying to include jurors with low-risk characteristics. Thus, the defense attorney did not strike members of racial minorities and persons under age 30. The prosecution, on the other hand, directed its peremptory challenges toward the same subgroups that the defense team was struggling to save during the *voir dire* session.

In the struggle to assemble favorable jurors, 7 of the 12 jurors finally selected were white (58.4%), 3 were black (25.0%), and 2 were Hispanic and other ethnic groups (8.3%, respectively). Of the 12 jurors, 9 were male (75.0%). No person under age 20 or over age 70 was selected to serve. All jurors had at least a high school education, and a majority (58%) had some college education. Most important, in the contest to find reasoning peers, the attorneys selected 3 of 12 jurors and 2 alternates with college postgraduate education. As the analysis indicated, education was one of the most important factors in predicting the potential verdict of the *Harris* jurors. That is, highly educated potential jurors were more likely to vote for life imprisonment than to sentence the defendant to death.

Another important point is that the racial composition of the selected jurors was very similar to the overall racial makeup of the Long Beach Superior Court judicial district and seemed to reflect the racial composition of the community: 59.5% white, 16.4% black, and 20.9% Hispanic, according to the 1980 U.S. Census. Although the proportion of black jurors on the final jury was higher than that in the community, the ratio of white to minority jurors in the jury box remained almost identical to the racial composition in the jurisdiction. Although racial minorities were generally underrepresented in jury pools, the scientific jury selection technique was useful in the selection of a final jury characterized by racial representativeness.

Surviving Trend: Markov Chain

There is another way of examining the effectiveness of scientific *voir dire* jury selection in systematically choosing the low-risk jurors and eliminating high-risk potential jurors. That is, the impact of *voir dire* can also be examined by showing the probability of various cognizable groups' "surviving" the *voir dire* screening process, that is, by the use of the Markov chain of jury selection (see Figure 6–1).[7]

Two kinds of important information were provided by the Markov chain in analyzing jurors' survival rates during *voir dire:* (1) the particular stages of elimination from the selection process and (2) the probability that each subgroup (note, not the total group) would survive through the chain of the elimination process. The main objective of this careful observation of subgroups throughout the *voir dire* screening process was to monitor the survival rate of the low-risk jurors and to develop a courtroom strategy for preserving the target population by eliminating high-risk jurors. Obviously, the passage of each low-risk subgroup through the net of a particular stage of the selection process meant that the defendant's chances of a favorable sentence were improved.

According to the Markov chain and the resultant survival probabilities of potential jurors, the analysis pointed out that 63.9% of whites successfully passed through the *voir dire* screening process, and 36% of them did not. Of the 64% of white jurors who had survived, 23.9% of them were selected, and the 76.1% remaining were either excused or challenged. Some 63.6% of the selected white jurors became the members of the jury panel, and 36.4% of them became alternates.

The survival probabilities for white prospective jurors were thus based on many factors; the chance of whites becoming jurors was 15 out of 100 (0.64 multiplied by 0.239), and 85 out of 100 white prospective jurors did not make the final jury (85%).

Besides whites, who else entered the retrial jury box? Here, several facts need to be examined. First, although the probability of all subgroups surviving *voir dire* is similar (except for those under age 20, of whom none were selected, because no impaneled jurors from such an age cohort were available), the likelihood of becoming an actual juror varied by group (see Table 6–4). Of Hispanics, 10% were selected, whereas 25% of the original prospective black jurors became actual jurors. The chance of males becoming jurors was three times higher than that of females. No person between ages 41 and 50 and over age 70 "survived" the *voir dire* screening process. Those with less than a high school education did not make it through to the jury box either. The important finding is that the higher the educational attainment of the prospective jurors, the greater was their chance of serving on the jury. For example, 9.6% of high school graduates became jurors, and 10.0% and 13.6% of jurors with some college postgraduate education were selected, respectively.

It is also important to note that the probability of whites' becoming final jurors was the lowest among all racial groups. However, their proportion on the jury (58.4%) was similar to their proportion in the commu-

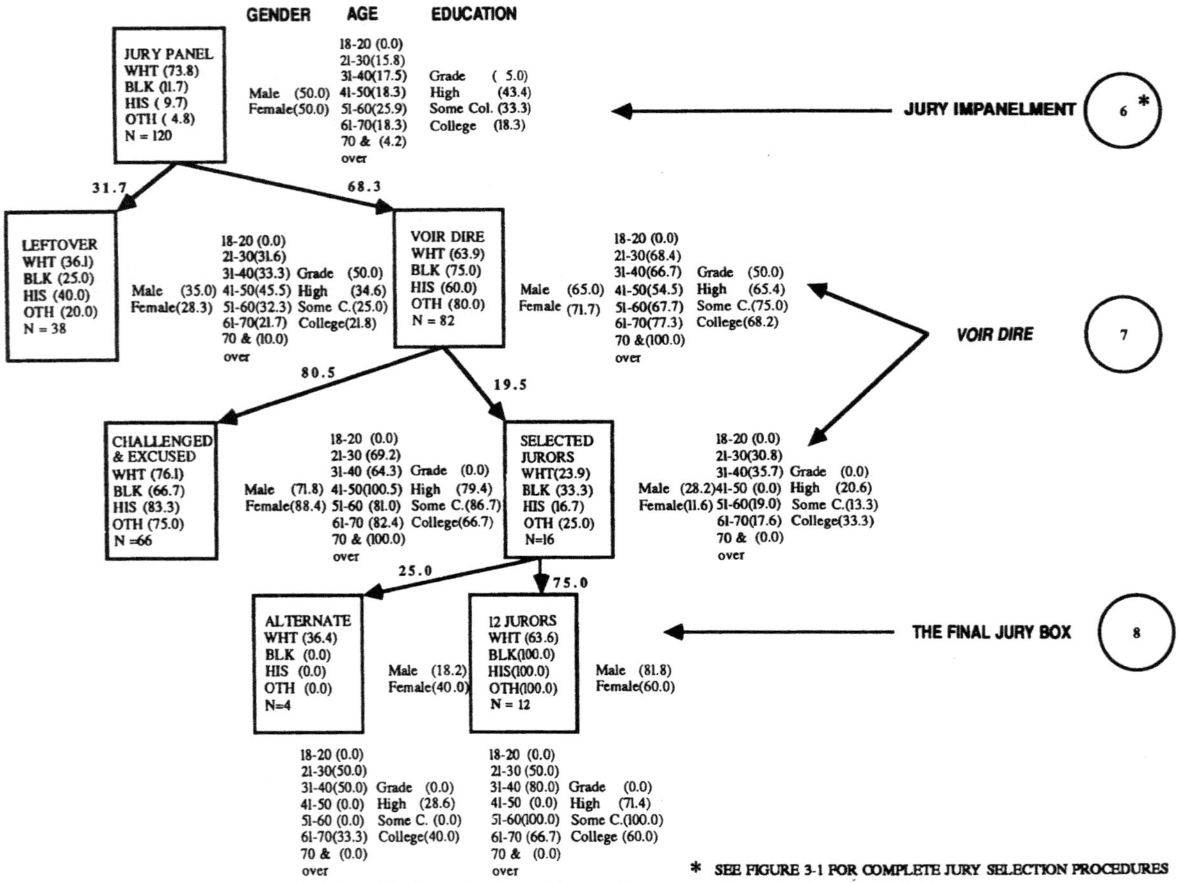

* SEE FIGURE 3-1 FOR COMPLETE JURY SELECTION PROCEDURES

FIGURE 6-1. Markov chains of jury selection and survival probabilities.

TABLE 6-4
Survival Probabilities of Cognizable Groups in Jury Selection

Variable	*Jury panel*	Voir dire	*Selected jurors*[a]	*Jury box*
Race				
Anglo	100.0 (73.8)[b]	63.9 (70.8)	15.3 (68.8)	9.7 (58.4)
Black	100.0 (11.7)	75.0 (13.8)	25.0 (18.8)	25.0 (25.0)
Hispanic	100.0 (9.7)	60.0 (9.2)	10.0 (6.2)	10.0 (8.3)
Others	100.0 (4.8)	80.0 (6.2)	20.0 (6.2)	20.0 (8.3)
Gender				
Male	100.0 (50.0)	65.0 (47.6)	18.3 (68.8)	15.0 (75.0)
Female	100.0 (50.0)	71.7 (52.4)	8.3 (31.2)	5.0 (25.0)
Age				
18–20	100.0 (0.0)	0.0 (0.0)	0.0 (0.0)	0.0 (0.0)
21–30	100.0 (15.8)	68.4 (15.9)	21.1 (25.0)	10.5 (16.7)
31–40	100.0 (17.5)	66.7 (17.1)	23.8 (31.3)	19.0 (33.3)
41–50	100.0 (18.3)	54.5 (14.6)	0.0 (0.0)	0.0 (0.0)
51–60	100.0 (25.9)	67.7 (25.6)	12.9 (25.0)	12.9 (33.3)
61–70	100.0 (18.3)	77.3 (20.7)	13.6 (18.7)	9.1 (16.7)
70 & over	100.0 (4.2)	100.0 (6.1)	0.0 (0.0)	0.0 (0.0)
Education				
Grade school	100.0 (5.0)	50.0 (3.7)	0.0 (0.0)	0.0 (0.0)
High school	100.0 (43.4)	65.4 (41.4)	13.5 (43.8)	9.6 (41.7)
Some college	100.0 (33.3)	75.0 (36.6)	10.0 (25.0)	10.3 (33.3)
College	100.0 (18.3)	68.2 (18.3)	22.7 (31.2)	13.6 (25.0)

[a]Sixteen jurors (12 actual jurors and four alternates).
[b]Percentages of subgroups in the jury panel are computed with respect to column totals of respective categories.

nity (59.5%). Because a large number of white jurors were originally summoned and appeared at the courthouse, the low selection probability did not stop them from having a numerically high number on the final jury.

As already noted, neither younger nor older jurors survived the selection process; all of those over age 70 were either challenged for cause or excused by stipulation, and no person under age 20 made it through the jury panel stage. A similar pattern was observed for those with less than a high school education. They were either peremptorily challenged by the defense attorney, challenged for cause, or excused by stipulation. Consequently, no person in that group served on the final jury.

Once *voir dire* was completed, it was clear that the jury selected from the 120 eligible candidates met the basic criteria of low-risk characteristics. Black jurors and jurors with high educational attainment were retained on the final jury. Female jurors—seen by the defense as likely to impose the death penalty—had the lowest probability of surviving through the *voir dire* process.

Does race still matter in selecting a jury, then? Postverdict interviews revealed that the first vote on the penalty was 9 to 3 in favor of death. The three jurors who voted against the death penalty were the *three black jurors*. The second vote was a unanimous vote in favor of life without possibility of parole. Postverdict interviews also indicated that one black male juror walked into the deliberation room after hearing all the penalty-phase evidence and said, "I'm not going to vote for the death penalty, and no one is going to change my mind." Ultimately, the assertiveness of that one black juror, working his chemistry with the others, significantly influenced their final verdict, eventually changing the first vote for death to a vote for life without the possibility of parole.

Voir Dire *and Its Social Significance*

The *voir dire* process is a fundamental guarantee of a defendant's Sixth Amendment right to trial by a fair and impartial jury.[8] *Voir dire* examination is designed to elicit information about each prospective juror that will indicate her or his ability to serve in an impartial and unbiased manner. Recently, however, *voir dire* techniques have become more extensive. As the following discussion shows, this extension has created controversy both within the legal community and among academicians.

Voir dire is the process in which an attorney, or a judge in some courts, questions a prospective juror. *Voir dire* literally means "to speak the truth." Based on the answers offered, an attorney attempts to pick the most favorable jury for his or her client by using two types of challenges to remove potentially unfavorable jurors: A challenge for cause is a challenge of a prospective juror in which an attorney must give the court legally cognizable grounds for disqualifying the juror, such as severe prejudice against either side. A peremptory challenge is a challenge of a prospective juror in which no explanation need be given for disqualifying a juror (*Swain v. Alabama*, 380 U.S. 202 1965).

Intelligent exercise of the cause and peremptory challenges, however, requires that information be elicited from the prospective juror regarding his or her life experiences and how these relate to the case at issue. A prospective juror's age, education, community status, personal experiences, and prejudices ultimately affect how that individual will deliberate (Van Dyke, 1977). A juror's impartiality was referred to as "indifference" during the common law period (Babcock, 1975). Yet, historical legal precedents have shown that indifference does not actually exist. Thus, the most effective way of dealing with the problem of juror bias is the use of extensive *voir dire* techniques, as demonstrated in the *Harris* trial.

Voir dire grew out of the common law practice of selecting men for a jury who were neighbors of the litigant parties (Moore, 1972). Communities were small, and people tended to live within limited geographic boundaries, so neighbors knew each other. The original intent of *voir dire,* under English law, was to elicit general information on factors such as blood ties to or familiarity with defendants or attorneys, incompetency, or criminality (Ryan & Neeson, 1981). The judge directed *voir dire* to determine if a prospective juror should be disqualified through the exercise of a challenge to his personal situation or characteristics, as known in the community. A prospective juror was challenged if he was classified as *propter honoris respectum,* a member of Parliament; *propter defectum,* incompetent; *propter affectum,* biased; or *propter delictum,* a convicted criminal (Moore, 1972, pp. 440–441).

In the United States, the 1986 U.S. Supreme Court decision in *Batson v. Kentucky* (106 S. Ct. 1712 1986) added another factor and became a landmark in establishing one of the guidelines for the contemporary *voir dire* screening process. It ruled that the equal-protection-of-the-law clause of the U.S. Constitution guarantees the defendant that the state will not exclude all members of his race from the jury box on account of race, or on the false assumption that members of his own race as a group are not qualified to serve as jurors (pp. 1716–1718). The Court also ruled that state prosecutors of a black defendant cannot use their peremptory challenges to dismiss all potential jurors simply because they are black and reaffirmed that a defendant has no right to a petit jury composed in whole or in part of persons of his own race, citing *Strauder v. West Virginia* (10 Otto 303, 305, 100 U.S. 303, 305 25 L.Ed. 664 1880).

Using such logic retroactively, there was no way that the Court could know the state prosecutor's real reasons for a peremptory challenge of any juror in the original *Harris* trial in 1979—because no reason need be given to the court for such a challenge. In such a case the Supreme Court majority would have to infer the use of *voir dire* from the pattern of excluding all 4 black jurors from the jury box and picking 12 white jurors who ultimately convicted the black man of burglary and receipt of stolen goods.[9]

The *voir dire* process has thus evolved today into a more complex technique. Whereas the original main goal of *voir dire* was to solicit minimal information from prospective jurors regarding their affiliation, the current practice of defense counsel has these four main practical goals: (1) to elicit information from jurors about their sociodemographic background and their attitudes and biases toward case-specific issues;

(2) to educate and persuade prospective jurors about the defense case and to neutralize negative factors of the prosecutor's case; (3) to develop an open rapport between the prospective juror and the defense attorney and the client; and (4) to build credibility for the defense attorney's quest to uncover the critical factors surrounding the case.

Research on Biases in Scientific Jury Selection

As demonstrated in the scientific jury-selection defense-strategy in the *Harris* trial, academicians and trial lawyers have, in the past, often come to similar conclusions in their evaluation of jurors. Social scientists have long believed that the composition of the jury is one of the major factors in predicting the final verdict (Hans & Vidmar, 1986; Hastie *et al.*, 1983; Lipton, 1979; Nietzel & Dillehay, 1986; Wrightsman, 1987). The examination of jurors' demographic and socioeconomic characteristics is of great significance because each juror's psychological attributes and proclivities, which will influence a particular verdict, are closely intertwined with the juror's ascriptive characteristics (e.g., age, race, and gender) and socially achieved status (e.g., education and income) (Brady, 1983, p. 242; Fukurai & Butler, 1991b; Fukurai *et al.*, 1991b; Kassin & Wrightsman, 1988; Nietzel, 1986; Simon, 1980; Van Dyke, 1977). In fact, a number of research studies have substantiated the close relation of jurors' backgrounds to their physical appearance and conditions and mental response patterns.

Race has played a major role in juror selection in the United States, particularly when a criminal trial involves racial minorities as defendants. In such trials, it has been assumed that acculturated racial prejudice and attitudes tend to predispose jurors to a particular type of verdict. For instance, past research has shown that black defendants have been treated more harshly by jurors when their victims were white than when the victims were nonwhite (Hans & Vidmar, 1986). The research further suggests that jurors of the same race as the victim are conviction-prone; and that jurors of the same race as the defendant are acquittal-prone (Dane & Wrightsman, 1982).

Racial prejudgment is likely to generate different outcomes in various types of trials as well. Research indicates that, in a criminal trial, the race and ethnicity of a defendant predisposes some jurors toward certain biases in their verdict (Poythress, 1981; Rokeach & McLellan, 1970). The effect of race on jurors' decisions in rape trials illustrates jurors' prejudice and the court milieu's influence on a particular verdict.[10] The all-black "Scottsboro Boys" case, in which they were accused of raping a white woman in the South, for instance, is a typical case in which a white jury returned a guilty verdict for the members of a racial minority. Chapter 4 provides numerous examples of cases involving black defendants who were tried by all-white juries.

Research also indicates that language, styles of expression, the demeanor of witnesses, and the cultural context of the incident may raise a major barrier to white judges' and juries' understanding and objectively evaluating the racial issues surrounding a case (Hans & Vidmar, 1986). Many jurors and judges evaluate a person's credibility on the basis of her or his sex, social class, and racial and ethnic background. Language, for example, affects how jurors perceive and evaluate witnesses, and racial minorities may be discriminated against because of their language and speech patterns (Conley, O'Barr, & Lind, 1978; Gumperz, 1982; Lind, Eriksen, & O'Barr, 1978; Swett, 1969). Given a significant number of trials involving racial minorities as defendants, it is not difficult to speculate how much more pronounced the effects must be when the witness speaks with the vocabulary of, for example, the black or Hispanic urban ghetto.

In addition to the effect that race and ethnic background have on jury verdicts, the age of a juror is also often associated with bias or prejudice that influences trial outcome. There is substantial evidence that a person's activities, attitudes toward life, relationships to family or to work, biological capacities, and physical fitness are conditioned by the age structure of the particular society or geographic areas in which the person lives. Different age cohorts have had dissimilar experiences that affect them in specific ways. All U.S. citizens, for instance, were affected by the war in Vietnam, but the age group drafted to fight the war was affected in a different way from the older age group who watched it on television and debated it over cocktails and coffee cups. This difference was also reflected in court cases at the time. Selective Service law violations committed by draft-age youths increased significantly between the years 1960 and 1970, and jurors asked to assess these violations belonged most often to older age cohorts and a different social milieu (as in the Camden 28 trials in New Jersey in 1972, for example). Further, research indicates that younger jurors tend to have fewer set notions about expected lifestyles and are likely to be more liberal, whereas older jurors are more likely to be conservative in attitude. Thus, these two groups reach different verdicts on similar cases (National Jury Project, 1983; Sealy, 1980).

There is also evidence that the sex of jurors predisposes them toward certain biases in verdicts. For instance, in Dr. Spock's trial regarding obstruction of the induction of draft-age candidates for the Vietnam war, the trial jury had no women, and he and other codefendants were found guilty (Simon, 1980). Dr. Spock's *The Common Sense Book of Baby and Child Care* had brought him great prominence among American mothers, but the jury consisted of all white males.[11]

Another example is the trial of Angela Davis. A member of the Communist Party, a black, and a Black Panther supporter, she was charged with murder and kidnapping growing out of a Marin County courthouse shooting in August 1970. In her 1972 trial in San Jose, California, she was permitted to act as her own counsel. She questioned prospective jurors during *voir dire,* argued some of the pretrial motions, and made an opening statement to the jury (Aptheker, 1975; Dorsen & Friedman, 1973, pp. 130, 196; Major, 1973).

With the help of five black psychologists, 12 jurors were selected from a panel of 116 in a nine-day effort, and an additional four days were required to pick 4 alternates (Simon, 1980, p. 134). The prosecution peremptorily challenged the only black in the *venire,* and when alternates were picked, the prosecution challenged a native American, the only other nonwhite to reach the jury box (Van Dyke, 1977, p. 155). The jury in the trial consisted of 12 white jurors, 7 women and 5 men: a maintenance electrician, once a schoolteacher; an accountant; a sales supervisor; two housewives (one of whom had a brother who had been an inmate of San Quentin); an IBM employee; a student; an unemployed person; a recently divorced woman; a medical research assistant; a retired librarian; and a collection agent (Major, 1973; Simon, 1980, p. 134). When the trial ended on June 2, 1972, the jury announced that they had reached a verdict of not guilty. This verdict also provides an excellent example of a trial outcome in which the jury's gender composition was influenced by the defense.

Other research indicates that the gender of jurors is strongly associated with the propensity to express their opinions and influence other members during deliberations. Conley *et al.* (1978) found that women are more likely to express their verdict opinions in a powerless style of speech and to be perceived as less convincing, less competent, less trustworthy, and less intelligent. The gender of chosen jurors may become the basis of a hierarchical system, strongly associated with the ability of each juror to convince other members of a jury.

The education of the prospective juror is another factor allowing a preview of possible sympathy with the accused and the defendant's attorney. The generally held assumption is that less educated persons are dogmatic and conservative, whereas better educated individuals are liberal and informed about various racial and political issues surrounding criminal cases (Simon, 1980, pp. 33–44). In many publicized trials, however, the political and ideological affiliation of the prospective jurors does not necessarily correlate with these assumptions. For example, the Harrisburg Seven trial in 1972 showed the exact opposite findings. This trial was connected with extensive wiretapping by federal authorities to investigate those whose loyalty to the government was doubted. Religious activists who opposed the war in Vietnam out of moral conviction were seen by the government as dangerous because of the influence they had among the religious laity. Members of the Catholic left were being watched, and two nuns, Joques Egan and Pat Chanel, had already been subpoenaed in a grand jury investigation of an alleged plot (Clark, 1975; O'Rourke, 1972). They refused to testify, even after receiving immunity against prosecution, claiming that they could not be compelled to answer questions that were based on illegally secured information, acquired by electronic surveillance, or wiretapping. They were cited for contempt and ordered imprisoned (Clark, 1975, p. 43).

Other religious activists broke into government Selective Service files and dumped blood on them as a symbol of what they believed to be a sacrilegious war in Vietnam. In the resulting Harrisburg trial, the defendants were charged with possessing contraband equipment, writing threatening letters, conspiring to raid federal offices, possessing substances for bombing government property, and planning to kidnap presidential adviser Henry Kissinger. Six were members of the Roman Catholic clergy, called the New Catholic Left; the seventh defendant was a Muslim from Pakistan.

The defense attorneys worked closely with social scientists in selecting the jury. Harrisburg was surveyed, and studies were made of the ideological affiliation and socioeconomic status of the entire population. Although the defense lawyers presumed that college graduates would be liberal and thus desirable defense jurors, survey analyses indicated that Harrisburg residents with a college education were quite conservative. Given the ideological profile of the prospective jurors, the defense attorneys proceeded with the *voir dire* screening session by excluding those with unfavorable profile characteristics. If undesirable jurors were not excused for cause, they were eliminated by peremptory challenges (O'Rourke, 1972, pp. 73–74). After seven days' deliberation, the jury was hung 10 to 2 for acquittal on the conspiracy and threatening letter counts. The Harrisburg trial revealed that higher educational attainment is not necessarily related to a liberal ideological affiliation. Nevertheless, the educational background of prospective jurors remains one basis for evaluating and selecting prospective jurors in the *voir dire* screening process.

Sequestration is also a factor that often plays an important role in influencing jury composition and jury verdicts. Sequestration is a procedure used by the government to insulate jurors from publicity about the trial and information about the defendants that is not admissible into evidence. Because jury service is a hardship involving loss of personal time and provides inadequate pay, this personal burden is likely to result in a jury that is not representative of the community. Due to small compensation, prospective jurors who have less education and less income, and who are in secondary labor markets, tend to be underrepresented (Fukurai & Butler, 1991a; Fukurai *et al.*, 1991b). Jurors who are likely to have higher education and thus higher paying jobs are more able to sit on a sequestered jury, rather than to ask to be excused for economic reasons (Fukurai & Butler, 1987). Thus, the resulting group of sequestered jurors are not likely to be representative of the community at large (Van Dyke, 1977, pp. 181–181).

Conclusions

The history of jury trials in capital cases has substantiated the influence of the racially demarcated jury, namely, a white-dominated jury that indicts and convicts a member of a racial minority. In *People v. Harris,* we found this pattern of racial domination in the judicial decision-making process. The trial took place in 1979 in the City of Long Beach, where approximately 40% of the residents were members of racial or ethnic minorities. However, the original trial in 1979 had an all-white jury, which sentenced the black defendant to death. In the 1985 retrial, the defense attorney decided to use scientific *voir dire* to screen prospective jurors. The final jury was composed of seven white and five minority jurors, including three blacks, one Hispanic, and one Asian.

Scientific defense *voir dire* is an important method of identifying high- and low-risk potential jurors whose ideological views and beliefs may influence the outcome of a trial. Using computerized data and analyzing the information by sophisticated statistical techniques, it is possible to assign "high" and "low" risks to potential jurors based on *voir dire* questionnaires and in-court behavioral assessment of each prospective juror.

Can this work be replicated by others? Several important findings need to be repeated. The prosecution systematically excluded the specific group of persons through the use of peremptory challenges. The cognizable groups that were systematically challenged and/or excluded by the prosecution were minorities and younger jurors (Dundee, 1972; Zeigler, 1978). Apparently, the prosecution believed that these groups were more likely to sympathize with the defendant.

To offset such narrowness, the defense attorney's strategy to preserve as many black jurors as possible was successful. The probabilities of a black juror's "surviving" the *voir dire* process was heightened by the use of systematic jury selection techniques. Also, the defense preserved some jurors believed to have negative attitudes toward the death penalty (i.e., the young, the male, and the well-educated). These "cognizable" groups came to constitute the target population preserved by the defense.

These analytical results also shed light on the understanding of the accused's intent in committing the criminal act. The selected jurors apparently believed that there was a strong relationship between a majority-dominated society's influencing the defendant's impoverished childhood experience and his resulting attitudes and beliefs which led to violent acts. As the favorable jurors seemed to share the belief that racial prejudice was still prevalent in our society, it was possible to predict their decision in advance.

There is a delicate balance between searching for a fair and impartial jury and searching for one that is partial and biased, that is, a balance between the narrow community that may best understand and favor the accused and the broad community, which may favor the prosecution. Following this line of argument, the balance struck by the "peers" picked by the defense and the "impartial" jurors picked by the prosecution may result in a fairer judgment of the accused than previously existed. The standards of a *narrowly defined peer group* would thus be tempered by those of *broadly based peers.*

Jury selection that has been revolutionized by computers and statistical methods does not necessarily make a mockery of the justice system. But will these latest methods become a game in which the prosecutor and the defense counsel try to feed the fastest computers with the best and most extensive data about each potential juror? And, in the name of advanced selection of the most favorable and unfavorable candidates, will there be an invasion of a prospective juror's privacy? Or will a kind of "star wars" mentality in aligning offenses and defenses be played out with selected jurors over the body of a defendant? The answers will emerge, not here, but in the course of the coming decades. What a jury of one's peers was in the past has already been changed somewhat, and its character in the future will undoubtedly involve further changes.

The results of greater effectiveness of the scientific jury selection method should encourage attorneys to increase their use of scientific defense *voir dire* in jury selection. Although the effectiveness of systematic jury selection has long been debated, the application of statistical methods to jury selection has now shown significant results. Future research should further validate the process and the result.

Notes

1. Jury trials have often revealed the strategic mechanisms of social control and political opposition in America. The jury that tried the defendants in the Boston Tea Party cases, for instance, acknowledged both material and forensic evidence of the alleged crime, that is, the factual violation of law. Yet, the jurors unanimously voted to acquit the defendants, signifying their power of jury *nullification*, which reflected people's strong dissatisfaction with England's mercantile controls. By contrast, black defendants from southern states who have been accused of raping white women have often been tried by all-white juries that have indicted and convicted them, thereby maintaining judicial dominance through systemic racial discrimination on juries.
2. In *Batson v. Kentucky*, the Supreme Court did not address the question of race-conscious peremptory challenges used by a defense lawyer; however, the Supreme Courts of California (1978), Massachusetts (1979), and Florida (1984) have ruled that, under their respective state constitutions, neither the defense nor the prosecution may use peremptory challenges to exclude blacks as a group.
3. Supreme Court Justice Thurgood Marshall may have unwittingly set a trap for defendants facing discriminatory *voir dire*. In *Batson v. Kentucky*, he called to eliminate peremptory challenges altogether on the basis of "the shameful practice of racial discrimination in the selection of jurors." Yet, once the shameful practice of excluding women, Seventh-Day Adventists, Jews, Vietnamese, Japanese, and so on, demands that *all* be included in the jury box, the defendant who seeks a narrow, "balanced" jury to render a fair decision will face a broad "unbalanced" jury that may understand little about the milieu from which the accused emerged and the mental frame and intent that led the defendant to perform a particular set of acts. Going beyond racial heritage, in 1987 Brooklyn District Attorney Elizabeth Holtzman sought the courts to declare that gender, religion, and national origin are impermissible bases for eliminating prospective jurors. She would have the courts almost eliminate the peremptory challenge—for which no cause need be given. That is, from a pattern of exclusion of jurors of any race, gender, religion, or national origin, she wanted the courts to determine that most peremptory challenges are improper. That would put the defense in the position of being unable to narrow the jury box to jurors who might favor the accused. Defense lawyers facing the best resources of the state would be hard put to winnow out prospective jurors they suspect—through hunches, stereotyped presumptions, background data, or statistical analysis—would vote to convict their clients.
   Thus, defense attorneys have countered Holtzman by attempting to narrow the jury box to the precise peers of the accused. They seem to argue that a jury of one's peers must be a panel of one's race, gender, and so on, so as to fulfill the defendant's, not the prosecution's, constitutional guarantee of a fair and impartial jury.
4. A three-way psychological interaction of intent and imputation takes place: (1) the defendant's actual intent; (2) the jurors' interpretation of the accused's intent, and finally, (3) the imposition of this perceived intent on each juror's imagined position in the situation the accused experienced. For the sake of the defending party, it is important to discover or uncover the prospective juror's last two psychological interplays, for such jury proclivities can be quantified in applying statistical *voir dire* strategies to identify "high-" and "low"-risk jurors.
5. An example may clarify the relationship of a defendant's acts, intent, and beliefs to those standing in judgment. Under the British system of colonialism, a so-called dual mandate that allowed the English to use colonial resources and exploit indigenous labor also promised protection of native people, who supposedly were permitted to maintain

their cultural ways (Burr, 1975; Chambliss, 1971; Cromer, 1910; Dutt, 1957; Green, 1985). Many African peoples living under this helotry, thinking they were performing righteous acts of protection, killed witches or other carriers of malevolence threatening their personal, or the community's, soul or physical body. Yet, when these people were arrested for causing the death of another, colonial judges tried them by the English standards established to judge an act of murder, say, on the streets of London.

As British judges neither believed in witches nor were judicially permitted to recognize the deceased victims as witches, rather than finding that the accused had acted in self-defense in killing a witch (an act that would block a determination of intent to kill), the British judges found the act of killing corroborated by the defendant's admission of intent (*mens rea*), or the court intuiting an intent to kill.

Thus, the elements of the act of killing and an intent to kill were used to hold Africans guilty of murder. In fact, royal governors regularly commuted these sentences in order to maintain the precepts of the dual mandate, to stop Africans' protest, and to keep the colonial production system operating smoothly. But one can also imagine that a jury of Africans who believed in witches would have returned an initial verdict of self-defense or defense of others in their community. From the accused's intent to kill a witch, then, they might imagine themselves having the same intent and performing the same act, viewing it as a heroic gesture and not an evil design.

6. The basic strategic model of scientific jury selection involved a direct comparison at the last three stages of the jury selection process (i.e., empaneling the jury [Stage 6], peremptory challenges by the defense, peremptory challenges by the prosecution, challenges for cause, excuses by stipulation [Stage 7], and composition of the jury box) of the potential jurors' demographic characteristics of race, gender, age, and education. (Stage 8).
7. The Markov chain is the method of predicting, from a target population, the probability that some phenomenon will occur. For example, the Markov chain has been used extensively to predict the probability of developing a certain type of cancer by exposure to a radioactive substance.
8. The Sixth Amendment of the U.S. Constitution provides that "In all criminal prosecutions, the accused shall enjoy the right to a speedy and public trial, by an impartial jury of the State and district wherein the crime shall have been committed. . . ."
9. The inconsistency of prior Supreme Court rulings under the 14th Amendment and the nature of *voir dire* required this inference; that is, (1) the 14th Amendment was designed to put an end to state governmental discrimination on account of race; (2) in *Strauder v. West Virginia* (100 U.S. 303 1880) the Court ruled that the State had denied a black defendant equal protection of the law when it put him on trial before a jury from which members of his race had been purposely excluded; and (3) that decision laid the basis for the Supreme Court to rule in future cases against racial discrimination in the procedures used to select the *venire* from which individual jurors are drawn. But *Strauder* recognized that a defendant has no right to a "petit jury composed in whole or in part of persons of his own race" (Id., at 305); thus, (4) to break through the secret veil of peremptory challenges of jurors—in which all black jurors are excluded from the jury box—the Supreme Court had no way of following law and precedent—(1), (2), and (3) above—except by inferring the misuse of peremptory challenges from the pattern of exclusion. (5) This misuse of peremptory challenges allowed the Court to gloss over the illogical proposition that the equal protection clause, which applies to determining whether there is discrimination in selecting the *venire*, also governs the state's use of peremptory challenges to strike individual jurors from the petit jury because, the Court said, (a) the prosecutor's exercise of peremptory challenges for any reason must be

related to his or her view concerning the outcome of the case to be tried, (b) but the equal protection clause forbids the prosecutor to challenge potential jurors solely on account of their race or on the assumption that black jurors as a group will be unable to give impartial consideration to the State's case against a black defendant (pp. 1718–1719). Yet, how could any court know what the prosecutor's sole goal or assumptions might be concerning the outcome of the case, unless the court infers these (i.e., sole goal or assumptions) from the pattern of exclusion of all black jurors from the petit jury? "Misuse of the peremptory challenge to exclude black jurors has become common and flagrant," concurred Associate Justice Thurgood Marshall in support of the six-judge majority.

10. See Hubert S. Feild (1979) and Shirley Feldman-Summers and Clark D. Ashworth (1981).
11. In the trial, the defense was allowed 15 peremptory challenges and the government 10. One observer stated that the judge and the prosecutor successfully influenced the jury composition and the verdict. For example, in the trial, "[T]en women find their way into the jury box and . . . one Negro; they are at once bounced by the government. It is hard to discern any real pattern in the challenges on the defense side and indeed there is open disagreement among the five legal interns over several jurors. The government is more predictable. . . . Those who are challenged stalk off with half-sheepish, half-angry expressions; during the recess one of the women excused by the government complains bitterly to the press. 'I'd have voted for the prosecution anyway!' she says" (Mitford, 1969, p. 100).

    Two women and a black were challenged by the government. The jury picked was composed of all white males: two were self-employed, six were white-collar employees, three were blue-collar workers, and one was a professional. This all-male jury deliberating for eight hours found all defendants guilty of all charges but conspiracy to turn in their draft cards.

7

The Optimal Design to Obtain a Racially Representative Jury

Cluster-Sampling Methods with the Probability Proportionate to Size Applied to Jury Selection[1]

Introduction

The Federal Jury Selection and Service Act was passed in 1968 guaranteeing that "all litigants in Federal courts entitled to trial by jury shall have the right to grand and petit juries selected at random from a fair cross-section of the community" (U.S., 1968, Section 1861).[2] Current federal law attempts to insure this goal by specifying two key concepts in forming the jury *venire*. During panel selection procedures, there must be (1) "a random" selection of jurors and (2) selection from an area that includes special geographic districts in which a particular court convenes (U.S., 1968, Section 1861).[3] At the state level, a similar standard applies.[4]

However, jury research throws doubt on the ability of these procedures alone to produce representative juries [*Hernandez v. Texas*, 347 U.S. 475 1954; *United States v. Fernandez*, 480 F.2d 726 732–33 (2d Cir. 1973)].[5] Although the jury is required to be composed of a fair cross section of the community, racial and ethnic minorities are consistently underrepresented in the vast majority of jury *venires* in both federal and state courts, even though the U.S. Supreme Court has given gender, race, and socioeconomic factors "cognizable" status so as to be protected against discrimination in jury selection. Also in depicting the neighborhoods of particular racial and economic groups, the Court has given geographic living areas the status of cognizable classes.

Other factors determine the ultimate composition of the jury, once a pool of jurors has been selected, including the use of peremptory challenges by prosecution and defense lawyers in *voir dire*. Nevertheless, the goal of guaranteeing defendants jury trial by a cross section of the community begins with a *randomly selected jury pool*. If the initial pool is biased or skewed, the legal principle on which jury trials are to be based is violated at the outset (see *Avery v. Georgia*, 345 U.S. 559 1953; *Atkins v. Texas*, 325 U.S. 398 1954; *Carter v. Jury Commission of Greene County*, 396 U.S. 332 1970).

Residential Factors and Jury Selection

In addition to socioeconomic and demographic characteristics of individual jurors that influence jury composition, research indicates that the presence of residential segregation also affects the chance of being selected for jury service (Fukurai, 1985; Fukurai *et al.*, 1991a). Other research further suggests that, in some cities, the overrepresentation of white-dominated neighborhoods contributes to a substantially greater chance of whites' serving on juries. Heyns (1979) and Fukurai (1985) substantiated that jury representation in eight superior courts in Los Angeles County between 1978 and 1985 showed similar jury composition and geographic distribution within the respective jurisdictions. Disproportionality was found even though the master list was supposedly composed of the following two lists: (1) registration of voters (ROV) and (2) motor vehicle registration (DMV) (CA, 1980, Sections 17, 18).

In order to obtain a truly representative list of prospective jurors, then, jury selection procedures must recognize the racial and socioeconomic factors affecting residential segregation, and the selection procedure must take these factors into account. Traditional methods of jury selection, which are based on simple random sampling, are inadequate because minority and ethnic groups are not equally distributed within a jurisdiction. Random sampling therefore generates unrepresentative juror pools.

Figure 7–1 shows the residential segregation in Los Angeles County, black residents of the county being highly concentrated in certain areas. With simple random sampling, there is no guarantee that areas with black concentration will be sampled and therefore no guarantee that the list of potential jurors will reflect the racial composition of the county.

It is our contention that cluster sampling with the probability proportionate to size (PPS) minimizes the effect of spatial biases on jury representativeness. Using this alternative method, this chapter examines the cluster sampling of prospective jurors, which incorporates racial and

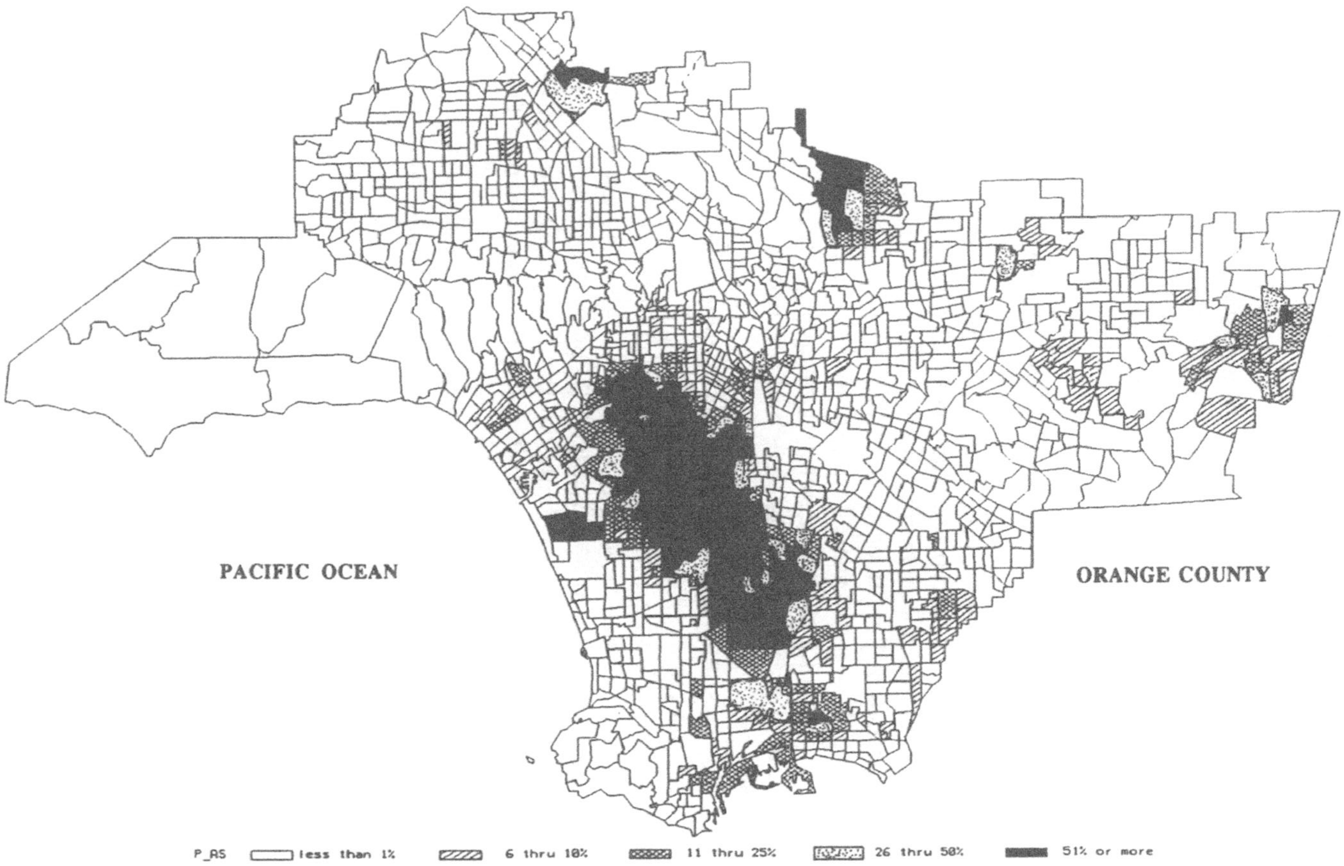

FIGURE 7-1. Residential segregation of black residents in Los Angeles County, 1980. Percentages of black residents in the census tracts.

socioeconomic factors affecting residential segregation and generates a pool of jurors that better reflects the cross section of the community.

The chapter also compares the two statistical methods, thus pursuing the following three specific objectives: (1) to evaluate jury representation based on simple random sampling; (2) to show how an alternative cluster-sampling strategy can effectively create an egalitarian system of juror representation; and (3) to show the extent to which the cluster-sampling method can help ensure racially balanced jury *venires*.

Cluster Sampling with the Probability Proportionate to Size

We argue that areal cluster sampling with PPS minimizes the effect of spatial biases on jury representativeness. The cluster-sampling method is designed to select prospective jurors based on an equal probability within a particular jurisdiction.

First applied in surveys by Kish in 1965, the PPS is an efficient method of obtaining multistage cluster sampling. Whenever the clusters sampled are of greatly differing sizes and compositions, it is appropriate to use PPS.

Cluster sampling with PPS assumes that each cluster will be given a chance for selection proportionate to its size. For example, each geographic unit, such as a census tract, has a different number of eligible jurors. A fixed number of eligible jurors—say, five—is selected from the census tract. Cluster sampling using PPS ensures that the selection procedure will offer each potential juror in the census tract the same probability of selection overall, the result being the selection of a fair cross section of the community population.

Cluster sampling of prospective jurors consists of two steps and is carried out in the following manner. In the first stage, the geographic units from which jurors are to be drawn are randomly selected. In the second stage, prospective jurors are randomly selected within the chosen geographic unit.

The computerized version of the cluster-sampling method is carried out in the following manner. In the first stage, each census tract within a jurisdiction is given a unique number. Then a series of random numbers is generated, identifying the fixed number of census tracts. This process is repeated each time a jury panel is assembled. Then, the frequency of clusters identified in jury panels is computed for each tract. The frequency of this census tract representation becomes equivalent to the expected number of prospective jurors from each census tract.

In the second stage, potential jurors are randomly selected from individual census tracts. Stratifying the jury selection by geographical units eliminates any potential selection biases arising from residential segregation and enhances the probability of assembling a more representative jury pool.

For example, consider the following situation. A particular judicial district has 1,000 census tracts and 1 million eligible jurors. When 1,000 jurors are to be assembled for jury duty, each juror has a 1,000/1 millionth, or .001, chance of selection. We can make this computation by first choosing 500 census tracts by random selection (the first stage). Each census tract will have approximately 2 eligible jurors to be selected.

A census tract containing 1,000 eligible jurors has a probability of selection equal to

$$\begin{matrix}500\\ \text{(tracts identified by}\\ \text{random selection)}\end{matrix} \times \frac{\text{1,000 (eligible jurors in the tract)}}{\text{1 million (eligible jurors in the district)}} = .5 \quad (1)$$

If this tract is represented, each eligible juror has a *second-stage* probability of selection equal to

$$\frac{\text{2 (to be selected from the tract)}}{\text{1,000 (eligible jurors in the tract)}} = .002 \quad (2)$$

By multiplying .5 times .002, we get an overall probability of selection equal to .001.

Now consider a census tract containing only 200 eligible jurors. The tract's chance of selection is only 500 times 200/1 millionth or .10, much less than that of the earlier example. If this tract is selected, each eligible juror has a chance of 2/200, or .01, of selection in the second stage. Overall in the sample, its probability of selection is .10 times .01, or .001; the same as in the earlier case and as demanded by the overall sampling design. The only difference in the two examples is *the number of eligible jurors in the two tracts,* but that number appears in both numerator and denominator, thus canceling itself out. No matter what the population size, then, the overall probability of an eligible juror's being selected is equal to 500 times 2/1 millionths, or .001.

The advantage of cluster sampling with PPS is that it takes relatively few eligible jurors from each census tract. Because the heterogeneity of the clusters (i.e., tracts) increases sampling variability, a large number of clusters is needed to reduce sampling errors (Sudman, 1976). Thus, a cluster-sampling design with a small cluster size and a large number of clusters is particularly useful because residential characteristics and racial representativeness are likely to be homogeneous and to affect sampling variability. For instance a cluster size of 5 is usually considered enough in the context of a large cluster sample (Babbie, 1989, p. 198) because the ratio of cluster to simple random-sampling error remains minimal (Sudman, 1976, p. 77). Obviously, a large number of eligible jurors in a single tract would improve the representation of the census tract slightly, but the cross-sectional representation of the judicial district as a whole would be more improved by the addition of more tracts to the sample than by the addition of eligible jurors in fewer tracts.

Given that the court needs only 1,000 potential jurors altogether, it would be better to select 2 jurors each from 500 census tracts than to select 20 each from 50 tracts. In addition to ensuring a fairer representation, cluster sampling with PPS allows an efficient use of limited sources.

The Empirical Model of Jury Representation

We used the following model of jury representation to evaluate the extent to which the cluster-sampling method creates a more egalitarian pool of potential jurors than simple random jury selection. In order to assess the influence of spatial biases on jury representation, the model includes the following four characteristics: (1) gender; (2) race; (3) socioeconomic positions; and (4) distance to the courthouse. In addition to the legally recognized variables, such as gender, race, and socioeconomic status, distance to the courthouse is included in the model because discrimination in jury representation may occur because of the distance and/or the travel time to the courthouse. These variables are the most important criteria to be used in an evaluation of the effectiveness of the two different sampling methods. The evaluative model of jury representation is shown in Figure 7–2.

If residential segregation affects jury representation, the four coefficients (β_1, β_2, β_3, and β_4) should be large and statistically significant. Statistically nonsignificant paths, however, indicate that residential segregation does not influence jury representation. Examination of the model thus allows an evaluation of the extent of potential discrimination and the anomalies of simple random jury selection. The model also enables a critical examination of the effectiveness of the alternative cluster-sampling model applied to jury selection. If individuals' areas of residence affect their chances of serving on juries, the statistically significant path would demonstrate the extent of discrimination in jury representation.

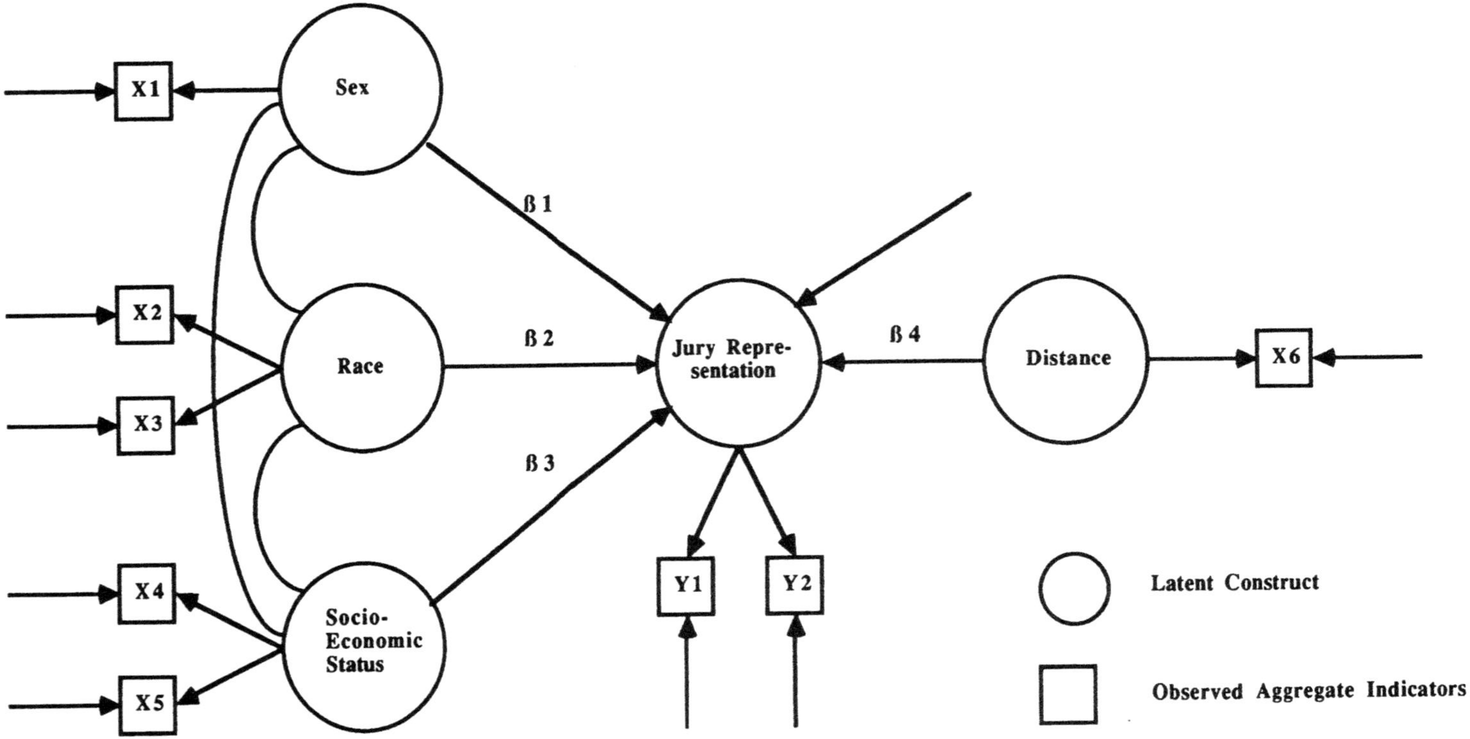

NOTE: X1, Male; X2, Black; X3, Spanish; X4, College; X5, Poverty; X6 Distance; Y1,No. of Peoples; Y2, No. of Panels

*: All the observed indicators are aggregate census variables by census tracts.

FIGURE 7-2. Evaluative model of jury representation.

Data

Two data sets were linked to serve as the foundation for an examination of the current jury representation model and the proposed cluster-sampling strategy: (1) jury impanelment lists for a retrial of a particular court case and (2) 1980 U.S. Census Bureau data.[6]

Ten jury impanelment lists, covering a period of 10 weeks, identified the neighborhoods (census tracts) from which jurors had been drawn to the Long Beach Superior Court, Los Angeles County, California. When compared with county demographic data, these lists also indicated whether the panels represented a fair cross section of the population in this court district.

Census tract information was used to compare the characteristics of the jurors on the impanelment lists with the sociodemographic characteristics of the population residing in the Long Beach Superior Court district. How to quantitatively determine the geographic definition of the judicial district remained an important issue. In the past, social scientists had relied on census tracts to evaluate jury representativeness and to examine the extent to which racial residential characteristics contributed to the representation of minority jurors. Kairys (1972), for instance, illustrated the practicality of using census tracts to generate a statistical index (chi-squares) and to examine the areal representation within a district. In California, as in most states, census tracts are used to evaluate judicial representation (*People v. Harris*, 36 Cal. 3d 36, 201 Cal. Rptr. 782 679 P. 2d 433 1984). For our analysis, the census tract is therefore used as a basis for delineating the judicial district. Jury impanelment lists enabled us to identify the census tracts in which eligible jurors resided.

The impanelments from which our lists came covered the period of April 4, 1985, through June 12, 1985. Hispanic jurors on the impanelment list were identified by a surname list provided by the U.S. Census Bureau. Census tracts on the lists also provided information on (1) the frequency of juror representation from each census tract and (2) the racial and ethnic compositions of the neighborhoods where potential jurors resided. There were 1,250 impaneled jurors during the 10-week period of the impanelment. The 10 panels drawn were typical of the panel data available for other time periods in the Long Beach Superior Court judicial district. Population and housing data were used to determine if there were disparities between the population composition and the representativeness of the jurors at the jury impanelment stage.

Methods

Covariance Structure Analysis

In assessing the jury representativeness model, we took advantage of the recent development of covariance structures and LISREL maximum-likelihood estimations to examine the overall goodness-of-fit test of the jury representativeness model. We used the likelihood ratio (chi-square) test statistic, and the likelihood-ratio indices (delta and rho) to compare fits in order to control for sample size (Bentler & Bonett, 1980; Bollen, 1989, pp. 271–276). Although failure to reject the null hypothesis may be taken as an indication that the model was consistent with the data, it is important to bear in mind that alternative models may also be consistent with the data (Fukurai, 1991; Joreskog & Sorbom, 1985). Moreover, because the chi-square test is affected by sample size, it follows that (1) given a sufficiently large sample, an overidentified model may be rejected even when it fits the data well, and (2) when the sample size is small, one may fail to reject the null hypothesis even when the model fits the data poorly (Long, 1983; Matsueda & Bielby, 1986). Therefore, a general null model based on modified independence among variables is also proposed to provide an additional reference point for the cluster evaluation of covariance structure models.[7]

We selected eight variables from 1980 U.S. Census to represent the five latent constructs so that we could examine the jury representation model. Gender was represented by the proportion of eligible male jurors in a given census tract. Race was measured by the proportions of black and Hispanic eligible jurors in the neighborhood. A socioeconomic factor was indicated by two measurements: (1) the proportion of prospective jurors with a college education and (2) the proportion of households under the poverty level. Distance was the absolute distance between the courthouse and the respective census tracts. Two variables represented the latent construct for jury representation: the number of times that the census tract had been chosen and the number of jurors living in the census tract who had been called to serve on juries.

Computer-Generated Graphics Analysis

The analysis also includes computer-generated graphics. The covariance structure analysis did not delineate the importance of particular spatial units such as residential segregation. Computer-generated graphics highlighted specific geographic locations and accurately reflected the impact of residential segregation on jury representation. We computed two statistical indices, chi-squares and Z scores, in order to evaluate the jury representation model. Those additional analyses assisted in our evaluation of the cluster-sampling method.

It was hypothesized that residential characteristics affect the jury composition most when simple random selection is used. That is, severe underrepresentation of racial minorities will be observed when potential jurors are selected with simple random sampling. We further hypothesized that cluster sampling reduces the effect of residential segregation on jury representation because every census tract has an equal probability of being selected. We also expected that cluster sampling with the probability proportionate to size (PPS) would ensure a more egalitarian pool of jury panels based on community populations.

Results

First, we examine simple random sampling and evaluate the relationship of residential characteristics to jury representativeness. Figure 7–3 shows the observed jury representation under the simple random-sampling method that was currently used by the court.

The social and racial compositions of the neighborhoods were associated with the opportunity to serve on juries. Note that the neighborhoods adjacent to economically prosperous Orange County had far greater chances of placing jurors on panels. Orange County, according to the 1980 U.S. Census, had 1.14% black and 12.50% Hispanic populations. The residents were predominantly white and were middle class or above. The Long Beach judicial district in Los Angeles County, on the other hand, had 16.4% eligible blacks and 20.8% Hispanics.

Some areas in the judicial district had no jurors on the panel, as would be expected in a random sampling. However, the nonrepresented areas included downtown Los Angeles and Long Beach, areas with the highest concentrations of racial minorities. The analysis further suggests disproportionality of representativeness within the impaneled neighborhood (see Table 7–1). One census tract was represented by potential jurors 22 times, whereas 117 census tracts were represented fewer than 4 times and 319 tracts had no representation. Half of the potential jurors came from 35 census tracts out of 538 tracts (6.5%) in the judicial district. The proportion of black and Hispanic jurors in nonrepresented areas (319) was higher than in the Long Beach judicial district as a whole. Further, the census tract with the highest representation had only 0.2% black and 5.9% Hispanic residents, far below the average in the jurisdiction.[8]

Neighborhoods that had below-average jury service representation

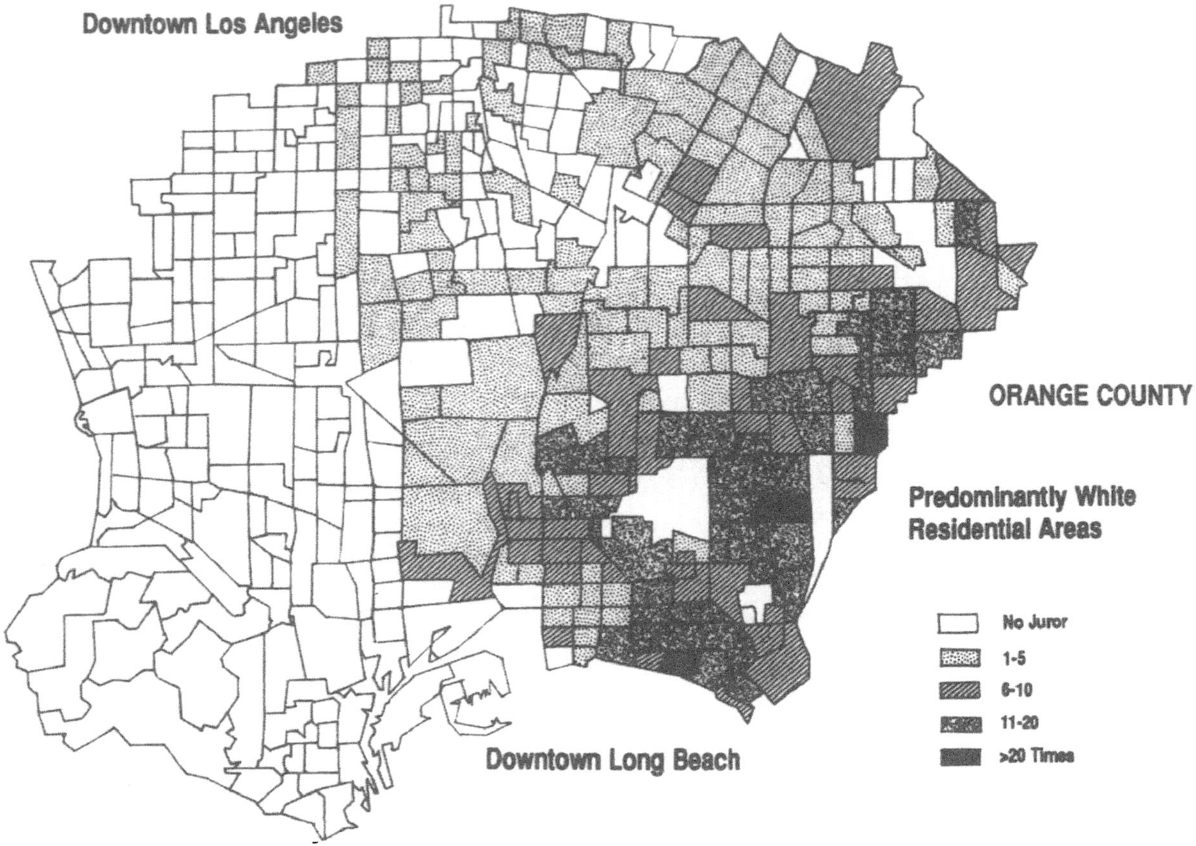

FIGURE 7-3. Simple-random-sampling jury selection and the frequency of census tract representation in the Long Beach jury panel.

TABLE 7-1
Census Tract Representation on 10 Panels: The Long Beach Judicial District[a]

Number of times census tracts represented	Frequency	Percentage[b]	Cumulative percentage	Minority composition: Black percentage	Minority composition: Hispanic percentage
				16.4	20.9
0	326	—	—	16.6	35.0
1	53	24.2	24.2	31.7	35.7
2	25	11.4	35.6	34.8	21.1
3	21	9.6	45.2	19.5	29.0
4	18	8.2	53.4	7.7	20.8
5	14	6.4	59.8	5.1	28.5
6	17	7.8	67.6	10.6	28.8
7	14	6.4	74.0	5.6	23.1
8	9	4.1	78.1	5.0	11.1
9	9	4.1	82.2	11.8	17.1
10	1	0.5	82.6	0.6	8.1
11	3	1.4	84.0	3.6	9.6
12	6	2.7	86.8	5.6	10.8
13	3	1.4	88.1	0.9	3.9
14	4	1.8	90.0	4.2	9.0
15	5	2.3	92.2	0.9	12.7
16	5	2.3	94.5	2.2	6.9
17	6	2.7	97.3	4.8	10.2
19	2	0.9	98.2	6.8	9.2
20	1	0.5	98.6	0.3	3.6
21	2	0.9	99.5	4.5	13.5
22	1	0.5	100.0	0.2	5.9

Median = 4
Mean = 10.28

[a]The table is identical to Table 2–7, showing the gerrymandering of the judicial district.
[b]Percentage is computed by the represented census tracts.

had far greater minority residents than those with above-average representation (19.3% and 26.6%, respectively, for black and Hispanic residents). Because jury representation was highly skewed, the median gives more meaningful information than the average for the location of observations in the distribution. The neighborhood based on the median substantiates that jury representation was highly disproportional. For instance, 26.1% of the residents in neighborhoods with below-median jury representation were black, in contrast to 6.0% of the residents in above-median neighborhoods. The same disproportionality was found for Hispanics (28.4% and 18.0% above and below the median, respectively).

This point can be illustrated if we posit alternative explanations and statistical proofs. For example, did underrepresented census tracts have a significantly lower percentage of qualified jurors? Juror qualification criteria, such as U.S. citizenship, language proficiency, residency requirement, and no prior felony conviction, are more likely to eliminate numbers of racial minorities and may affect the overall representation on jury impanelment lists. Disqualifying certain jurors, however, did not explain the geographical biases found here. For instance, 19.0% of all the potential jurors in the entire judicial district (538 census tracts) were qualified after a qualification screening process, and 19.8% of potential jurors who lived in the impaneled neighborhoods (212 tracts) were also qualified. Juror qualification thus does not explain the true extent of racially demarcated representation (see Table 2–9 for more detail).

We examined the current jury selection model for whether place of residence influenced one's chance of being included in the juror pool. We generated and examined coefficients of correlation (see Table 7–2). Two sets of the correlation matrix were the overall (538 tracts) and impaneled districts (212 tracts).[9] The overall goodness-of-fit of the model for the entire judicial district reflected the extent to which one's residence influenced one's chance of serving on a jury. The goodness-of-fit for impaneled tracts showed the effect of racial segregation only on the selected jurors. Thus, the similarity and difference of these two samples show the overall goodness-of-fit for the jury representation model with simple random jury selection.

Chi-square goodness-of-fit tests are shown in Table 7–3. For both overall and impaneled neighborhoods, the model in Figure 7–1 did not fit the observed covariance matrix. After six unique factor correlations were allowed, Model 3 in the table shows an excellent fit. For the entire judicial district, Model 3 explained 99.3% of the chi-square values. Model 3 also explained 91.6% of the chi-square values after the degrees of freedom were controlled for. By the same token, the model for impaneled districts explained 98.0% and 71.1% of the chi-square values.[10]

The standardized parameter estimates for both overall and impaneled districts are shown in Table 7–4. All path coefficients between four factors (gender, race, socioeconomic status, or SES, and distance) were significant, indicating that one's residential characteristics did influence jury representation. As previous analyses suggest, race has a statistically significant negative impact on the chance to serve. That is, the greater the proportion of black and Hispanic residents in a given neighborhood, the less chance a resident has to participate in jury service. The distance from the courthouse also indicated a significantly negative im-

TABLE 7-2
Simple Random Selection: Coefficients of Correlation among Causal Variables in Represented[a] (above Diagonal) and Total[b] Census Tracts (below Diagonal)

Variables	*X1*	*X2*	*X3*	*X4*	*X5*	*X6*	*Y1*	*Y2*	*Mean*	*SD*[c]
X1 Male	—	−.435	.241	.113	−.339	−.063	.132	.150	.475	.055
X2 Black	−.294	—	−.187	−.253	.643	.168	−.362	−.405	.185	.309
X3 Spanish	.109	−.263	—	−.631	.267	.341	−.350	−.335	.278	.177
X4 College	.189	−.227	−.653	—	−.585	−.389	.606	.588	.318	.177
X5 Poverty	−.153	.598	.316	−.621	—	.068	−.403	−.403	.146	.121
X6 Distance	−.049	.177	.272	−.206	.152	—	−.386	−.432	12.94	4.95
Y1 No. of people	.015	−.175	−.263	.296	−.233	−.470	—	.927	2.32	4.31
Y2 No. of panels	.013	−.174	−.265	.266	−.220	−.505	.956	—	1.49	2.44
Mean	.474	.176	.208	.355	.132	10.28	5.90	3.80	—	—
SD	.026	.291	.183	.154	.110	4.96	5.11	2.53	—	—

[a]*N* = 212.
[b]*N* = 538.
[c]Standard deviations.

pact on representation, suggesting that the impaneled neighborhoods were mostly located in the area close to the courthouse. Note, however, that many minority neighborhoods immediately adjacent to the courthouse were not represented.

Cluster-Sampling Methods

The First Stage

Our analyses substantiate that simple random jury selection fails to control for residential and geographic biases and thus results in discrimination. Therefore, the jury panel shows racially disproportionate representation and does not reflect the overall characteristics of the general population in the judicial district.

The first-stage cluster sample selection assumes that one person is randomly selected from each identified census tract for a jury panel. By the use of 125 random numbers, 125 prospective jurors were identified in the panel from 125 census tracts. We performed this proce-

TABLE 7-3
Simple Random Selection: Chi-Square Goodness-of-Fit Test of the Juror Representation Model

Model[a]	*Degrees of freedom*	X^2	p *level*	*Rho (%)*	*Delta (%)*
Total neighborhoods[b]					
1. Model in Figure 7–2	8	250.66	.000	69.32	91.03
2. Model with correlations[c] X2–X4, X2–X5, X3–X4, X3–X5	4	66.56	.000	84.18	97.61
3. Model with correlations X1–X2, X1–X3	2	18.61	.000	91.60	99.33
4. Model with restriction[a]	6	76.98	.000	88.03	97.24
5. Null model[e]	28	2,796.60	.000	—	—
Represented neighborhoods[f]					
1. Model in Figure 7–2	8	186.64	.000	40.56	82.71
2. Model with correlations X1–X4, X2–X4, X4–X6, X5–X6	4	60.15	.000	62.63	94.43
3. Model with correlations X1–X2, X1–X3	2	21.39	.000	71.19	98.01
4. Model with restriction[d]	6	64.06	.000	87.55	96.84
5. Null model	28	1,080.03	.000	—	—

[a]X1 = male; X2 = black; X3 = Spanish; X4 = college; X5 = poverty; X6 = distance.
[b]$N = 538$.
[c]Residual correlations for observed variables.
[d]$\beta = 0$.
[e]See Bentler & Bonett (1980) for further references.
[f]$N = 212$.

dure 10 times, as there were 10 lists to be impanelled. Then we computed the number of times each census tract was observed in the sample. Thus, using the cluster-sampling procedure, we *re-created* a pool of jurors ($N = 1{,}250$).[11]

The geographic distribution of jurors selected by cluster sampling is shown in Figure 7–4. The difference between simple random selection and cluster sampling is clear. The latter method pulls jurors from the entire judicial district, creating a pool of potential jurors that appears to reflect the overall population of the area (compare to Figure 7–3).

The next question is: Do the residential characteristics of the selected jurors significantly impact their chance for jury representation so that imbalanced juries are created?

Again, the goodness-of-fit of the jury representation model was put to the test. The jury representation model explained 98.5% and 99.8% of the total chi-square values for the overall district. After we controlled for

TABLE 7-4

Simple Random Selection: Standardized Parameter Estimates for the Structural Model

	Total areas (N = 538) Model 3			Represented areas (N = 212) Model 3		
Factors and variables	*Factor loadings*	*Standard error*	*Critical ratio*	*Factor loadings*	*Standard error*	*Critical ratio*
Factor correlations						
Rsex–race	–.18	.03	5.80	–.24	.05	4.61
Rsex–SES[a]	.30	.02	13.04	.47	.04	10.93
Rsex–dist.[b]	–.09	.02	3.33	–.12	.04	2.85
Rrace–SES	–.94	.03	27.67	–.96	.05	18.82
Rrace–dist.	.53	.03	15.14	.61	.05	10.89
RSES–dist.	–.32	.03	10.32	–.30	.05	5.76
Regression weights						
βsex–rep.	–.25	.00	45.45	–.36	.02	6.42
βrace–rep.	–.23	.01	12.77	–.27	.04	5.86
βSES–rep.	.25	.04	11.01	.54	.05	9.63
βdist.–rep.	–.87	.04	19.77	–.47	.06	6.86
Residual variances						
Representation	.78	.04	19.12	.72	.04	14.79

[a]Socioeconomic status.
[b]Distance.

the degrees of freedom, similarly 93.6% and 99.3% of the total chi-square values described the designated neighborhoods. Of the 538 census tracts in the jurisdiction, 492 (91%) were chosen to represent potential jurors by cluster sampling. Note that only 212 (39%) census tracts were represented when simple random jury selection was used.

We examined whether a resident's origin would affect his or her chance of being selected for jury service (see Model 4 in Table 7–5, which assumed no causal paths between exogenous factors and jury representation). For the entire district, we failed to reject the null hypothesis, a finding suggesting that with cluster sampling, one's residential origin does not impact his or her chance of jury representation.

The standardized parameters of the cluster-sampling model for Model 3, the best fitted model, are shown in Table 7–6. All the critical ratios equivalent to a student *t*-test statistic were less than 1.96. The set of four structural factors—gender, race, SES, and distance—thus did not influence the jury representativeness. This finding shows that SES or racial factors did not affect the representativeness of juror pools when cluster sampling was used. Thus, every potential juror in the district had a more-or-less equal chance of being included on a jury panel.

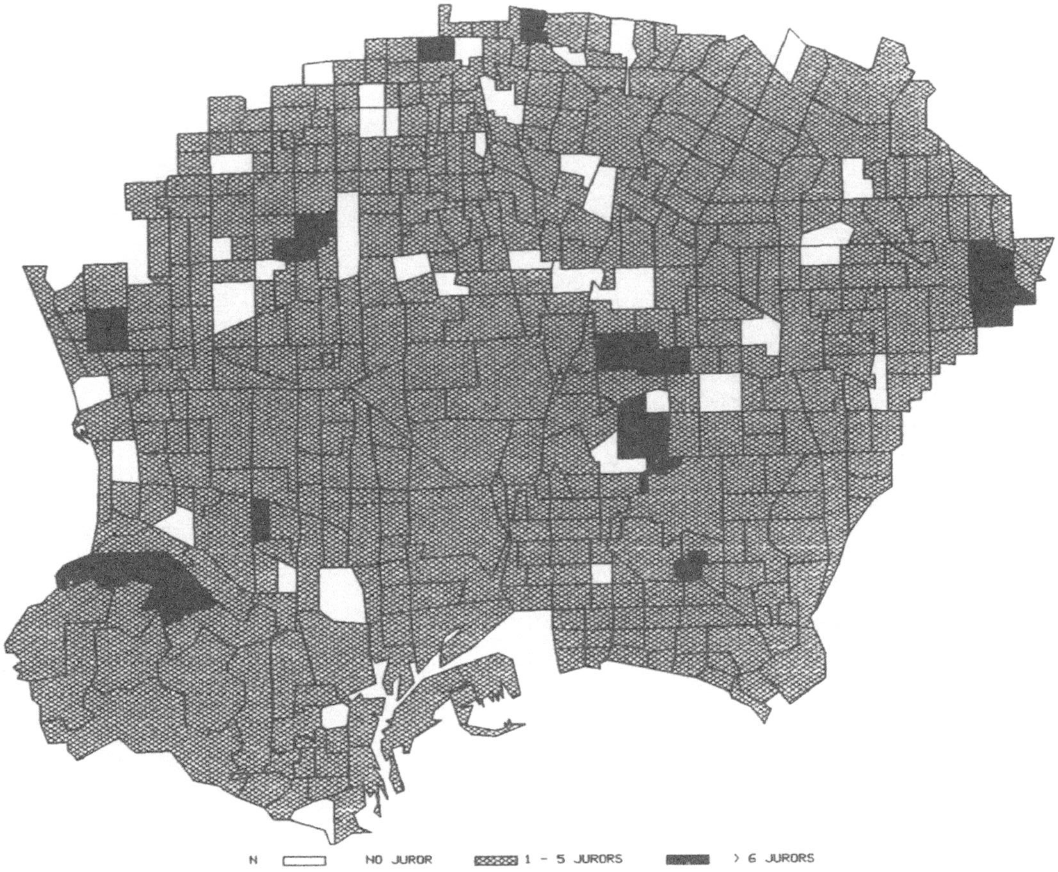

FIGURE 7-4. Cluster-sampling jury selection—the first stage—with PPS (Probability Proportionate to Size).

The Second Stage

The above analysis demonstrates that a cluster-sampling strategy is superior to the currently used simple-random-selection method in two ways: (1) racially segregated residential patterns have no bearing on the potential for jury representation (i.e., there is no "systematic selection" of neighborhoods based on residential characteristics), and (2) the cluster-sampling method ensures an equal probability of jury representation within the geographic boundary of the jurisdiction. We then examined the second stage of the cluster-sampling method. Once the census tracts were identified, the selection of eligible jurors with the probability proportionate to size (PPS) was carried out within individual census tracts.

In order to evaluate the ability of the cluster-sampling method to accurately reflect the individual's potential choice to become a juror, we needed to ask the following two questions. First, would the cluster-

TABLE 7-5
A Cluster-Sampling Strategy: Chi-Square Goodness-of-Fit Test of the Juror Representation Model

Model	*Degrees of freedom*	X^2	*p level*	*Rho (%)*	*Delta (%)*
Total neighborhoods[b]					
1. Model in Figure 7–2	8	230.01	.000	68.09	90.66
2. Model with correlations X2–X4, X2–X5, X3–X4, X3–X5	4	45.51	.000	88.07	98.15
3. Model with correlations[c] X1–X2	3	4.51	.211	98.55	99.81
4. Model with restriction[d]	7	12.49	.052	99.09	99.49
5. Null model[e]	28	2,463.79	.000	—	—
Represented neighborhoods[f]					
1. Model in Figure 7–2	8	345.98	.000	44.22	83.90
2. Model with correlations X1–X4, X2–X4, X4–X6, X5–X6	4	59.14	.000	81.80	97.24
3. Model with correlations X1–X2	3	17.46	.000	93.63	99.31
4. Model with restriction[d]	7	38.75	.000	94.01	98.19
5. Null model	28	2,149.23	.000	—	—

[a]X1 = male; X2 = black; X3 = Spanish; X4 = college; X5 = poverty; X6 = distance.
[b]$N = 538$.
[c]The addition of the unique factor correlation, X1–X3, did not reduce χ^2 values. Thus, this residual correlation was not respecified in the model estimation.
[d]$\beta s = 0$.
[e]See Bentler & Bonett (1980) for further references.
[f]$N = 492$.

TABLE 7-6
A Cluster-Sampling Strategy:
Standardized Parameter Estimates for the Structural Model

	Total areas (N = 538) Model 3			*Represented areas (N = 492) Model 3*		
Factors and variables	*Factor loadings*	*Standard error*	*Critical ratio*	*Factor loadings*	*Standard error*	*Critical ratio*
Factor correlations						
Rsex–race	−.19	.03	6.33	−.59	.03	18.54
Rsex–SES[a]	.29	.02	13.18	.37	.02	14.06
Rsex–dist.[b]	−.10	.02	3.70	−.15	.02	5.83
Rrace–SES	−.91	.03	26.00	−.95	.03	30.44
Rrace–dist.	.50	.03	14.28	.71	.03	20.71
RSES–dist.	−.31	.03	10.00	−.45	.03	14.14
Regression weights						
βsex–rep.	−.03	.00	6.00	−.00	.01	.11
βrace–rep.	−.09	.01	5.00	−.00	.02	.03
βSES–rep.	.05	.04	2.20	.00	.03	.17
βdist.–rep.	−.01	.04	0.22	−.00	.04	.19
Residual variances						
Representation	.91	.04	22.19	.99	.02	34.13

[a]Socioeconomic status.
[b]Distance.

sampling method accurately reflect the racial and socioeconomic composition of *each* geographical unit (i.e., each census tract)? Second, would the method result in a more egalitarian jury pool of prospective jurors for the entire judicial district?

For the first question, about the individual's chance to become a juror, we used a Z-test statistic to examine the jury representativeness *within* each census tract. The Z score tests whether the characteristics of a sample will be consistent with those of the total population from which the sample is drawn. For example, if the sample (e.g., the jury panel) contains a fair cross section, the proportion of selected Hispanics in it will be similar to the proportion of Hispanics in the given tract (see Ott, Mendenhall, & Larson , 1987, pp. 257–258, for a further discussion of the Z score and binomial distribution).

For the second question, about the overall representativeness of a cognizable group, we used a goodness-of-fit chi-square test to examine the overall proportionality of such a group. A chi-square goodness-of-fit test examines whether observed probabilities differ from expected probabilities. For example, consider the observed and expected numbers of potential jurors of different racial or ethnic groups in an *entire* judicial district. The expected probabilities for racial groups were calculated from the census population (Kairys, 1972). The chi-square, then, was used to examine whether the observed individual probabilities to become a juror in the chosen census tracts were equal to the racial makeup of the judicial district as a whole. A significant chi-square test, for example, pointed out that the observed racial composition of the panel was statistically different from the racial distribution for the whole district. Thus, there was systematic selection of potential jurors in the jurisdiction (see Ott *et al.*, 1987, pp. 270–276, for a further discussion of the one-sample goodness-of-fit chi-square test).

Our analysis of juror representation also focused on Hispanic-surname jurors and their chance of being included in jury impanelment lists. The deviation of the proportion of Hispanic jurors in jury panels from the Hispanic composition in the entire district and each individual census tract showed the extent of the systematic exclusion of Hispanic jurors under the guidelines prescribed by the simple-random and cluster-sampling methods. Thus, the relationship between chi-square and z values showed the extent of this systematic discrimination against individual Hispanic jurors.

First, we computed a chi-square distribution of juror representation under the simple-random-selection method. This distribution is spatially displayed in Figure 7–5. The analysis suggests that areas adjacent to downtown Long Beach (the south part of the district) and downtown Los Angeles (the northeastern portion of the map) had the greatest concentration of large chi-square values, indicating that there were greater disparities in Hispanic participation on jury panels. Which direction did this disparity show? A Z test shows the strength and the direction of Hispanic representation in the census tract.

Comparing the Hispanic proportions in each census tract shows that the areas with high chi-square values had the largest negative Z scores. Many Z scores ranged from 0 to –10. The Z scores substantiated the considerable underrepresentation of Hispanic jurors, as the Z value of –1.96 indicates a statistically significant underrepresentation ($p < .05$ two-tailed). Thus, given the number of Hispanic jurors for each census tract, the highly represented areas had a statistically significant underrepresentation of Hispanics.

In cluster sampling the chi-square distribution was notably smaller than in simple random sampling (see Figure 7–6). Similarly, the analysis suggested that the Z-test statistics were more equally and evenly distributed over the entire judicial district. For instance, many Z values ranged from +2 to –4. The average Z score for cluster samples was –0.24, in contrast to –0.95 for simple random samples (see Table 7–7). Similarly, the

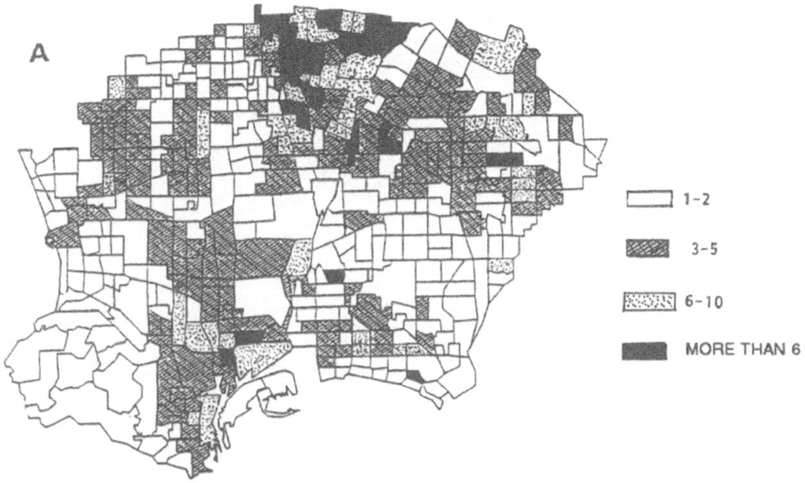

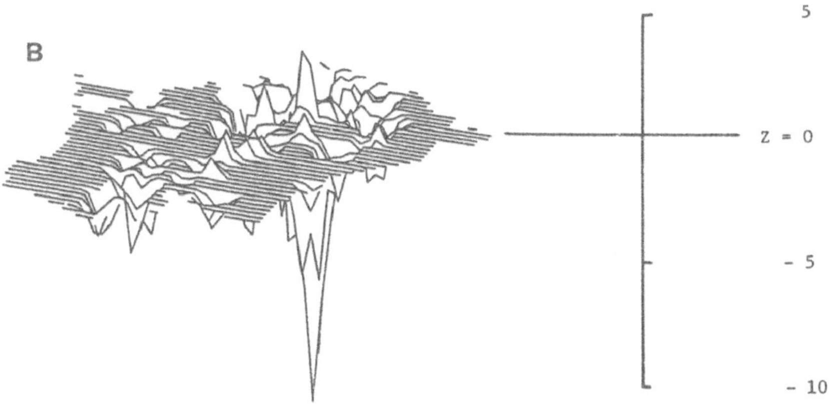

FIGURE 7-5. Simple-random-sampling jury selection. **a.** Chi-square and **b.** Z-test statistics for the evaluation of jury representation in the Long Beach Judicial District.

average chi-square values were 1.86 and 2.21 for the respective sampling methods. In addition, both maximum and minimum values for Z scores and chi-square values were notably smaller for cluster samples than for random sampling.

We believe that the negative Z values, particularly for cluster sampling, were partly attributable to the underestimation of the actual numbers of Hispanic jurors in the jury panels. In our analysis, Hispanic jurors were identified by the surname list provided by the U.S. Census Bureau, rather than by the self-identification method. It has been shown that the

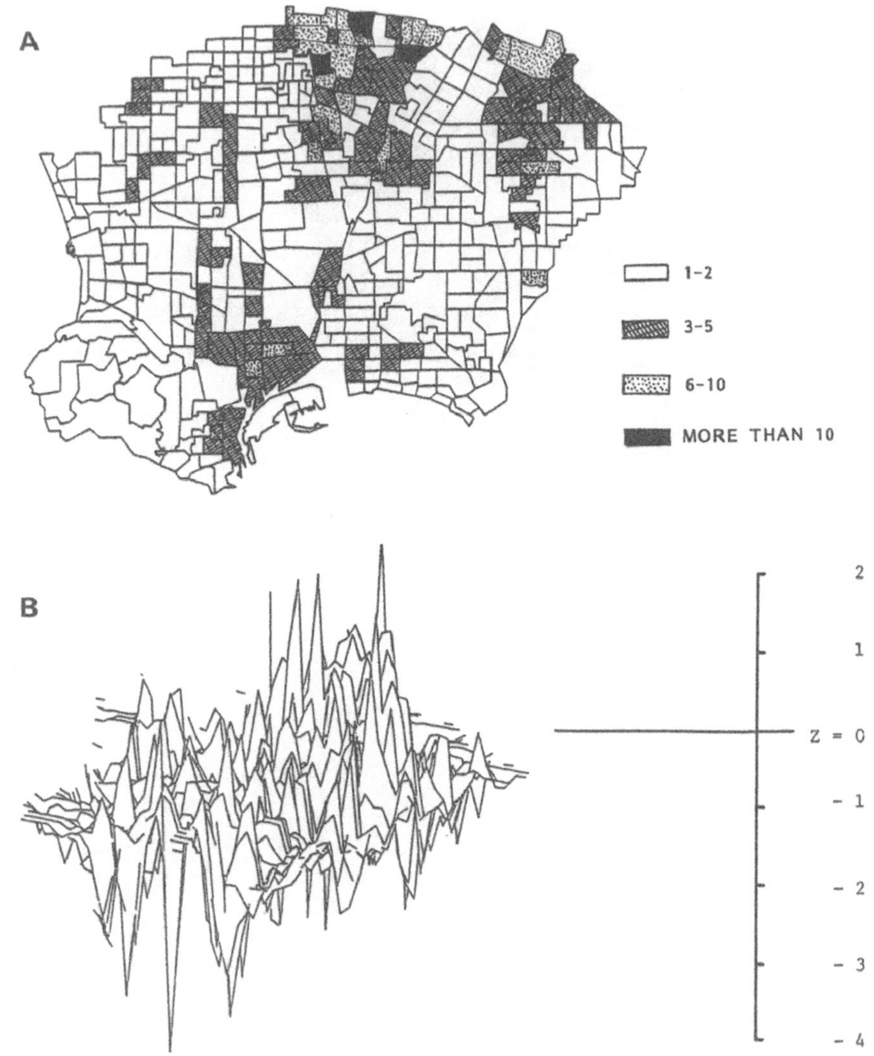

FIGURE 7-6. Cluster-sampling jury selection with PPS (Probability Proportionate to Size). **a.** Chi-square and **b.** Z-test statistics for the evaluation of jury representation in the Long Beach Judicial District.

census surname list tends to undercount people of Hispanic origin (Bean & Tienda, 1987; Butler & Fukurai, 1984; Fukurai *et al.*, 1991b). We believe that if we had used the self-identification method, the negative *Z* value would have been very close to zero. Nevertheless, the *Z* value for His-

TABLE 7-7
Chi-Square and Z-Score Distributions for Simple Random Selection and Cluster-Sampling Strategies

Statistical index	*Mean*	*Standard deviation*	*Minimum*	*Maximum*
Simple random sampling[a]				
Chi-square	2.21	2.75	0.00	21.20
Z score	−0.95	1.40	−10.26	4.70
Cluster sampling[b]				
Chi-square[c]	1.86[d]	1.94	0.00	13.06
Z score	−0.24	0.62	−4.41	1.81

[a]The correlation coefficient between χ^2 and z is −0.781.
[b]The correlation coefficient between χ^2 and z is −0.143.
[c]N = 421.
[d]When the analysis included the census tract with no representation of Hispanic jurors in the panels the mean and standard deviation was reduced to 1.46 and 1.72, respectively.

panic representation was not statistically significant for the cluster jury selection method. Our analysis further suggests that the mean of the estimated Z values was likely to have been a mere sampling fluctuation around a zero population parameter; that is, there were no significant discrepancies in Hispanic representation between the census tract and the judicial district as a whole.

In sum, under the simple-random-sampling method, there was a statistically significant underrepresentation of Hispanic jurors at two levels: (1) in the entire judicial district and (2) within each individual census tract. The greater values of chi-squares indicated a statistically significant underrepresentation of Hispanic jurors for given census tracts under simple random sampling ($r = -.781$). The cluster-sampling method, however, shows that such systematic underrepresentation was not significant ($r = -.143$).[12] Thus, the cluster-sampling method is clearly superior to the random-sampling procedure in reaching the goal of equal racial representation.

Discussion and Policy Implications

One question, of course, is whether cluster sampling is allowable under current federal and state statutes. The California Code of Civil Procedure does not spell out detailed jury-selection methods between jury impanelment and jury panel stages. Thus, it would be possible to use the proposed cluster selection method (see CA, 1980, Sections 17, 18, and 19). In the federal courts, it would also be possible to use the cluster-sampling method to generate more egalitarian jury pools. The Federal and Uniform Jury Selection statute of 1968 states that "the jury commission or the clerk shall publicly draw at random from the qualified jury wheel such number of names of persons as may be required for assignment." The statutes *do not mandate the random selection of qualified jurors' names.* Rather it emphasizes the number of jurors to be drawn for assignment to jury panels. Thus, it is possible for the federal courts to incorporate the cluster-sampling method with PPS, as our proposed jury selection technique provides more racially representative juries than the selection method used in Los Angeles County. Particularly in federal courts using registered-voter rolls as a sole source list, cluster-sampling selection should prepare more racially balanced jury *venires* than the method currently exercised (see Carp, 1982).

However, two types of argument may be made against the proposed cluster-sampling method of jury selection. First, because jury qualifications vary by district, the numbers of qualified jurors in different neighborhoods vary, and these discrepancies may affect the cross-sectional representation of racial groups. However, our evaluation of actual juror qualifications for Los Angeles County compared with those for the Long Beach District (a 20-mile radius from the courthouse) showed that the proportion of potential jurors qualified for jury service was virtually identical. Even if there had been some variation, this variation could be fitted into the system because the cluster-sampling technique with PPS is designed specifically to control for the different numbers of qualified jurors in different census tracts. The cluster selection method further guarantees that potential jurors in selected neighborhoods will be of the same proportion in the selected jury panel and the overall population.

Second, the cluster selection process would increase the overall mileage traveled by jurors to the courthouse. Any system that results in a fair cross section will require more aggregate miles traveled because of the very fact that the jurors would come from all areas of the district rather than from a few neighborhoods. This increased mileage, however, is a necessary part of a system that results in the selection of a fair cross section of the community: Jurors must come from all parts of the community. The proposed system, then, does away with the idea of selecting jurors only from the areas closest to the court and, in fact, requires just the opposite, so that jurors are drawn from all areas of the district. However, the district still could fall within the state-law-mandated 20-mile region for Los Angeles County.

In Los Angeles County, a particular problem that also must be dealt with is the overlapping of judicial district boundaries. This problem is one amenable to statistical sampling methods (see Chapter 3 for detailed discussions of overlapping judicial districts and their effects on racial representation). However, even if some overrepresentation should occur, it would be substantially less than is now occurring with the use of the simple random jury selection method.

Finally, the analysis presented here covered only a part of one year and thus might be considered relatively static. A dynamic jury selection process involves selecting jurors over a long period of time. However, jurors are also qualified periodically. Thus, a dynamic system of jury qualification could use the same technique described in the cluster-sampling method. That is, the jury qualification process could also be accomplished by, first, randomly selecting census tracts within the jurisdiction and then mailing qualification questionnaires to prospective jurors in the tracts periodically throughout the year. In addition, the cluster-sampling method with PPS is applicable to any geographically bounded area.

Conclusions

This chapter focused on the anomalies of simple random jury selection procedures and proposed an alternative sampling technique for obtaining more egalitarian jury pools. Specifically, we examined cluster and simple random jury selection methods to determine their relative abilities to produce jury lists that reflect the racial and ethnic composition of the community. The racial composition of impaneled census tracts under simple random sampling indicates that (1) selected census tracts are clustered in regions with high concentrations of majority groups, and (2) as a result, Hispanic and black prospective jurors are systematically underrepresented.

One possible explanation is that those highly and consistently represented neighborhoods had more qualified jurors than the excluded areas in the judicial district. Yet, our analysis shows that this assumption is false. The examination of the jury representation model indicates that, under the simple random jury selection method, each resident's geographic location and ethnic origin significantly influenced his or her chance of being selected for jury service.

We suggested an alternative sampling strategy: the cluster selection of jurors, which provides a list of cross-sectional representations of geographic areas within a jurisdiction. We examined whether this sampling method creates a jury pool that reflects a cross section of the population in the district. Two test statistics, chi-square and Z, substantiated that cluster sampling is superior to the simple random selection method, because potential minority jurors indicated by Hispanics have a more equal chance of participating on panels when the cluster method is used.

The generalizability of our findings on random sampling to other communities is an empirical question. We believe, however, that cluster sampling would enhance any community's cross sectional representation of potential jurors. Implementation of the cluster-sampling method would be a significant step toward reducing the representative bias of jury pools, because the method is congruent with the requirements established by the 1968 Federal Jury Selection and Service Act. In California, the basic notion of this cross-sectionality is also congruent with the 1981 California Code of Civil Procedure.

Notes

1. An earlier version of this chapter appeared in the *Journal of Criminal Justice.* We appreciate the comments of Jo-Ellan Huebner-Dimitrius at California State University at Los Angeles, Ray Jessen at the University of California at Los Angeles, and anonymous reviewers of the journal for their helpful comments and suggestions in completing the section on the application to jury selection of cluster sampling with the probability proportionate to size.
2. For more information, see *Thiel v. Southern Pacific Co.* (328 U.S. 217 1946); *State v. Holstrom* (43 Wis. 465, 168 N.W. 2d 574 (1969); and *State v. Cage* (337 So. 2d 1123 La. 1976). The Federal Act requires that selection procedures "ensure that each county, parish or similar political subdivision within the district or division is substantially proportionally represented in the master jury wheel for that judicial district, division, or combination of divisions" [U.S., 1968, Section 1863(b)(3)].
3. In the U.S., the historical footing for a panel of jurors drawn from the community is known. The first provision for a jury trial in a vicinage can be found in Article III, Section 2, of the Constitution: "The Trial of all Crimes, except in Cases of Impeachment, shall be by Jury; and such Trial shall be held in the State where the said Crimes shall have been committed; but when not committed within any State, the Trial shall be at such Place or Places as the Congress may by Law have directed."
4. For example, California law specifically states that persons listed for service in the court "shall be fairly representative of the population in the area served by the court and shall be selected upon a random basis" (Section 9, 203). For more detailed discussions, see *People v. White* (43 Cal. 3d 740 1954); *People v. King* (49 Cal. Rptr. 562 1966); *People v. Sirhan* (7 Cal. 3d 258 1978); *People v. Wheeler* (148 Cal. Rptr. 890 1978); *People v. Estrada* (155 Cal. Rptr. 731 1979); *People v. Graham* (160 Cal. Rptr. 10 1979); and *People v. Harris* (36 Cal. 3d 36, 201 Cal. Rptr. 782 679 P.2d 433 1984). For the U.S. Supreme Court, see *Alexander v. Louisiana* (405 U.S. 625 1972); *Peters v. Kiff* (407 U.S. 493 1972); *Taylor v. Louisiana* (419 U.S. 522 1975); *Duren v. Missouri* (439 U.S. 357 1979); and *City of Mobile, Ala. v. Bolden* (466 U.S. 55 1980).
5. For further discussion, see Alker and Barnard (1978); Alker *et al.* (1976); Benokraitis and Griffin-Keene (1982); Butler (1980a,b, 1981); Chevigny (1975); De Cani (1974); Fukurai (1985); Fukurai and Butler (1991a,b); Fukurai *et al.* (1987, 1991a); Hans and Vidmar (1986); Heyns (1979); Kairys *et al.* (1977); Staples (1975); Wishman (1986); and "The case for black juries" (1970).
6. See *People v. Harris* (36 Cal. 3d 36 201 Cal. Rptr. 782 679 P.2d 433 1984). Empirical analyses of *People v. Harris* were performed at the University of California at Riverside. In *People v. Harris,* the motion of the respondent for leave to proceed in *forma pauperis*

was granted; however, a writ of *certiorari* by the prosecution to the U.S. Supreme Court was denied on October 29, 1984, effectively requiring a retrial in California.

7. Two indices, delta and rho, are calculated in the following equations.

$$\text{delta} = \frac{\text{chi-square (null)} - \text{chi-square (model)}}{\text{chi-square (null)}}$$

$$\text{rho} = \frac{\dfrac{\text{chi-square (null)}}{df\,\text{(null)}} - \dfrac{\text{chi-square (model)}}{df\,\text{(model)}}}{\dfrac{\text{chi-square (null)}}{df\,\text{(null)}} - 1.0}$$

8. Table 7–1 is identical to Table 2–7. This chapter attempts to examine the feasibility of applying cluster sampling with probability proportionate to size (PPS) to jury selection procedures. This chapter also introduces the new cluster-sampling strategy in order to rectify the discriminatory systematic selection of white-dominated census tracts and the arbitrary elimination of minority-dominated areas from the defined boundaries of the judicial district, that is, the gerrymandering of the judicial district.
9. The variables, X1 through X5, represent the proportion of the cognizable groups in given census tracts. We created gender and racial variables by dividing the absolute number of respective groups by the total population. The percentage of college graduates was computed by the total number of college graduates divided by the population over 25 years of age. The percentage of poverty was judged by the number of poverty households divided by the total number of households in given census tracts.
10. Unique-factor correlations generally arise from a number of factors related to the nature of the data. The two most common factors are data collection procedures and the sharing of the same denominator in the indices for statistical analyses (Fukurai, 1991; Hayduk, 1987, p. 188). The survey technique used by the U.S. Census Bureau is generally a mixture of several data collection methods, including telephone and person-to-person interviews and mail surveys. It is possible that the mixture of these data collection methods had some effect on the variables included in our analysis. A second factor in possible residual correlations is the use of the same denominator to construct the three variables X1, X2, and X3. In fact, two unique-factor correlations (X1–X2 and X1–X3) suggested by the partial derivatives from LISREL are attributed to the use of the same denominator in the measurement constructions. Similarly, three additional residual correlations are allowed by the evaluation of the partial derivatives. We are aware of the *post hoc* freeing of error covariances and the danger of such heuristic model fittings. Nevertheless, the freeing of the unique-factor correlations was performed only for exogenous indicators, and the path coefficients did not significantly change. We thus believe that the above procedures would not pose serious problems in the interpretation of the theoretical substance on the causal relationship between a set of exogenous factors and an endogenous factor in the covariance structural model.
11. Those 10 individual simulations ($N = 1{,}250$) were conducted to correspond to the actual 10 impanelments as previously analyzed and used in the *Harris* retrial. This procedure assumed that each juror had (1) an equal probability of being selected and (2) an identification number that corresponded to an assigned number of a particular census tract in the district.
12. The r represents the correlation coefficient between the Z score and a chi-square value. The coefficient is merely used as an index to show the relationship between the discrepancies in expected and observed Hispanic representation in the census tract and the direction of the Hispanic representation (over- and/or underrepresentation) in the jurisdiction. The coefficient, however, does not offer a test statistic.

8

The McMartin *Trial*

Race and Scientific Jury Selection[1]

Introduction

Sexual abuse of children became a national preoccupation in the 1980s and early 1990s. In 1985, the Meese Commission claimed that the child-pornography industry grossed $675 million per annum. The National Broadcasting Company (NBC) estimated the figure at $3 billion in the white paper *The Silent Shame*. Many social scientists claimed that sexual abuse of children had become more pervasive than in the past (Committee on Public Safety, 1987; McGraw & Timnick, 1985; U.S. Department of Justice, 1984).

Throughout the 1980s, the topic of sexual abuse of children made the headlines of many major newspapers and national magazines. One of the most publicized child-molestation cases was the *McMartin* case. The prosecution spent $15 million and took nearly six years making a criminal case against seven day care workers—only to have the jurors declare them not guilty.

As we have discussed in previous chapters, the race of prospective jurors has become an important determinant of the outcome of a trial. The *McMartin* trial, the longest and costliest criminal trial in American history, was no exception. The defendants in the *McMartin* trial, both whites, were charged with molesting young children at a day care center owned by Peggy McMartin Buckey.[2] The alleged crime took place at a preschool in Manhattan Beach, Los Angeles County, California. Because it was assumed that the race of the prospective jurors would play a crucial role in the outcome of the trial, both a pretrial community survey and pre–*voir dire* questionnaires were examined by the authors to assess prospective jurors' attitudinal, demographic, and socioeconomic characteristics and to develop juror profiles for the trial.

The investigation of potential jurors was considered crucial because the pretrial community survey revealed that approximately 90% of the residents in Los Angeles County already believed that two of the defendants, Raymond Buckey and Peggy Buckey McMartin, were guilty of child molestation. Because massive publicity about preindictment materials on the defendants had greatly influenced the perceptions of prospective jurors, a fair trial was perceived to be in jeopardy if the traditional method of jury selection was used. Thus, scientific jury-selection techniques were used to obtain impartial jurors to try the unpopular defendants.

The Trial Background

A background synopsis of the *McMartin* child-molestation case will afford a better understanding of scientific defense jury selection in the trial. The jury trial was held in the Central Superior Court Judicial District, Los Angeles County, California.

The McMartin Pre-School was located in Manhattan Beach, the outer reach of suburbia in Los Angeles County, California. In 1984, this middle-class day care center was placed under police surveillance when one of its clients, Judy Johnson, said that she believed her 2½-year-old son had been molested by school aide Raymond Buckey. It was later found that the boy had attended McMartin preschool 14 times over a three-month period and had been in Buckey's class no more than two afternoons. Raymond Buckey was arrested but released because of lack of evidence. The complaining mother continued to make charges, one being that her son and the family dog had both been sodomized by her estranged husband, an AWOL U.S. Marine. In a letter to the district attorney, Ms. Johnson maintained that Peggy Buckey was involved in ritualistic practices featuring both "goatman" and church being the alleged mode of occult worship. "Peggy drilled a child under the arms" and "Ray flew in the air," she said. Less than a month later, police sent letters to approximately 200 parents naming Buckey as a suspected child molester.[3]

In 1985, Judy Johnson was found to be an acute paranoid schizophrenic, and she died of alcohol-related liver disease in 1986, a year before the actual trial took place (Timnick, 1986d; Timnick & McGraw, 1986). In the six months following the initial accusation, nearly 400 children who had attended the school were interviewed, and 41 were listed as victims in a complaint filed by the state. The district attorney filed charges after interviewing one third of the children. Claiming that the McMartin Pre-School was linked to a child-pornography ring, authorities armed with search warrants then visited 11 school locations in three counties but found nothing.

On February 2, 1984, Los Angeles station KABC-TV broadcast the allegations. One of its television reporters, Wayne Satz, reported that more than 60 children "have now each told authorities that he or she had been keeping a grotesque secret of being sexually abused and made to appear in pornographic films while in the Pre-School's care—and having been forced to witness the mutilation and killing of animals to scare the kids into staying silent" (McMartin: Anatomy of a witch-hunt, 1990).

On March 22, 1984, a grand jury indicted Raymond Buckey; his mother, Peggy McMartin Buckey; his sister, Peggy Ann Buckey; his grandmother, Virginia McMartin; and three McMartin teachers charged with abusing children over a ten-year-period. The two Buckeys, held without bail, pled not guilty. The charges alleged a decade of rape and other sexual molestation involving dozens of children and accusations of drugging and death threats, physical torture, and using toddlers for pornography and forced prostitution. The prosecutors alleged that much of the brutality had taken place at the Virginia McMartin Pre-School, where all seven defendants had taught (Arnold & Decker, 1984).

On April 2, the *Los Angeles Times* reported on the use of therapeutic puppets to obtain the children's stories about molestation—rape, sodomy, oral copulation, fondling, slaughter of animals to scare them into silence, and threats against them and their parents. *Times* reporter Cathleen Decker said that the reports were based strictly on the children's accounts to their parents and to social workers.[4]

A preliminary hearing began on June 6, 1984, and lasted 18 months (Timnick, 1986e). Defendants' lawyers cross-examined 13 child witnesses, one of whom testified that he and other children had played "naked games." Other children's testimony included satanic rituals, cemetery visits, animal sacrifices, and molestations in caves, a market, and even a car wash ("Grocer joined sex games, McMartin witness says," 1985; McGraw, 1985; McGraw & Timnick, 1985; Timnick, 1985a,b; Timnick & McGraw, 1985). The testimony was, however, uncorroborated: The hearing produced no photographs; no evidence of secret tunnels, rooms, or doors that the children had said existed; no outside adult witnesses of children being molested; and no defendant willing to testify against the others in a deal with the D.A. that would grant immunity or leniency.

With 135 counts against the seven defendants, the judge ordered all seven to stand trial (Timnick, 1986a, 1986f). Citing insufficient evidence, the newly elected district attorney, Ira Reiner, then dropped the charges against all defendants except the two Buckeys, citing the "incredibly weak" evidence against them, and saying on the radio that it was "not likely" that there had been "massive molestation" at the McMartin school ("Exhaustive sex case inquiry told: McMartin flaw—gap in evidence," 1986). The five released defendants had had irregular contact with the school when the acts had allegedly occurred (Chambers, 1986d; Feldman & Timnick, 1986). But the charges remained for Raymond and Peggy Buckey, both of whom had been continuously present at the school (Timnick, 1987e).[5]

The parents of the children saw news coverage momentarily turning against them, and many McMartin parents dropped their pursuit of legal action. Once the sensational headlines stopped, major media like *Newsweek* and *Time* and the TV program "20/20" questioned if there was ever any substance behind the original charges (Rosenberg, 1985). A few smaller publications did in-depth investigations of the Buckeys' past, revealing that they were not monsters but ran a preschool because they loved children (Timnick, 1989). However, a "prodefense" newspaper, the *Daily Breeze* in Torrance—a daily covering the area where those most directly involved in the *McMartin* case lived—had a picket line of angry parents and supporters surrounding its office.

Meanwhile, Mrs. Buckey was released on bail after 10 months in jail, but Raymond Buckey, at first unbailable, could not raise the $3 million bail and remained in jail nearly five years (Timnick, 1987a).[6]

Prepublicity and Political Motives

From the beginning, it was an open question whether the charges were based on sufficient evidence. It is important to note that, at the time Los Angeles District Attorney Robert Philibosian leveled them against the Buckeys, he was facing reelection. His campaign was not going well. Later, his assistant, Deputy District Attorney Glenn Stevens, lost confidence in the prosecution's case, quit the prosecuting team, joined the defense, and reported that the former DA had deliberately attempted to use this case to create massive publicity to favor his political bid (Chambers, 1986b; Shaw, 1984; Timnick, 1987).[7]

In March 1984, for example, television cameras were allowed to accompany the police who arrested Raymond Buckey and his mother, Peggy McMartin Buckey, at home. Ray's sister, Peggy Ann Buckey, was arrested in front of the La Palma High School classroom where she taught deaf children. Only the crippled grandmother, Virginia McMartin, age 82, was allowed to surrender voluntarily (Arnold & Decker, 1984). Though Philibosian lost the election and denied that his motives had been political, the trial had nonetheless gone forward (Timnick, 1986b). Nearly four years after the first arrest in the *McMartin* case, defendants Raymond Buckey and Peggy McMartin Buckey finally were put on trial on July 13, 1987 (Timnick, 1987e).

The chief prosecutor, Lael Rubin, was the only early DA staff member to stay on the case to the end. But her influence may have extended beyond the courtroom. She took a strong stand against child abuse and found an ally in *Los Angeles Times* staff writer Lois Timnick, who had been a pre–*McMartin*-case critic of child molestation. During the case, Rubin reportedly gave Timnick out-of-court "evidence" that Raymond Buckey had been counseled for "sexual problems involving young children" by Frank Richelieu, a pastor of the Church of Religious Science in Redondo Beach, California (Timnick, 1987). Richelieu denied this allegation in and out of court, and Rubin did not produce corroborating evidence. In July 1988, Rubin also met David Rosenzweig, *Times* metropolitan editor during most of the case, who had kept running stories setting the critical tone of the paper's stance toward the defendants. When a romance started between Rubin and Rosenzweig just a few months before the defense began to present its case at trial, critics argued that this liaison explained the *Times* biased and inattentive coverage of the defense. But soon after, the *Times* said, Rosenzweig removed himself from any role in the trial coverage.[8]

With the public following and being influenced by these reports, the possibility of finding an impartial jury was greatly reduced. Could one find a jury that represented a fair cross section of the community where the crimes were alleged to have been committed? The defense attorneys, Dean Gits and Danny Davis, thought not, and marshaled good reasons.

Jury Selection: Community Cross Section and Biases

The logic of the jury selection process is based on screening—from a target population to those who finally enter the jury box. The purpose of the selection procedure is to choose a jury that reflects a cross section of the community where the crimes have allegedly been committed. This purpose is legally accomplished by a random selection of jurors from the geographic district in which a particular court convenes. Thus, all qualified residents are given an equal opportunity to serve. Once the jurors are chosen, they are viewed as being both impartial and qualified to represent the community's collective sentiments and interests.

The step-by-step process involves defining the population eligible for jury service, sending jury qualification questionnaires to randomly selected candidates, constructing a qualified-jurors' file of those meeting various requirements, assigning potential jurors to the court, placing those who actually show up for jury service on the qualified jury panel, screening the jurors by *voir dire* challenges to eliminate potential jurors who may be biased and unacceptable to the prosecution and/or the defense attorneys, and finally selecting specific jurors for the particular case.

Though the rationale of the jury system is to lend legitimacy to decisions through verdicts reached by a cross section of the community, the shortcomings of the process are known, and the factors that lead to nonrepresentative juries have been fully elaborated in the previous chapters. How closely juries reflect a cross-section of the community depends on the success of the procedures by which the jurors are chosen. At each stage of the selection process, many factors and informal filtering techniques influence egalitarian participation, and these have a cumulative effect on the racial, ethnic, gender, and attitudinal composition of jury panels.

In California, one of the statutory situations authorizing a *voir dire* challenge for cause is that the prospective juror has a "state of mind" preventing her or him from acting with impartiality and without prejudice. Even so, there is evidence that, despite the explicit objective of exposing juror biases in order to identify and obtain impartial jurors, *voir dire* may elicit, accentuate, and even enlarge juror partiality. In criminal cases, the reason is that the prosecution tends to look for prospective jurors with certain characteristics, such as being middle aged, middle class, and white. This type of juror is assumed to identify with the government rather than with the defendant and will therefore be more likely to convict. By contrast, defense attorneys tend to seek jurors who have no views, who are least "offensive to the jury," who can approach the particular case without prejudice against the defendant charged, or who look like, act like, and think like the defendant and can therefore comprehend and empathize with the defendant. Those jurors are assumed to be more likely to find for the defendant. For both prosecution and defense, *voir dire* becomes a fight to enlarge the jury's bias toward one position, thereby undermining jury impartiality and the statutory requirements for a jury that represents a fair cross section of the community.

Pretrial Publicity and Its Influence on People's Perceptions

In the initial *McMartin* case, the defense sought to impanel jurors with particular qualities, using its peremptory challenges (i.e., those without cause) and challenges for cause to eliminate jurors with certain biases.

Rather than using their own subjective and intuitive judgment to evaluate prospective jurors and influence the jury composition, the defense attorneys mobilized social scientists and criminologists as jury consultants to prepare scientific questionnaires to be submitted to the potential jurors and to determine their preconceptions, biases, feelings, and abilities to reason logically and "legally" about a hypothetical situation that approximated the one in question.

The analysis was considered necessary because a telephone survey in 1986 revealed that pretrial publicity had exerted significant influence on public perceptions of the case. The defense attorneys requested testimony from two Duke University professors to substantiate the biases due to the massive pretrial publicity. Robert M. Entman analyzed how the press had covered the case between 1985 and 1987, and John B. McConahay conducted a telephone survey of approximately 500 people in the Los Angeles area. After reviewing several thousand pages of newspaper clippings and eight hours of television coverage, Entman concluded in a written statement that "the early coverage of the McMartin Pre-School case was extraordinary in amount, scope, sensationalism and negativity toward the defendants," and that, although "later coverage was more balanced," assembling an impartial jury was unlikely (Timnick, 1986b).

McConahay's telephone survey found that 96% of those queried had heard of the case, more than 97% of those with an opinion thought that Raymond Buckey was "definitely or probably guilty," and nearly 93% felt that Peggy McMartin was also guilty. In addition, more than 80% of the surveyed respondents believed that Raymond Buckey had mutilated animals to scare the children into silence, that he was part of a child pornography ring, and that the five defendants against whom charges had been dropped were guilty (Timnick, 1986d). As a result of the survey and analyses, the defense made a motion for a change of venue to a district where such biases would be minimized (Timnick, 1986c). But the court denied the motion, and the McMartin attorneys moved to the next logical stage of defense (Timnick, 1987c).

A list of the potential jurors was obtained from the Jury Service Division, Los Angeles County, and those jurors were already placed in the master file to be called into jury service. A survey questionnaire was then filled in by eligible jurors who resided in the Los Angeles Central Superior Court judicial district in 1986. A total of 407 prospective jurors responded to the questionnaire. The responses to the questionnaire survey were then quantified and computerized. The questionnaire was similar to the jury qualification questionnaire in the sense that those who had moved or were classified as "undeliverables" were automatically screened out from jury selection, simply because they did not receive the questionnaire. By the same token, the recalcitrant who was unwilling to respond to the questionnaire was also eliminated from the subsequent jury selection. Both groups were less likely to serve on juries and were thus eliminated from the analyses.

Table 8–1 shows the results of the community survey. The findings indicate that prospective jurors were fully aware of the pretrial publicity surrounding the *McMartin* case. During the period between 1984 and 1986, 98.5% of the respondents said that they had heard or read about child sexual abuse. Similarly, 96.7% of the respondents said that they had specifically heard or read about the *McMartin* case over the same period. Almost all respondents said that they believed that children involved in the *McMartin* case had been sexually abused (97.1%). This belief was of great significance because the trial was not to start until the following year. The results further suggested the extent to which the massive publicity had exerted an influence on the general perception by the prospective jurors; the general tone of the mass media was against the defendants. Similarly, although the charges against five of the original seven McMartin Pre-School teachers had been dropped, the majority of the respondents (58.2%) still believed that they were guilty of molesting children (Stein, 1986). Though many eligible jurors could not state whether Peggy McMartin Buckey was guilty of the crime, 86% of those who had already decided the outcome of the trial said that she was guilty.

Another significant finding was that more than two thirds of the respondents (70.4%) were not satisfied with current California law dealing with sexual abuse such as in the McMartin case. The majority of the respondents further questioned the credibility of testimony by children. The survey results showed that 63.6% of the respondents thought that children could be trained to testify about things, such as sexual abuse, that had not really occurred. Critical analyses of the community survey thus revealed that significant influence had been exerted by the publicity surrounding the *McMartin* case.

Analyses for Developing Juror Profiles

To search out those who might still be unbiased in the court district, the defense hoped to gain help in selecting jurors for the case by using both statistical analysis and observational methods. Through the services of a consulting firm, Los Angeles Central District survey data were examined to identify the sociodemographic and behavioral characteristics of the potential jurors who were least likely to be influenced by the pretrial publicity, or those who had yet to make up their minds about the trial outcome.

TABLE 8-1
Community Survey Results:[a]
The Los Angeles Central Superior Court Judicial District[b]

Questions	*Responses*	N	*Percentage*	*Valid percentage*
1. During the past two years, have you heard or read about the subject of child sexual abuse?	Yes	394	98.5	98.5
	No	6	1.5	1.5
	N/A[c]	7	—	—
2. During the past two years, have you heard or read about the *McMartin* preschool case?	Yes	385	96.7	96.7
	No	13	3.3	3.3
	N/A[c]	9	—	—
3. Do you think that most of the children involved in the *McMartin* preschool case were sexually abused, or some of them were, or a few of them were, or do you think that none of them were sexually abused?	Most	94	23.7	33.3
	Some	146	36.9	51.8
	Few	36	9.1	12.8
	None	6	1.5	2.1
	Don't know	114	28.8	—
	N/A[c]	11	—	—
4. Have you heard that the charges against five of the seven *McMartin* preschool defendants were dropped?	Yes	320	82.5	82.5
	No	68	17.5	17.5
	N/A[c]	19	—	—
5. Do you believe that the dismissed defendants were guilty?	Yes	120	41.4	58.2
	No	86	29.7	41.8
	Don't know	77	29.0	—
	N/A[c]	124	—	—
6. Have you heard about or read anything about the Peggy McMartin Buckey preschool case?	Yes	277	72.1	72.1
	No	107	27.9	27.9
	N/A[c]	23	—	—
7. Based on what you know about Peggy McMartin Buckey, do you think she is:	Guilty	110	29.6	86.0
	Not guilty	18	4.9	14.0
	Don't know	243	65.5	—
	N/A[c]	36	—	—
8. Do you feel that children can be trained to testify about things that really did not happen?	Yes	238	60.3	63.6
	No	51	12.9	13.6
	Not sure	85	21.5	22.7
	Don't know	21	5.3	—
	N/A[c]	12	—	—
9. Are the laws of California adequate to deal with the problems of sexual abuse?	Yes	94	26.2	29.6
	No	223	62.1	70.4
	Don't know	42	11.7	—
	N/A[c]	48	—	—

[a]The community survey questionnaire was filled in by eligible jurors who lived in the Central Superior Court judicial district in 1986.
[b]The total number of respondents was 407.
[c]No answer.

In order to develop the *McMartin* jury profile, additional survey data were collected from a court-distributed questionnaire filled out by the 205 prospective jurors who had been assigned to the case. Similarly, during the pre–*voir dire* screening session, behavioral observations were made, and the information was computerized for an evaluation of possible hidden prejudices among individual jurors. The additional observational information was given numerical values and almost simultaneously prepared for the analysis by round-the-clock preparation.

Those sources of information were merged for further analyses. Juror profiles were developed from the result of the community survey, the pre-*voir dire* questionnaires, and the observational data by means of statistical and mathematical models: (1) multiple-regression analysis; (2) discriminant analysis; (3) logit regression techniques; and (4) factor analysis.

The *multiple-regression technique* is perhaps the most widely used analytical model in the behavioral and social sciences. The multiple-regression model treats a continuous measurement as a dependent variable and treats a set of continuous independent measurements as predictor variables. The statistical model is able simultaneously to control the effects of the predictor variables on a dependent or criterion variable. The basic assumption of multiple regression is that the variables have a multivariate normal distribution. That is, all the variables must be normally distributed and measured on a continuous scale, that is, a ratio or at least interval levels of measurement. Some of the significant predictors of the final verdict were categorical variables, such as race and employment status (full-time, part-time, etc.). These categorical measures were converted into a set of dummy variables and were included in the model so that their effects on the probable outcome of the trial could be estimated.

A three-item ordinal scale (guilty, not sure, and not guilty) was also developed as a criterion variable so that the probable outcome of the trial could be assessed and juror profiles could be developed. The scale was not continuous, and thus it may have violated a statistical assumption of the multivariate normal distribution for multiple-regression analyses. Nevertheless, the three-item variable was treated as a continuous dependent variable and was regressed against a set of predictor variables. The multiple-regression analyses were performed to develop the profile of prospective jurors by identifying a set of predictor variables that significantly explained the large variance of the probable outcome of the trial.

In addition to multiple regression, *discriminant analysis* was performed to provide an additional reference for the assessment of the prospective jurors and overcome the methodological shortcoming of the multiple-regression analyses: The criterion variable was not truly a continuous measure, but a three-item nominal scale. Discriminant analysis is a sophisticated classification method based on the measured items in a dependent variable, for example, in this case, the prospective jurors who said the defendants were guilty as charged, those who said they were not guilty, and those who were not sure. To distinguish between those groups, a set of discriminating variables was identified in the statistical model that measured the attitudinal and socioeconomic characteristics on which the groups differed. Because the mathematical objective of discriminant analysis is to weight and linearly combine the discriminating variables so that the groups are forced to be as statistically distinct as possible, the analyses were performed to identify those discriminating predictors that significantly separated the three-item dependent variable.

Although multiple-regression techniques were able to identify a set of predictor variables that explained the large variance of the outcome variable, discriminant analysis provided additional information diagnosing the discriminating variables that significantly distinguished the three groups: Those who believed that the defendants were guilty, those who believed they were not guilty, and those who were unsure of the outcome before all the evidence was presented and thoroughly examined. The statistical theory of discriminant analysis assumes that the discriminating predictor variables have a multivariate normal distribution and equal variance–covariance matrices within each itemed group. Although the statistical technique of discriminant analysis is robust, another statistical model was used to examine the relationship between the outcome variables and a set of predictor variables: logit regression.

Logit regression treats a dichotomous categorical indicator as a dependent variable and a set of both dichotomous and continuous variables as predictors. The advantage of logit regression over multiple regression and discriminant analysis in the *McMartin* case was its ability to identify the set of predictor variables by dichotomizing the outcome variable into two groups: (1) those who said the defendants were guilty and (2) those who said otherwise. The latter group was created by combining prospective jurors who said not guilty and those who were unsure of the trial outcome before all the evidence was presented. Thus, the outcome variable measured in a dichotomous fashion was regressed against a set of independent variables that were believed to influence the perceptions of the possible trial outcomes in the *McMartin* case.

Lastly, *factor analyses* were used to examine the level of jurors' prejudice and biases about their perceptions on child sexual abuse that might prevent them from evaluating the case impartially. The use of factor analyses was of great importance because a single question on the potential outcome of the trial may not be sufficient to evaluate jurors' perceptions about the trial. It was important to look at an array of related variables and questions designed to capture some elements of potential jurors' biases in child molestation and sexual abuse. In the present analysis, a factor analytic approach was used to address whether the related variables could be explained by the existence of a hypothetical variable, called "prejudice," as a distinct underlying dimension of the questions in the questionnaire. The factor analysis thus became the important empirical tool in measuring and examining prejudice and evaluating jurors' impartiality in the trial.

The questions used to evaluate the underlying dimension of prejudice included the following:

- Has anyone ever told you about having been sexually touched in a manner they felt was wrong?
- Has anyone ever talked to you about having been spoken to in a sexual manner they felt was improper or wrong?
- Do you think being exposed to sex or sexual acts at a very early age (two to ten years) has any effect on a child?
- Do you think it is possible that early exposure to sexual acts could have a benefit for a child?
- Do you know people who collect what has been generally labeled by society as pornography?
- Do you believe all pornography is evil?
- Has anyone ever made accusations about you relating to sexual misconduct?
- Has anyone ever made accusations about anyone you know regarding sexual misconduct?
- Are you, or have you ever been, associated in any manner with a group, society or organization which advocates or supports the revision of the laws of the United States or of any state concerning child sexual abuse?

These analyses were performed on the community survey, and the results were superimposed on the pre–*voir dire* survey collected from the court-distributed questionnaire filled in by the 205 prospective jurors assigned to the *McMartin* case. In addition, the same analyses were carried out on the observational information and the results from community survey data in order to give a better understanding of possible hidden prejudices among individual jurors. The observational information was given numerical values. With the results from the community survey, the pre–*voir dire* questionnaires, and the observational data, the 205 prospective jurors were rank-ordered from the least partial to the most partial, Number 1 being the least biased and Number 205 being the most biased.

Comparisons of Eligibles in the Central District and Impaneled Jurors

Before examining the actual screening strategies used by the defense attorneys, it is important to understand the general characteristics of community residents in the Los Angeles Central Superior Court judicial district where the *McMartin* trial was to be held. The critical assessment of both the socioeconomic and the demographic characteristics of the prospective jurors provided additional information for developing an effective screening strategy for scientific defense *voir dire* jury selection.

The Central Superior Court is located in the city of Los Angeles, and its 20-mile radius court jurisdiction covers most of the metropolitan areas of Los Angeles County (see Figure 8–1).

In order to develop a profile of the prospective jurors, Table 8.2 was prepared and assessed. The table shows the eligible jurors' profiles in several stages of jury selection in the *McMartin* trial: (1) the eligible population for the trial; (2) the prospective jurors who responded to the community survey; and (3) the jurors who appeared at the Central Superior Courthouse and were assigned to the *McMartin* trial.

The eligible population in the Central Superior Court judicial district was characterized by a large proportion of racial and ethnic minorities. For instance, whereas 34.7% of the prospective jurors were black and Hispanic, the same groups made up 42.3% of the district's population. Other demographic proportions were similar, yet education differed significantly. For example, there were larger numbers of prospective jurors with less than a high school education in the judicial district than in Los Angeles County as a whole. Similarly, the judicial district had a smaller number of prospective jurors with a college education, perhaps because the high concentration of minority jurors may have lowered the average educational attainment among the eligible jurors in the jurisdiction.

In comparing the composition of those in the community survey with the composition of the population of the Central Superior district, there was overrepresentation of white and black jurors (+10.0 and +5.0% for whites and blacks, respectively). However, the proportion of Hispanic jurors was significantly lower than that in the eligible population (–19.8%). Similarly, females were overrepresented in the survey. There was a significant underrepresentation of younger jurors, especially those under age 30. However, the educational comparison revealed that the underrepresented groups were more likely to be less educated. For example, whereas 34.1% of the eligible population had less than a high school education, the same group had only 4.9% representation in the survey.

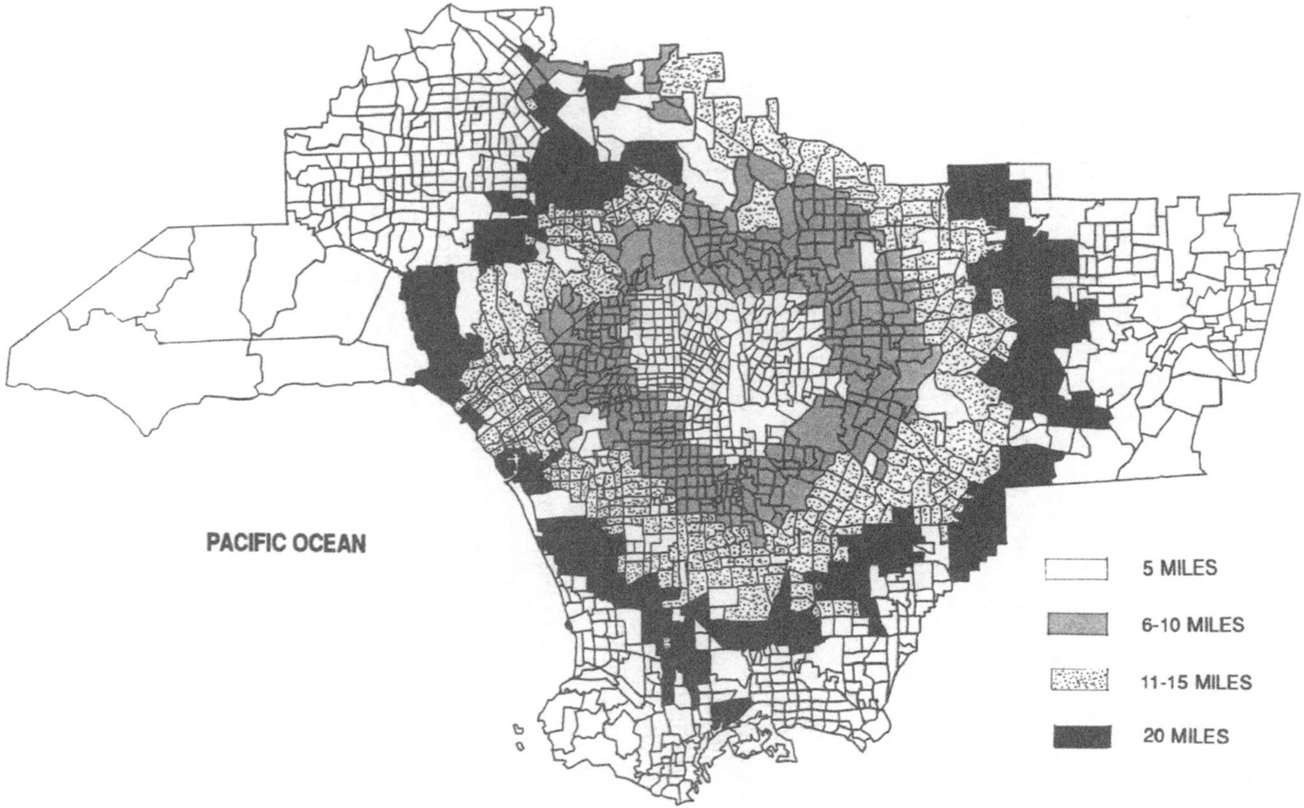

FIGURE 8-1. Los Angeles Superior Court district and distances from the courthouse.

TABLE 8-2
Eligible Jurors' Profile in Several Stages of Jury Selection for the McMartin *Trial in 1986 (%)*

Variable	*L.A.*[a] *County*	*Central*[a] *district*	*Community*[b] *survey*	*Prospective*[c] *jurors*
Race				
White[d]	58.3	50.8	61.8	43.4
Black	11.4	14.6	19.6	31.2
Hispanic	23.3	27.7	7.9	4.9
Gender				
Male	47.9	47.5	43.5	53.2
Female	52.1	52.5	56.5	46.8
Age				
18–20	7.7	7.6	0.8	3.4
21–29	24.1	24.5	18.5	17.6
30–44	27.9	27.1	32.2	34.1
45–54	13.9	13.4	19.6	19.0
55–64	12.9	12.9	16.3	15.7
65+	13.5	14.5	12.6	10.2
Education				
Less than high school	30.1[e]	34.1[e]	4.9	4.9
High school	30.2	29.5	25.8	21.5
Some college	21.2	19.7	33.3	55.6
College	18.5	16.6	31.1	18.1

[a]Figures are based on the 1980 U.S. Census survey.
[b]Figures are based on the 1986 community survey in the Los Angeles Central Superior Court Judicial District.
[c]Figures are based on the 1987 pre-*voir dire* screening questionnaires administered at the Los Angeles Central Superior Courthouse.
[d]Calculated by subtracting the total nonwhite population from the total population (18 years or older) and dividing it by the total eligible population.
[e]Based on the total population aged 25 or older.

On the other hand, those with a college education were overrepresented. In fact, two thirds of the community survey respondents had some college experience or had completed a college education.

At the next stage of jury selection, prospective jurors who appeared at the courthouse and were assigned to the *McMartin* trial, the composition of the pool took on a different character. These assigned jurors were more likely to be black, male, younger, and more educated. For example, there was a significant overrepresentation of blacks (31.2%), and whites (43.4%), and Hispanic (4.9%) jurors were underrepresented. Similarly, male jurors dominated the jury *venire* by 53% to 47%. There were also more younger and middle-aged jurors in the jury pool. On the other hand, jurors aged 45 or older were underrepresented. Approximately 74% of the prospective jurors in the *venire* had a college education, a sizable increase over the education of Los Angeles Central Superior Court district residents or those responding to the community survey.

Importance of Race in Screening Prospective Jurors

Statistical analysis of the results of both the community survey data and *voir dire* questionnaires revealed that, despite the massive media coverage, the *race* of the prospective jurors was one of the most crucial factors differentiating those who expressed the opinion that the defendants were guilty and those who were not sure about the trial outcome. The analysis suggested that Hispanics and native Americans were more likely to be decided on guilt, and that blacks, Asians, and whites were more likely to be unsure of the verdict.

This finding from the survey was somewhat unexpected. Whereas racial minorities are generally believed to be more sympathetic to the accused and less sympathetic to the prosecution, the statistical analyses gave this different result. The two ethnic minority groups, Hispanics and native Americans, were found to be more likely to render a guilty verdict in the *McMartin* case than were other groups, perhaps because the defendants were white and did not share the racial or ethnic background of the prospective jurors, and/or child molestation may have had significant cultural and ideological meaning to the Hispanics and the native Americans.

Other important characteristics distinguished impartiality and bias, that is, those who had already decided the verdict on the basis of the mass media reports. These characteristics included (1) age, with older prospective jurors more likely to believe the defendants guilty, and the younger more likely to believe otherwise; (2) gender, with females more likely to render a guilty verdict and males not; (3) educational background, with those with less than a high school education more likely to render a guilty verdict, and those who were college graduates not; and (4) income, with those with lower income more biased toward guilt, and those with higher income not.

Still other behavioral and nondemographic variables differentiated the two groups (i.e., those favoring guilt and those being unsure). The battery of inquiries in the *voir dire* questionnaire included two central questions:

- At what age do you feel that children can reliably describe things that actually happened to them?
- Do you feel that children can be trained to testify about things that really did not happen?

Those who answered "No" to the last question were more likely to render a verdict of guilty, and those who answered "Yes" or "Don't know" were more likely to be unsure.

Other questions focused on sexual abuse to identify those with such a strong emotional response that they might convict anyone thus charged even without proof:

- Exactly how would you define child sexual abuse?
- Has a relative or close friend been a victim of child sexual abuse?
- Are the laws of California adequate to deal with the problems of sexual abuse?
- During the past two years, have you heard or read about the subject of child sexual abuse?
- When you were a child, can you remember having any experiences you would consider sexual abuse?

Next were a series of statements, to which the respondents were asked to circle their responses of "Strongly Agree," "Agree," "Not Sure," "Disagree," or "Strongly Disagree":

- If the prosecution goes to the trouble of bringing someone to trial the person is probably guilty.
- Even the worst criminal should be considered for mercy.
- Regardless of what the law says, a defendant in a criminal case should be required to prove his or her innocence.
- The rights of persons charged with child sexual abuse are better protected than the rights of the alleged child victims.
- Too often people accused of serious crimes are treated lightly by the courts.
- If a person is allowed to get out of jail on bail, then that person is probably not guilty.
- In a child sexual abuse case, medical evidence is very useful in deciding whether a person is guilty or not guilty.
- Due to a great deal of media coverage, sometimes the public assumes that a person is guilty when in fact they are not.
- Sometimes political officials prosecute individuals for political gain.
- If a group of persons is charged with a crime and later charges against some of them are dropped, then those still charged are probably guilty.
- Children aged 7–11 almost always tell the truth about their sexual experiences that happened when they were aged 2–6.
- It is highly unlikely that a female would sexually abuse a child.
- Testimony by a child in sexual abuse cases should be confirmed by other evidence.

After the lengthy *voir dire* process in evaluating and examining hidden prejudices of each prospective juror assigned to the trial, the majority of the jurors who finally reached the jury box were those ranked high in impartiality. They were largely young and middle-aged jurors, most with a relatively high level of education. After illness and financial pressure caused some of the selected jurors in the jury box to retire, the remaining 12 jurors were made up of 1 Hispanic, 2 Asians, 3 blacks, and 6 whites; these characteristics were distributed among 4 women and 8 men. The age range was 23 to 27 on the low end, reaching 47 in the middle range and 73 at the high end. These selected 12 jurors and 6 alternates met the basic sociodemographic and behavioral characteristics of exhibiting the least prejudice, according to both the survey data and pre–*voir dire* answers to the questionnaire.

Eleven members of the final jury were the members of racial or ethnic groups that had been found to lean less toward a guilty verdict, namely, Asians, blacks, and whites. The age distribution of the final jurors was skewed toward the young and middle-aged groups. The majority of the final jurors had a college education, and their average educational attainment was higher than the level found in the jurisdiction. It is important to note that the trial was held in the Central Los Angeles Superior Court district. Because the judicial district covers most of the census tracts in downtown Los Angeles, where a high concentration of qualified black jurors were found, the largest number of potential jurors in the jurisdiction were black and Hispanic (14.6 and 27.7%, respectively).

In addition to sociodemographic characteristics associated with impartiality, the final jurors also met the basic behavioral characteristics found to be more associated with impartiality and less prejudice. They made up a largely well-balanced, unbiased jury, though the prosecution had also used private jury-selection consultants in an effort to impanel a jury that would convict. The prosecution team, however, did not use the scientific jury-selection method to evaluate individual jurors during the *voir dire* screening session but relied on intuitive and subjective judgment to evaluate prospective jurors.

The Verdict

After hearing 124 witnesses and 60,000 pages of testimony, the jurors retired without a clear sense of events. "When I went into the jury room I was as confused and uncertain as I was on the first day of the trial," concluded Brenda Williams, a black juror and a Pacific Bell service representative (Timnick & McGraw, 1990).

The 12 jurors agreed: It was impossible to convict the defendants on 52 of the counts charged; on the other 13 counts, they could offer only a deadlocked vote. Judge William Pounder, who presided over the 2½ years of actual trial, said that the case "poisoned everyone who had contact with it"—children, parents, witnesses, litigants, and judicial officers. The editorial column of the *Los Angeles Times* also asked, "How could investigators, even onlookers, miss the many warning signals on the trail along which this case plunged like some wayward tank? A disaffected prosecutor called the case 'junk' months ago" (Timnick & McGraw, 1990).

Finally the decision was made. Right after the verdict of acquittal, a Fox television call-in poll found that viewers, by nearly a 7-1 margin, believed that justice was not served. After 2½ years of isolation and 9 weeks of secret deliberations, the *McMartin* jurors were thrust into the public eye. Two jurors appeared on "Nightline" and 2 others on "A.M. Los Angeles." All 12 were blitzed by reporters' telephone calls (Rainey, 1990).

Mrs. Buckey immediately filed suit in the Los Angeles Federal District Court to recoup her losses (Timnick, 1990a). The defendants included the city of Manhattan Beach, whose police department had sent letters to approximately 200 parents describing the allegations of a single child; Los Angeles County and its former district attorney, Robert Philibosian, who had pressed the case without adequate evidence and possibly for political purposes; the Children's Institute International, which had concluded that the children had been abused at the McMartin Pre-School and had pressured the children to modify their stories to corroborate one another; former Children's Institute International employee Kathleen MacFarlane; and Capital Cities–ABC, Inc., along with former reporter Wayne Satz, who on February 2, 1984, had created the public panic and made allegations against the Buckeys, based on children's accounts describing dozens of alleged sexual acts at the McMartin Pre-School (Timnick, 1990a, 1990b).

In April 1990, Virginia McMartin and Peggy Ann Buckey also filed claims against Los Angeles County, asserting that their lives were ruined because they had been unjustly prosecuted (Rohrlich, 1990a). And in May 1990, a former defendant, Bette Raidor, and her husband, Milan Raidor, filed a similar suit against Los Angeles County (Timnick, 1990b).

Media Event and the Aftermath

After the verdict, the parents of the alleged victims were outraged. The press reported that the defendants had been assumed guilty by association with the purported crime. "At the early stages, they were tried and convicted and sentenced by the media," said Mrs. Buckey's lawyer Dean R. Gits pointing to the extraordinary nature of both mass hysteria and legal prosecution (Rohrlich, 1990b).

For six years, the *Los Angeles Times* had minimized and given late coverage to important trial developments that raised questions about the prosecution's case—stories that smaller local media had covered promptly and prominently. "We all recognize how important the *Times* is," said Walter Urban, who represented one of the defendants against whom all charges were dropped. "I think that had the *Times* done a major, long article, solid investigative work showing there was no child pornography, no child prostitution, no animal mutilation, maybe it would have stopped the case a lot sooner" (Shaw, 1990). David Shaw, a *Times* staff reporter, reported that editors of the *Times* strongly felt the coverage was, overall, fair and balanced. But two prosecutors, the defense attorneys and their supporters, rival reporters, and even some critics inside the *Times* pointed to flaws, large and small, in the *Times* coverage that they said added up to unfairness to the defendants and imbalance in the coverage of the trial. Barbara Palermo, who covered much of the case for *Daily News* in the San Fernando Valley, similarly stated that "*Times* coverage of the McMartin case has been the laughingstock of the press corps. No one could understand how *Times* coverage could differ so drastically [from the other media's] for so long without anyone at the *Times* noticing" (Shaw, 1990).[9]

Although the media in general had used their constitutional 1st Amendment rights of free speech and press to report what they selected as McMartin news, they had also created a climate of hysteria that helped jeopardize the defendants' 4th Amendment rights to be secure against unreasonable searches and seizures of persons, houses, papers, and effects. Media coverage made their 6th Amendment rights to a fair trial by an impartial jury of their peers almost impossible and had undermined their 14th Amendment rights to due process of law before depriving them of liberty and property.[10]

For the media-battered public, even after the trial nothing much changed. Reported cases of sexual abuse of young children had gained broad media attention, and nationally reported instances of such sex abuse had jumped from 24,900 in 1980 to 138,000 in 1986 (just before the *McMartin* trial began), annually rising thereafter. The November 2, 1986, "60 Minutes" interview with Raymond Buckey and five of the other six original defendants was sympathetic to them. But this telecast was long forgotten on the day the *McMartin* decision was rendered, when some 87% of nearly 13,000 respondents to a Los Angeles TV station still thought that the Buckeys were guilty—a drop of a few percentage points from the views of those surveyed before the trial began.

Some of the 13 charges undecided by the deadlocked jury were later pressed by the DA against Raymond Buckey; the result was a hung jury in August 1990, and the prosecution opted not to seek another trial ("Buckey case ends; he files suit," 1990). The criminal case was also over for Peggy McMartin Buckey. She left the courthouse—again facing a jeering crowd of parents and children, some screaming lewdly, others "giving her the finger." The Los Angeles police department made no arrests for lascivious behavior this time. "I did not look at their faces," Peggy McMartin said, turning her back to them, eyes welling. "God forgive them. They know not what they do" ("McMartin case verdicts," 1990).

Recipe for Reform

The *McMartin* case illustrates a variety of situational dilemmas that call for possible future reforms of the judicial system in child abuse cases. We propose the following six specific reforms in order to ensure a fair trial in well-publicized cases that touch on sensitive issues such as children and sexual molestation. These suggestions are of critical importance because preindictment materials exerted significant influence on the public perception of the *McMartin* case. After a careful review of the evolution of the *McMartin* trial, it was not easy to overlook the significant role played by both the DA and the mass media in building a negative criminal case against the day care workers.

First, in highly charged and emotion-laden situations such as the *McMartin* case, we suggest that police investigations should proceed without political interference by the district attorney or the media's excessive involvement.

Second, the district attorney should proceed to convene a grand jury hearing only if there are witnesses, strong forensic and material evidence, and reasons to believe that a felony has been committed and that those suspected have perpetrated the crime. Explicit state or federal legislation should make it a crime for a DA to use his or her office for political or personal gain.

Third, the media should not be contacted by either police investigators or the DA before grand jury hearings are convened to consider both the evidence and the basis of the charges leveled against the suspects. Laws thus need to be passed to make it a felony for a DA or investigators to build their case by using the media to bring charges, indict the suspects, and act as judge and jury.

Fourth, when the DA and the media violate the rights of the accused, the defense should be legally empowered to move to change the venue of the trial.

Fifth, the defense should also be funded by the court in such cases to carry out community surveys to find unbiased population sectors to act as impartial jurors, and to design a three-tier system that (1) expands the geographic area by including census tracts from neighboring jurisdictions in which unbiased jurors may be sought; (2) makes it legally obligatory for the judge to grant a change of venue if unbiased jurors cannot be found in census tracts within the jurisdiction of the court; and (3) allows a random selection of qualified jurors on the basis of the procedures set down in Chapter 7 (cluster sampling with PPS) once the census tracts have been randomly selected.

Sixth, in child molestation cases, the defense should be legally empowered to (1) use pretrial discovery of the DA's records to review any and all forensic evidence, confessions, or child testimony; (2) move to have the judge review so-called forensic evidence and child testimony before its presentation to the jury; (3) move to immediately sequester the jury to insulate it from the media, the public, and the DA's office; (4) move successfully for mistrial if children's testimony is *not* corroborated by adults' testimony, forensic evidence, or other circumstantial proofs; and (5) move to have the judge review the merit of scheduled expert testimony before the expert appears before the jury.

Conclusions

In the *McMartin* trial, the race of prospective jurors played an important role in identifying the jurors' perceptions of the case. Scientific *voir dire* jury selection was particularly important because the pretrial publicity exerted a significant influence on the perceptions of the general population, and thus prospective jurors. In the 1986 survey, well over 90% of the prospective jurors in Los Angeles County thought that both Raymond and Peggy Buckey were guilty of child molestation. The trial did not even start until the following year. Pretrial publicity exposed the public to preindictment investigative materials.

In a criminal trial, the prosecutors generally have a great deal of leeway in deciding where the defendants will be tried, in regulating the extent of the information to be released (or not to be released) to the media, and in deciding which regulations or laws will be applied to the case. Theoretically speaking, the prosecution in criminal cases represents the general interest of the State and its judicial apparatus, including governmental functions and regulations, all the statutory laws, the judges, and other legal functionaries. The prosecution is also concerned with procedural regulations such as how to select jurors, what to tell jurors before they go to the deliberation room, and when to sequester the jurors, if necessary, during the course of the trial. For example, the procedure of sequestration is used by the government to shield jurors from publicity about the trial and information about the defendants that is not admissible as evidence.

Although sequestration is used to enable the court to conduct a fair trial without putting limits on the freedom of the press, its impact on the jury composition is known: the hardship due to the loss of time and pay is likely to result in a jury that is not representative of the community. Indeed, because of small compensation, the underrepresented may be those in the less stable secondary labor markets, racial minorities, and women with small children. The overrepresented may be those with high incomes and prestigious occupations, who are more likely to identify with the judges and the prosecutions. Research indicates that the resulting nonrepresentative jury may show a consistent bias in trial outcomes (Van Dyke, 1977, pp. 181–183).

Whereas the prosecution has a great deal of leeway in many trials, the defense has little leeway to overcome its handicaps. Scientific jury selection is one of few options available to the defense to influence jury composition and the trial outcome. In fact, less systematic but similar jury selection methods were used in earlier criminal cases, including the 1968 trial of Black Panther Huey Newton, the 1972 trial of the Harrisburg Seven, the Vietnam Veterans against the War case in 1972, the Attica Prison rebellion trial in 1974, the Wounded Knee trial of Indian activists in 1975, the trial of former U.S. Attorney General John Mitchell and Maurice Stans in 1974, the trial of Joan Little in 1975, and other trials that touched on sensitive political and racial issues.

As shown in the *McMartin* trial, when pretrial publicity exerts significant influence on the perceptions of the general population and therefore of prospective jurors, the development of jurors' profiles and the identification of impartial prospective jurors become crucial aspects of scientific defense jury selection.

Although there are some objections to using systematic jury selection techniques, the method used in the *McMartin* trial was effective in developing juror profiles and in identifying prospective jurors' partiality and perceptions of the probable outcome of the trial. In fact, in the pretrial community survey, almost all of the surveyed prospective jurors said that the defendants were guilty of the crime. Because the survey was conducted in the Central Superior Court judicial district, where the trial was to take place, the prosecution was confident in indicting and convicting the defendants. However, social survey analyses combined with observational assessments of prospective jurors assigned to the *McMartin* case were used effectively to create a ranking scale of jurors' partiality and, along with sociodemographic information, to assess individual jurors for their ability to judge the case without prejudice.

There are two main concerns regarding the use of the scientific jury-selection technique: (1) its effectiveness and (2) the ethical issues of "intentionally" influencing jury composition by coding individual jurors into mere numbers and analyzing them with objective statistical and mathematical techniques.

With regard to the first concern, although research has shown that many well-publicized trials in which scientific jury selection was used have resulted in favorable awards, acquittal, or, at worst, convictions on lesser charges (Hans & Vidmar, 1986), there are reasons to be skeptical about the effectiveness of scientific jury selection. First, the success may be due to other factors in the trial rather than the jury selection method. For example, analyses of the scientific jury selection method used in the Watergate trial involving John Mitchell and Maurice Stans revealed that the technique itself was not directly related to the acquittal of the defendants (Zeisel & Diamond, 1976). As stated earlier, many trials that have used the scientific jury selection technique were political, racial, or social in nature. For example, the Chicago Seven trial dealt with the issue of conspiracy. Van Dyke (1977) pointed out that conspiracy is a difficult charge to prove. In many cases against anti–Vietnam activists that used systematic jury-selection techniques, the political nature of the trial made it relatively more difficult to convict the defendants.

Second, the carefully studied preparation of jurors and their profiles by the attorneys in some cases may have been responsible for the favorable results. For example, Angela Davis, a defendant also acting as her own attorney, showed that her careful observation and her skillful *voir dire* technique of revealing jurors' biases, without using any high-powered computers and statistical inference, may have been responsible for her acquittal.

The second question underlying the use of scientific jury selection is the ethical issue: Is it ethically permissible to use scientific techniques to influence the jury composition, and thus possibly the outcome of the trial? Many researchers justify their involvement in the trial on the grounds that it is otherwise impossible for the defendants to get a fair trial. In fact, a large number of the defendants in criminal cases are members of racial minorities. Because minorities are underrepresented in the jury pool, the scientific jury-selection technique enables the defense attorney to evaluate the proclivities of assigned jurors and to obtain jurors who are capable of inferring the defendants' motives, understanding their life conditions, and possibly identifying with defendants' gender, race, and class background. Although some critics maintain that the legitimacy of the trial and the resulting verdict may be undermined by the use of scientific jury selection, scientific jury selection is essential when a fair trial is perceived to be in jeopardy if the traditional method of jury selection is used. The *McMartin* trial was a particularly important case because it touched on the very sensitive issues of children and sexual abuse. Scientific jury selection allowed the defense to obtain impartial jurors to try the unpopular defendants and thus to obtain a fair trial.

Another ethical problem surrounding scientific jury selection is its use in civil cases. Systematic scientific jury-selection techniques are becoming increasingly demanded and used by major corporations and wealthy clients who have economic resources at their disposal and seek a "favorable" jury rather than an "impartial" jury.

Should the motion of a fair trial be translated to a favorable jury towards the acquisition of certain economic means or to an impartial jury which consists of jurors without prejudice or biases? Under the former system, is justice served in such trials? Obviously the client with tremendous economic resources can hire social and behavioral scientists to use the technique and thus to influence both the jury composition and the outcome of the trial. When there is an unequal distribution of resources, the major ethical questions about the use of scientific jury selection and participation by social scientists in the courtroom become crucial. Although it is not easy to answer these ethical questions, they should be addressed and carefully assessed both by the social scientists who use the technique and by those who hire them.

Notes

1. This chapter was made possible by the cooperation of the Jury Service Division, the Superior Court, and the Public Defender's Office, Los Angeles County, California. We would also like to thank Jo-Ellan Huebner-Dimitrius for her cooperation and work in carrying out scientific defense jury selection in the *McMartin* trial. The authors also wish to thank two defense attorneys, Dean Gits and Danny Davis, who represented Peggy McMartin Buckey and Raymond Buckey in the trial.
2. Peggy McMartin Buckey was acquitted of all charges. For Raymond Buckey, her son, the jury offered deadlocked votes on 13 of the original 52 counts. He was later charged with some of the 13 charges, but the second trial resulted in a hung jury. The prosecution finally opted not to pursue another trial.

3. Testimony by former Deputy District Attorney Glenn Stevens revealed that, by the time Judy Johnson called him, she had already made child molestation allegations against her former husband, employees at a local gym, and a Los Angeles school board member. She had also reported that defendant Raymond Buckey could fly, that her son had been forced to drink blood and take part in satanic rituals, and that McMartin teachers had put staples in his ears and scissors in his eyes (Timnick, 1986f).
4. Terms such as "young victims," "tormented secrecy," and "the assailant" were used with an absence of qualifying adjectives such as *charged* or *alleged*. Most of the press in the Los Angeles area wrote about the case using similar terminology (Shaw, 1990).
5. Defense attorney Dean Gits argued that the evidence against Peggy McMartin Buckey was no different from that against the five other teachers no longer facing charges. He noted that "there is no material difference between the six . . . after reviewing the children's testimony, videotaped interviews with therapists and other information available to the prosecution and defense." Similar arguments on behalf of defendant Raymond Buckey were presented to the court, and it was asked to consider dismissal of the case (Timnick, 1987b).
6. Peggy McMartin Buckey was freed on $295,000 bail. After Raymond Buckey had stayed in jail almost five years, Judge William Pounder moved in December 1988 to cut his bail in half, to $1.5 million (Timnick, 1988). Raymond Buckey was finally released in February 1989, after Judge Pounder determined that he had met the $1.5 million bail by pledging real estate worth twice that amount, as required by law (Himmel, 1989).
7. The *Los Angeles Times* reported on December 17, 1986 (Chambers, 1986b), that Myra Mann, a screenwriter who was writing a book and a movie script about the *McMartin* case, testified that Glenn Stevens, a former prosecutor in the McMartin Pre-School child molestation case, had agreed to tell her the inside story of the case for $1,000 and 5% of the project's profits.

   Stevens testified under a grant of immunity from the prosecution that the prosecution office had not only suppressed information suggesting Johnson's mental imbalance but had also failed to investigate whether she had already been troubled when she made her first report of child molestation. After completing his testimony, Stevens reiterated his belief in "the innocence of the McMartin Seven," including the remaining defendants, Raymond Buckey and Peggy McMartin Buckey (Rohrlich & Timnick, 1986).

   In November 1986, the defense attorneys moved for the dismissal of all charges against the two defendants, Raymond Buckey and Peggy McMartin Buckey. Specifically, the motion alleged the following six acts of governmental misconduct:

   a. The two defendants had been held without bail on a charge on which the district attorney never intended to proceed and a grand jury indictment had been superseded by a broader criminal complaint. Chief prosecutor Lael Rubin had lied to the court as a ploy to keep Peggy McMartin Buckey in jail for nearly two years, although bail had been set for her on the larger complaint.

   b. The prosecutors had intentionally suppressed and withheld from the grand jury material evidence that tended to exonerate the defendants. The evidence consisted of notes of interviews with Judy Johnson, who had initiated the McMartin investigation. Ms. Johnson had had a history of mental illness, and some of the molestations that she alleged took place had occurred while Raymond Buckey was in jail and remained "completely unproved."

   c. To keep the defendants from being released, the prosecutors had announced that they were ready to begin the preliminary hearing, when in fact they were still putting their case together. They then "filled" court time with unnecessary witnesses to stall for time.

d. To gain their cooperation and consent, Rubin had "intentionally misrepresented" to parents of children allegedly molested at the Manhattan Beach nursery school that the children would never have to testify in front of the defendants.

e. Rubin had "intentionally misrepresented" to the court that specific children were available to testify by closed-circuit television, when in fact they were not. The result was a delay in the proceedings of more than four months. Eventually, one child testified by television.

f. Rubin arranged with the sheriff's department to keep Peggy McMartin Buckey and three other former female defendants from having any contact with each other or other inmates at Sybil Brand Institute for Women and then lied to the court about her action ("McMartin attorneys charge misconduct, seek case dismissal," 1986).

8. Lois Timnick worked as a reporter for 18 years, seven at the *Times*. David Shaw, a *Times* reporter, said that Timnick was "a single mother who felt even more strongly than most about child abuse. She has spoken publicly on the subject and was interested in it before McMartin hit headlines; she wrote nine by-lined stories on child abuse the year before McMartin—a major reason she was assigned to the story in the first place. She knew—and cared—about the subject" (Shaw, 1990).

9. There were five other instances of imbalance in the reporting of the *McMartin* trial.

a. In 1985, during the preliminary hearing, two vital prosecution witnesses—Kee MacFarlane, the social worker who conducted most of the original interviews with the *McMartin* children, and Astrid Heger, the pediatrician who said she found signs of molestation—refused under oath to disclose if they had been molested as children themselves. The defense said that if they had been molested, the experience might have tainted their evaluation of the *McMartin* children. Both the *Herald Examiner* and the *Daily Breeze* in Torrance covered this development the day after each testified. The *Times* did not report MacFarlane's testimony until two days later—in the last half of a story about the closure of another South Bay preschool. The *Times* did not report Heger's testimony at all. It is ironic that when defendant Peggy McMartin Buckey testified during the trial that she had been molested as a child four years later, the *Times* put the story on page 1 of the Metro Section.

b. The now defunct *Herald Examiner, Daily Breeze, Daily News*, and *Orange County Register* all published stories in 1988 when MacFarlane testified that she and reporter Wayne Satz of KABC had a "boyfriend/girlfriend" relationship, and again when Judge Pounder said that it was relevant for the jury to hear that information. *The Times* published no story on either development.

c. Judy Johnson initially made many bizarre charges. Many skeptics questioned Judy Johnson's stability and the legitimacy of her accusations. But early in the case, a *Times* story said that the *McMartin* allegations stemmed from "one parent's alertness," not elaborating on her mental problems.

d. Unlike *Easy Rider*, an alternative weekly in Hermosa Beach, Los Angeles County, the *Times* did not cover the case's medical testimony in detail and reported only briefly the difficulty the defense was having in finding a medical expert willing to testify in its behalf.

e. When former Deputy District Attorney Glenn Stevens lost confidence in the prosecution's case, *California* magazine ran a lengthy excerpt and the *New York Times* quoted from the tape-recordings he made with movie producer Abby Mann and Mann's wife, Myra who were interested in making a movie about the McMartin trial. The *Los Angeles Times* ran no excerpts and made only brief references to the content of the tapes.

David Shaw, a *Los Angeles Times* writer, also reported that Bob Williams, another *Times* reporter, became so upset by what he perceived as the bias in the *Times' McMartin* coverage that he wrote memos criticizing Lois Timnick, the paper's primary *McMartin* reporter. Williams, a 20-year veteran, was a reporter in the paper's South Bay section when he wrote several *McMartin* stories himself, including the paper's first coverage of the *McMartin* case (Shaw, 1990).

10. Nevertheless, the media gradually changed sides from favoring the children's charges to favoring the defendants. Several weeks before the court verdict, the press as jury would have unanimously exonerated Peggy McMartin Buckey and by a majority found Raymond Buckey not guilty either. The press almost unanimously found the *Los Angeles Times* guilty of unremitting bias in reporting.

References

Abbott, A. (1990). *A brief for the trial and civil issues before a jury.* Rochester, NY: Lawyers' Co-Operative Publishing Co.

Adams, G. B. (1934). *Constitutional history of England.* New York: Henry Holt.

Alker, H. R., Jr., & Barnard, J. J. (1978). Procedural and social biases in the jury selection process. *The Justice System Journal, 3,* 220–241.

Alker, H. R., Jr., Hosticka, C., & Mitchell, M. (1976). Jury selection as a biased social process. *The Law and Society Review, 9,* 9–41.

Alvarez, N. L. (1982). Racial bias and the right to an impartial jury: A standard for allowing voir dire inquiry. *The Hastings Law Journal, 33,* 959–983.

American Bar Association. (1983). *ABA Standards for Criminal Justice.* ABA: Standing Committee on Association Standards for Criminal Justice.

Apktheker, B. (1975). *The morning breaks: The trial of Angela Davis.* New York: International Publishers.

Arnold, M. (1974). How Mitchell-Stans jury reached acquittal verdict. *New York Times,* May 5.

Arnold, R., & Decker, C. (1984). Teachers seen as upstanding citizens or predators—McMartin case: A community divided. *Los Angeles Times,* April 29.

Autoworker acquitted of rights violation in Asian's death. (1987). *Chicago Tribune,* May 2.

Avins, A. (1967). *The Reconstruction amendments' debates: The legislative history and contemporary debates in Congress on the 13th, 14th, and 15th amendments.* Richmond, VA: Commission on Constitutional Government.

Babbie, E. (1989). *The practice of social research.* Belmont, CA: Wadsworth.

Babcock, B. A. (1975). Voir dire: Preserving "its wonderful power." *Georgetown Law Journal, 16,* 545–565.

Baldus, D., Pulaske, C., & Woodsworth, G. (1983). Judicial review of death sentences. *Journal of Criminal Law and Criminology, 74,* 661–753.

Barkan, S. E. (1985). *Protestors on trial: Criminal justice in the Southern civil rights and Vietnam antiwar movement.* New Brunswick, NJ: Rutgers University Press.

Baron, J. N. (1984). Organizational perspectives on stratification. *Annual Review of Sociology, 10,* 37–69.

Barrera, M. (1979). *Race and class in the Southwest: A theory of racial inequality.* Notre Dame: University of Notre Dame Press.

Barth, F. (1969). *Ethnic groups and boundaries.* Boston: Little, Brown.

Bean, F. D., & Tienda, M. (1987). *The Hispanic population of the United States.* New York: Sage.

Becker, T. L. (1971). *Political trials.* Indianapolis: Bobbs-Merrill.

Benokraitis, N. (1975). *Institutional racism: An empirical study of blacks and jury selection process in ten southern states.* Unpublished doctoral dissertation, University of Texas, Austin.

Benokraitis, N., & Griffin-Keene, J. A. (1982). Prejudice and jury selection. *Journal of Black Studies, 12*, 427–449.

Bentler, P. M., & Bonett, D. G. (1980). Significance tests and goodness-of-fit in the analysis of covariance structure. *Psychological Bulletin, 88*, 588–606.

Bermant, G. (1977). *Conduct of the voir dire examination: Practices and opinions of federal district judges.* Washington, DC: Federal Judicial Center.

Bermant, G. (1978). *The voir dire examination, juror challenges, and adversary advocacy.* Washington, DC: Federal Judicial Center.

Bermant, G. (1982). *Jury selection procedures in the United States district courts.* Washington, DC: Federal Judicial Center.

Bermant, G. & Shapard, J. (1981). *The voir dire examination, juror challenges, and adversary advocacy.* Washington, DC: Federal Judicial Center.

Black, H. C. (1990). *Black's Law Journal.* St. Paul, MN: West.

Blackstone, S. W. (1884). *Commentaries of the laws of England.* Chicago: Callaghan.

Blauner, R. (1972). *Racial oppression in America.* New York: Harper & Row.

Boags, C. D., & Boags, R. M. (1971). The misuse of a so-called psychological examination for the selection of jurors. In C. Thomas (ed.), *Boys no more: A black psychologist's view of community* (pp. 48–64). Beverly Hills, CA: Glencoe.

Bollen, K. A. (1989). *Structural equations with latent variables.* New York: Wiley.

Bonacich, E. (1972). A theory of ethnic antagonism: The split labor market. *American Sociological Review, 37*, 547–559.

Bonacich, E. (1973). A theory of middleman minorities. *American Sociological Review, 38*, 583–594.

Bonacich, E. (1980). Class approaches to ethnicity and race. *The Insurgent Sociologist, 10*, 9–23.

Bowers, W., & Pierce, G. (1980). Arbitrariness and discrimination under post-Furman capital statutes. *Crime and Delinquency, 26*, 563–635.

Bowles, R. A. (1980). Juries, incentives and self selection. *British Journal of Criminology, 20*, 368–376.

Brady, J. (1983). Fair and impartial railroad: The jury, the media, and political trials. *Journal of Criminal Justice, 11*, 241–263.

Brodie, I. (1982). Putting the brake on wheels of justice. *Daily Telegraph,* March 1, p. 15.

Buckey case ends; he files suit. (1990). *Press-Enterprise,* August 2.

Burr, G. L. (1975). *Narratives of the witchcraft cases, 1648–1706.* New York: Barnes & Noble.

Butler, E. W. (1980a). *Torrance Superior Court panels and population analysis.* Riverside: University of California.

Butler, E. W. (1980b). *Van Nuys Superior Court panels and population analysis: May 7, 1979 through September 24, 1979.* Riverside: University of California.

Butler, E. W. (1981). *The 1980 Los Angeles County jury selection study: Compton Superior Court.* Riverside: University of California.

Butler, E. W., & Fukurai, H. (1984). An evaluation of jury panel selection procedures: The North Valley Superior Court, Los Angeles County. Riverside: University of California.

Butler, E. W., & Kaiser, E. J. (1971). Prediction of residential movement and spatial allocation. *Urban Affairs Quarterly, 6*, 477–494.

Butler, E. W., & Fukurai, H., Huebner-Dimitrius, J., & Krooth, R. (1992). *The McMartin trial: Anatomy of the jury.* New Brunswick, NJ: Rutgers University Press.

Cannon, L. (1991). White jury's comment on cop brutality: Not guilty. *San Jose Mercury News,* May 21.

Carmichael, S., & Hamilton, C. (1967). *Black power: The politics of liberation in America.* New York: Random House, Vintage Books.

Carp, R. A. (1974). The Harris County grand jury—A case study. *Houston Law Review, 12*, 90–120.

Carp, R. A. (1982). Federal grand juries: How true a "cross section" of the community. *The Justice System Journal, 7*, 256–277.

Carter, D. T. (1979). *Scottsboro: A tragedy of the American South.* Baton Rouge: Louisiana State University Press.

Casanova, P. G. (1965). Internal colonialism and national development. *Studies in Comparative International Development, 1*, 27–37.

Case comments: Voir dire limitations as a means of protecting jurors' safety and privacy. (1980). *Harvard Law Review, 93*, 782–792.

The case for black juries. (1970). *Yale Law Journal, 79*, 531–550.

Chambers, M. (1986a). Officials drop case against 5 on child abuse. *New York Times*, January 18.

Chambers, M. (1986). Screenwriter says ex-prosecutor made a deal in child abuse case. *Los Angeles Times*, December 17.

Chambliss, W. J. (1971). *Law, order, and power.* Reading, MA: Addison-Wesley.

Chevigny, P. G. (1975). The Attica case: A successful jury challenge in northern city. *Criminal Law Bulletin, 11*, 157–172.

Clark, L. (1975). *The grand jury: The use and abuse of political power.* New York: The New York Times Book Co.

Clark, W. A. V. (1986). *Human migration.* Beverly Hills, CA: Sage.

Cochran, W. (1954). "Some methods for strengthening the common Chi-square tests." *Biometrics, 10*, 417–451.

Cocke, A. K. (1979). Constitutional law—Sixth Amendment right to trial by jury—Five jurors are not enough. *Tennessee Law Review, 46*, 847–864.

Cole, G. (1973). *Politics and the administration of justice.* London: Sage.

Cole, J. (1972). Justice is a man wearing a hard hat. *Memphis Commercial Appeal*, December 24.

Colson, B. (1986). *Jury selection: Strategy and science.* Wilmette, IL: Callaghan.

Committee on Public Safety. (1987). *Investigating child molestation cases: Interim hearing.* Sacramento, CA: Legislature Assembly.

Comparing voters and drivers lists. (1982). *Center for Jury Studies News Letter. 4*, 1–8.

Conley, J., O'Barr, W., & Lind, A. (1978). The power of language: Presentation style in the courtroom. *Duke Law Journal*, 1375–1399.

Cox, O. (1976). *Race relations: Elements and social dynamics.* Detroit: Wayne State University Press.

Cromer, E. (1910). *Ancient and modern imperialism.* New York: Longmans, Green.

Cullen, F. T., & Link, B. G. (1980). Crime as an occupation. *Criminology, 18*, 399–410.

Cummings, J. (1983). Detroit Asian-Americans protest lenient penalties for murder. *New York Times*, April 26.

Dane, F., & Wrightsman, L. (1982). Effects of defendants' and victims' characteristics on jurors' verdicts. In N. L. Kerr & R. M. Bray, (Eds.), *The psychology of the courtroom.* New York: Academic Press.

Danielski, D. (1971). The Chicago conspiracy trial. In T. Becker (Ed.), *Political trials.* New York: Bobbs-Merrill.

Daughtery, M. (1975). Cross sectionalism in jury selection procedures after Taylor v. Louisiana. *Tennessee Law Review, 43*, 62.

De Cani, J. S. (1974). Statistical evidence in jury discrimination cases. *The Journal of Criminal Law and Criminology, 65*, 234–238.

The defendant's right to object to prosecutorial misuse of the peremptory challenge. (1979). *Harvard Law Review, 92*, 1170–1789.

Deosaran, R. (1981). The jury system in a post-colonial, multi-racial society: Problems of bias. *The British Journal of Criminology, 21,* 305–323.

Diamond, W. H. (1980). Federal remedies for racial discrimination in grand jury selection. *Columbia Journal of Law and Social Problems, 16,* 85–117.

DiPerna, P. (1984). *Juries on trial: Faces of American justice.* New York: Dembner.

Doeringer, P., & Piore, M. (1968). *Internal labor markets and manpower analysis.* Lexington, MA: D. C. Heath.

Dorsen, N., & Friedman, L. (1973). *Disorder in the court: Report of the association of the bar of the City of New York.* Special committee on courtroom conduct. New York: Pantheon Books.

Duncan, R. (1987). Putting a cap on voir dire: We can turn out fair verdicts and save time by letting judges ask the questions. *California Lawyer, 7,* (March 3) 28.

Dundas, P. B., Jr. (1972). The constitutionality of excluding young people from jury service. *Washington and Lee Law Review, 29,* 131–142.

Dutt, R. P. (1957). *The crisis of Britain and the British Empire.* London: Lawrence & Wishart.

Edward R., Reich, M., & Gordon, D. (1975). *Labor market segmentation.* Lexington, MA: D. C. Heath.

Erlanger, H. S. (1970). Jury research in America. *Law and Society Review, 5,* 345–370.

Exhaustive sex case inquiry told: McMartin flaw—gap in evidence. (1986). *Los Angeles Times,* January 27.

Feagin, J. R. (1984). *Racial and ethnic relations.* Englewood Cliffs, NJ: Prentice-Hall.

Featherman, D., & Hauser, R. (1978). *Opportunity and change.* New York: Academic Press.

Feild, H. S. (1979). Rape trials and juror's decisions: A psychological analysis of the effects of victim, defendant, and case characteristics. *Law and Human Behavior, 3,* 261–284.

Feild, H. S., & Bienen, L. B. (1980). *Jurors and rape: A study in psychology and law.* Lexington, MA: Lexington Books.

Feldman, P., & Timnick, L. (1986). D.A. won't try 5 in McMartin case. *Los Angeles Times,* January 9.

Feldman-Summers, S., & Ashworth, C. D. (1981). Factors related to intentions to report a rape. *Journal of Social Issues, 37,* 53–70.

Foley, L. A., & Powell, R. S. (1982). The discretion of prosecutors, judges, and juries in capital cases. *Criminal Justice Review, 7,* 16–22.

Frankel, M. E., & Naftalis, G. P. (1975). *The grand jury: An institution on trial.* New York: Hill & Wang.

Fukurai, H. (1985). *Institutional racial inequality: A theoretical and empirical examination of the jury selection process.* Unpublished doctoral dissertation, University of California, Riverside.

Fukurai, H. (1991). Japanese migration in contemporary Japan: Economic segmentation and interprefectural migration. *Social Biology,* 38, 28–50.

Fukurai, H., & Alston J. (1990). Divorce in contemporary Japan. *Journal of Biosocial Science, 22,* 453–464.

Fukurai, H., & Butler, E. W. (1987). *Jury selection: Institutionalized racial inequality.* Book manuscript.

Fukurai, H., & Butler, E. W. (1991a). Organization, labor force, and jury representation: Economic excuses and jury participation. *Jurimetrics,* 32, 49–69.

Fukurai, H., & Butler, E. W. (1991b). Race or social class? Determinants of judicial inequality. Submitted for publication.

Fukurai, H., & Butler, E. W. (1992). Computer-aided evaluation of racial representation in jury selection. *Computers, Environment and Urban Systems,* 16, 131–155.

Fukurai, H., Butler, E. W., & Huebner-Dimitrius, J. (1987). Spatial and racism imbalances in voter registration and jury selection. *Sociology and Social Research, 77,* 33–38.
Fukurai, H., Butler, E. W., & Krooth, R. (1991a). A cross-sectional jury representation or systematic jury representation? Simple random and cluster-sampling strategies in jury selection. *Journal of Criminal Justice, 19,* 31–48.
Fukurai, H., Butler, E. W., & Krooth, R. (1991b). Where did black jurors go? A theoretical synthesis of racial disenfranchisement in the jury system and jury selection. *Journal of Black Studies, 22,* 196–215.
Geschwender, J. A. (1978). *Racial stratification in America.* Dubuque, IA: Wm. C. Brown.
Ginger, A. (1969). *Minimizing racism in jury trials.* Berkeley, CA: The National Lawyers Guild.
Ginger, A. F. (1984). *Jury selection in civil and criminal trials.* Berkeley, CA: Lawpress.
Glazer, N. & Moynihan, D. P. (1975). *Ethnicity: Theory and experience.* Cambridge: Harvard University Press.
Goffman, E. (1959). *The presentation of self in everyday life.* New York: Doubleday Anchor.
Gordon, D. (1972). *Theories of poverty and underemployment.* Lexington, MA: D. C. Heath.
Green, T. A. (1985). *Verdict according to conscience: Perspectives on the English criminal trial jury, 1200–1800.* Chicago: University of Chicago Press.
"Grigsby vs Mabry": A new look at death qualified juries. (1980). *American Criminal Law Review, 18,* 145–163.
Grocer joined sex games, McMartin witness says. (1985). *Los Angeles Times,* February 16.
Gumperz, J. (1982). Facts and inference in courtroom testimony. In J. Gumperz (Ed.), *Language and social identity.* London: Cambridge University Press.
Hagan, J. (1974). Extra-legal attributes and criminal sentencing: An assessment of a sociological viewpoint. *Law and Society Review, 7,* 357–383.
Hans, V., & Vidmar, N. (1986). *Judging the jury.* New York: Plenum Press.
Hastie, R., Penrod, S. D., & Pennington, N. (1983). *Inside the jury.* Cambridge: Harvard University Press.
Hayduk, L. A. (1987). *Structural equation modeling with LISREL: Essentials and advances.* Baltimore: Johns Hopkins University Press.
Hepburn, J. R. (1978). Race and the decision to arrest: An analysis of warrants issued. *Journal of Research in Crime and Delinquency, 15,* 54–73.
Heyns, B. (1979). 1979 jury analysis, Superior Court, County of Los Angeles, No. A-344097, Joseph Piazza, defendant.
Himmel, H. (1989). Buckey freed on $1.5-million bail after 5 years in jail. *Los Angeles Times,* February 16.
Horowitz, I. A. (1980). Jury selection: A comparison of two methods in several criminal cases. *Journal of Applied Social Psychology, 10,* 86–99.
Hosch, H. M., Beck, E. L., & McIntyre, P. (1980). Influence of expert testimony regarding eyewitness accuracy on jury decisions. *Law and Human Behavior, 4,* 287–296.
Huebner-Dimitrius, J. (1984). *The representative jury: Fact or fallacy?* Unpublished dissertation, Claremont College.
Hurst, W. (1977). *Law and social order in the United States.* Ithaca, NY: Cornell University Press.
Inverarity, J. M., Lauderdale, P., & Feld, B. C. (1983). *Law and society: Sociological perspectives on criminal law.* Boston: Little, Brown.
Johnson, G. T. (1981). *Mobility, residential location, and urban change: A partially annotated bibliography.* Chicago, IL: CPL Bibliographies.
Joreskog, K. G., & Sorbom, D. (1985). *LISREL VI: Analysis of linear structural relationships by the method of maximum likelihood.* Chicago: National Educational Resources.
Judicial Council of California. (1978). *A report to the judicial council on ways to improve trial*

jury selection and management. San Francisco, CA: National Center for State Courts, Western Regional Office.

Jury-duty fear discourages voter registration. (1990). *New York Times*, September 28.

"Jury-mandering": Federal jury selection and the generation gap. (1973). *Iowa Law Review, 59*, 401–419.

Justice proposes fewer challenges. (1984). *Chicago Daily Law Bulletin.* 6, 1, January 3.

Kadane, J. B., & Lehoczsky, J. P. (1976). Random juror selection from multiple lists. *Operations Research, 65*, 207–219.

Kairys, D. (1972). Juror selection: The law, a mathematical method of analysis, and a case study. *American Criminal Law Review, 12*, 771–806.

Kairys, D. (1974). Juror selection. *American Criminal Law Reviews, 10*, 122–129.

Kairys, D., Kadane, J. B., & Lehoczky, J. P. (1977). Jury representativeness: A mandate for multiple source lists. *California Law Review, 65*, 776–827.

Kalven, H., Jr., & Zeisel, H. (1966). *The American jury.* Boston: Little, Brown.

Karlen, D. (1964). *The citizen in court.* New York: Holt, Rinehart & Winston.

Kassin, S. M., & Wrightsman, L. S. (1988). *The American jury on trial: Psychological perspective.* New York: Hemisphere.

Kaufman, J. I. (1984). Verdict on juries. *New York Times Magazine*, April 1, p. 47.

Kaye, D. (1980). And then there were twelve: Statistical reasoning, the Supreme Court, and the size of the jury. *California Law Review, 46*, 461–474.

Keating, E. (1970). *Free Huey.* New York: Dell.

Kerr, N. L., & Bray, R. M. (1982). *The Psychology of the courtroom.* New York: Academic Press.

Kish, L. (1965). *Survey sampling.* New York: Wiley.

Kraft, I. (1982). Happy New Year—You're a juror. *Crime and Delinquency, 28*, 582–600.

Kramer, R. C. (1982). From "habitual offenders" to career criminals. *Law and Human Behavior, 6*, 273–293.

Law Enforcement Assistance Administration. (1987). *Criminal victimization in the United States.* Washington, DC: Department of Justice.

Lichter, D. T. (1989). Race, employment hardship and inequality in the American nonmetropolitan south. *American Sociological Review, 54*, 436–446.

Lind, A., Eriksen, B., & O'Barr, W. (1978). Social attribution and conversation style in trial testimony. *Journal of Personality and Social Psychology, 36*, 1558–1567.

Lipset, J.M., & Bendix, R. (1959). *Social mobility in industrial society.* Berkeley: University of California Press.

Lipton, J. P. (1979). *Sociocultural and personality perspectives on jury behavior and decision making.* Unpublished dissertation, University of California.

Locin, M. (1984). Rights-case jurors hear officer, stripper. *Chicago Tribune*, June 14.

Loh, W. D. (1982). Perspectives on psychology and law. *Journal of Applied Social Psychology, 11*, 314–355.

Long, L. E. (1988). *Migration and residential mobility in the United States.* New York: Sage.

Lowman, Z. (1981). *Jury modernization in Las Vegas.* A report prepared for Supreme Court testimony.

Mahoney, B., & Sipes, D. A. (1988). Toward better management of criminal litigation. *Judicature, 4*, 29–37.

Major, R. (1973). *Justice in the round: The trial of Angela Davis.* New York: Third Press.

Matsueda, R. L., & Bielby, W. T. (1986). Statistical power in covariance structure models. *Sociological Methodology, 16*, 120–158.

McAllister, R. J., Kaiser, E. J., & Butler, E. W. (1971). Residential mobility of blacks and whites: A national longitudinal survey. *American Journal of Sociology, 77*, 445–456.

McGraw, C. (1985). Forced to drink blood: Witness claims. *Los Angeles Times*, February 21.

McGraw, C., & Timnick, L. (1985). Witness, 9, gives detailed account of alleged abuse. *Los Angeles Times*, March 14.
McKay, J. (1982). An exploratory synthesis of primordial and mobilizationist approaches to ethnic phenomena. *Ethnic and Racial Studies, 5*, 395–420.
McMartin: Anatomy of a witch-hunt. (1990, June). *Playboy*, pp. 45–49.
McMartin attorneys charge misconduct, seek case dismissal. (1986). *Los Angeles Times*, November 13.
McMartin case verdicts. (1990). *Los Angeles Times*, January 19.
Miles, R. (1980). Class, race, and ethnicity: A critique of Cox's theory. *Ethnic and Racial Studies, 3*, 169–187.
Mills, E. S. (1969). A statistical profile of jurors in a United States district court. *Law and the Social Order*, 329–339.
Mistrial in officers' beating of motorist in '89. (1991). *New York Times*, May 6.
Mitford, J. (1969). *The trial of Dr. Spock, The Rev. William Sloane Coffin, Jr., Michael Ferber, Mitchell Goodman, and Marcus Raskin*. New York: Knopf.
Moore, L. E. (1972). *The jury: Tool of kings palladium of liberty*. Cincinnati: W. H. Anderson.
Morse, S. J. (1982). Reforming expert testimony. *Law and Human Behavior, 6*, 45–47.
Munsterman, G. T. (1978). *Multiple lists for jury selection: A case study for San Diego Superior Court*. Washington, DC: National Institute of Law Enforcement and Criminal Justice.
Murguia, E. (1975). *Assimilation, colonialism, and the Mexican American people*. Mexican American Monograph Series 1. Center for Mexican American Studies, University of Texas at Austin.
National Jury Project. (1983). *Jury work: Systematic techniques*. New York: Clark Boardman.
Nemeth, C. R. (1976). Governing jury deliberations: A consideration of recent changes. In G. Bermant & N. Vidmar, (Eds.), *Psychology and the law: Recent frontiers*. Lexington, MA: D. C. Heath.
Nemeth, C. R. (1977). Interactions between jurors as a function of majority vs. unanimity decision rules. *Journal of Applied Psychology, 7*, 38–56.
Neubauer, D. W. (1984). *America's courts and the criminal justice system*. Monterey, CA: Brooks/Cole.
Newman, S. J. (1985). *Federal policy and the mobility of older homeowners: The effects of the one-time capital gains exclusion*. Ann Arbor: Survey Research Center, Institute for Social Research, University of Michigan.
Newton, H. (1968). *Revolutionary suicide*. New York: Harcourt, Brace & World.
Nietzel, M. T., & Dillehay, R. C. (1982). The effects of variations in voir dire procedures in capital murder trials. *Law & Human Behavior, 6*, 1–13.
Nietzel, M. T., & Dillehay, R. C. (1986). *Psychological consultation in the courtroom*. New York: Pergamon Press.
Note: Restricting inquiry into racial attitudes during the voir dire. (1982). *American Criminal Law Review, 19*, 719–750.
Note: The peremptory challenges in a criminal case after United States v. Barnes. (1980). *Journal of Criminal Law and Criminology. 71*, 173–180.
O'Rourke, W. (1972). *The Harrisburg 7 and the New Catholic Left*. New York: Thomas Y. Crowell.
Ott, L., Mendenhall, W., & Larson, R. (1987). *Statistics: A tool for the social sciences*. Boston: Duxbury Press.
Palen, J., & London, B. (1984). *Gentrification, displacement, and neighborhood revitalization*. Albany: State University of New York Press.
Pollakowksi, H. O. (1982). *Urban housing markets and residential location*. Lexington, MA: Lexington Books.

Portes, A., & Sassen-Koob, S. (1987). Making it underground: Comparative material on the informal sector in western market economies. *American Journal of Sociology, 93*, 30–61.

Poythress, N. G., Jr. (1982). Concerning reform in expert testimony. *Law and Human Behavior, 6*, 39–43.

Probing racial prejudice on voir dire: The Supreme Court provides illusionary justice for minority defendants. (1981). *Journal of Criminal Law and Criminology, 72*, 1444–1460.

Rainey, J. (1990). McMartin jurors feel ire of public over their verdicts. *Los Angeles Times*, January 20.

Reston, J. (1977). *The innocence of Joan Little: A Southern mystery*. New York: Times Books.

Robinson, W. S. (1950). Bias, probability and trial by jury. *American Sociological Review, 15*, 73–78.

Rohrlich, T. (1990a). 2 in McMartin case file damage claims against L.A. County. *Los Angeles Times*, April 1.

Rohrlich, T. (1990b). Local experts believe case was bungled. *Los Angeles Times*, January 19.

Rohrlich, T., & Timnick, L. (1986). McMartin flaw: gaps in evidence. *Los Angeles Times*, January 27.

Rokeach, M., & McLellan, D. D. (1970). Dogmatism and the death penalty: A reinterpretation of the Duquesne poll data. *Duquesne Law Review, 81*, 125–129.

Roper, R. T. (1980). Jury size and verdict consistency: "A line has to be drawn somewhere." *Law and Society review, 1414*, 977–995.

Rose, S. J. (1986). *The American profile poster: Who owns what, who makes how much, who works where, and who lives with whom*. New York: Pantheon Books.

Rosenberg, H. (1985). 20/20 takes a limited view of McMartin case. *Los Angeles Times*, January 2.

Rosenfeld, R. A., & Kalleberg, R. L. (1990). A cross-national comparison of the gender gap in income. *American Journal of Sociology, 96*, 69–106.

Rowland, C. K. (1979). The relationship between grand jury composition and performance. *Social Science Quarterly, 60*, 323–327.

Ryan, D. J., & Neeson, P. J. (1981). Voir dire: A trial technique in transition. *American Journal of Trial Advocacy, 4*, 523–557.

Sabagh, G., Van Arsdol, M. P., & Butler, E. W. (1969). Some determinants of intrametropolitan residential mobility, conceptual considerations. *Social Forces, 48*, 88–98.

Saltzburg, S. A., & Powers, M. E. (1982). Peremptory challenges and the clash between impartiality and group representation. *Maryland Law Review, 41*, 337–383.

Scott, J. (1984). *Jury selection and the right to a fair trial: The genesis, implementation and impact of the jury selection acts*. Unpublished dissertation. University of California, Riverside.

Sealy, A. P. (1980). Another look at social psychological aspects of juror bias. *Law and Human Behavior, 5*, 187–200.

2d rights trial opens in 1982 beating death. (1987). *New York Times*, April 23.

Seidman, R. (1969). Witch murder and mens rea: A problem of society under radical social change. In William Chambliss (Ed.) *Crime and the legal process*. New York: McGraw-Hill.

Shaw, D. (1990). Times McMartin coverage was biased, critics charge. *Los Angeles Times*, January 22.

Shelton, B. A. (1987). Variations in divorce rates by community size: A test of the social integration explanation. *Journal of Marriage and the Family, 49*, 827–832.

Silas, F. A. (1983). A jury of one's peers: Peremptory challenges of minorities raise fairness issues. *American Bar Association Journal, 69*, 1607–1609.

Simon, R. (1967). *The jury and the defense of insanity*. Boston: Little, Brown.

Simon, R. J. (1980). *The jury: Its role in American society*. Lexington: Lexington Books.

Sixth Amendment—trial by an impartial jury—the breadth of the basis for excluding veniremen under the Witherspoon doctrine. (1982). *American Criminal Law Review, 10,* 47–63.
Strodbeck, F. L., James, R. M., & Hawkins, C. (1957). Social status in jury deliberations. *American Sociological Review, 22,* 713–718.
Sudman, S. (1976). *Applied sampling.* New York: Academic Press.
Summers, M. R. (1961). A Comparative study of the qualifications of state and federal jurors. *Wisconsin Bar Bulletin, 34,* 35–42.
Swett, D. (1969). Cultural bias in the American legal system. *Law and Society Review, 4,* 79–110.
Tandon, R. L. (1979). Jury preconceptions and their effect on expert scientific testimony. *Journal of Forensic Science, 24,* 681–691.
Tell, L. (1987). From jury selection to verdict in hours. *Business Week,* September 7.
Timnick, L. (1985a). "Naked games" described by child in McMartin case. *Los Angeles Times,* January 23.
Timnick, L. (1985b). McMartin witness alleges rape by Raymond Buckey. *Los Angeles Times,* February 27.
Timnick, L. (1986a). All 7 McMartin defendants are ordered to stand trial. *Los Angeles Times,* January 10.
Timnick, L. (1986b). Educator's study stirs new McMartin case controversy. *Los Angeles Times,* November 12.
Timnick, L. (1986c). Judge won't quit McMartin school case. *Los Angeles Times,* November 15.
Timnick, L. (1986d). Key McMartin case accuser found dead. *Los Angeles Times,* January 9.
Timnick, L. (1986e). Testimony ends in McMartin child-abuse hearing. *Los Angeles Times,* January 9.
Timnick, L. (1986f). Withheld facts in McMartin case—Ex-prosecutor. *Los Angeles Times,* January 21.
Timnick, L. (1987a). After 4 years in jail, Buckey has bail set at $3 million. *Los Angeles Times,* December 18.
Timnick, L. (1987b). Bias in prosecution of Peggy Buckey charged. *Los Angeles Times,* February 5.
Timnick, L. (1987c). Judge rejects defense bid to move McMartin trial. *Los Angeles Times,* March 27.
Timnick, L. (1987d). McMartin attorneys to seek relocation of trial. *Los Angeles Times,* February 23.
Timnick, L. (1987e). McMartin trial to begin, 4 years after first arrest. *Los Angeles Times,* July 13.
Timnick, L. (1987f). No image of ex-McMartin D.A. emerges. *Los Angeles Times,* January 29.
Timnick, L. (1987g). Raymond Buckey known as molester, D.A. says. *Los Angeles Times,* September 11.
Timnick, L. (1988). Judge halves bail to $1.5 million for Raymond Buckey. *Los Angeles Times,* December 7.
Timnick, L. (1989). Ran "happy, loving" school McMartin defendant asserts. *Los Angeles Times,* May 18.
Timnick, L. (1990a). McMartin case defendant sues for millions. *Los Angeles Times,* January 20.
Timnick, L. (1990b). 3 ex-McMartin defendants file suit for millions. *Los Angeles Times,* May 30.
Timnick, L., & McGraw, C. (1985). 2 sides in McMartin case claim support in boy's testimony. *Los Angeles Times,* February 25.

Timnick, L., & McGraw, C. (1986). McMartin figure's death cause unclear: Mother's complaints triggered molestation investigation. *Los Angeles Times*, December 21.

Timnick, L., & McGraw, C. (1990). Justice: The jury's findings close the longest and costliest criminal trial in history: No decision has been made on retrying Raymond Buckey on 13 undecided counts. *Los Angeles Times*, January 19.

Trefousse, H. L. (1987). Teach 13-year olds Lincoln freed slaves. Letter to the editor. *New York Times*, November 8.

Ugwuegbu, D. (1979). Racial and evidential factors in juror attributions of legal responsibility. *Journal of Experimental Social Psychology, 15*, 133–146.

U.S. Bureau of the Census. (1981a). Voting and registration in the election of November, 1980 (Advanced Report). *Current population reports*. Series P-20, No. 359. Washington, DC: Government Printing Office.

U.S. Bureau of the Census. (1981b). Voting and registration in the election of November, 1980. *Current population reports*. Series P-20, No. 370. Washington, DC: Government Printing Office.

U.S. Bureau of the Census. (1984). Geographic mobility: March 1982 to March 1983. *Current population reports*. Series P-20, No. 393. Washington, DC: Government Printing Office.

U.S. Bureau of the Census. (1987). *Geographic mobility: November 1986 to March 1987*. Washington, DC: Government Printing Office.

U.S. Bureau of the Census. (1989). Voting and registration in the election of November, 1988. *Current population reports*. Series P-20, No. 370. Washington, DC: Government Printing Office.

U.S. Congress. (1967). *Hearings, federal jury service*. 90th Congress, 1st Sessions, March 21–July 20. (Quoted in Van Dyke, 1977, p. 90.)

U.S. Congress. (1975). *Use of voter registration lists for jury selection*. 94th Congress, 1st Sessions (Congressional Record, Section 5985), April 15. (Quoted in Van Dyke, 1977, p. 108.)

U.S. Department of Justice. (1983). *Report to the nation on crime and justice*. Washington, DC: Department of Justice.

U.S. Department of Justice. (1984). *National symposium on child molestation*. Washington, DC: Department of Justice.

U.S. 90th Congress House Report. (1968). No. 1076.

Van Arsdol, J., Maurice, D., Sabagh, G., & Butler, E. W. (1968). Retrospective and subsequent metropolitan residential mobility. *Demography, 5*, 249–267.

Van den Berghe, P. L. (1974). Bringing the beast back in. *American Sociological Review, 39*, 777–788.

Van Dyke, J. M. (1977). *Jury selection procedure*. Cambridge: Ballinger.

A verdict in a very sad case: Editorials (1990). *Los Angeles Times*, January 19.

Voir dire limitations as a means of protecting jurors' safety and privacy: United States v. Barnes. (1980). *Harvard Law Review, 93*, 720.

Weakliem, D. L. (1990). Relative wages and radical theory of economic segmentation. *American Sociological Review, 55*, 574–590.

Why some trials go on and on and on. (1939). *U.S. News & World Report*, February 13.

Wilderson, I. (1987). Asian-American acquittal in rights case arouses outrage and fear. *New York Times*, May 6.

Wishman, S. (1986). *Anatomy of a jury: The system on trial*. New York: Times Books.

Wright, E. O. (1979). *Class structure and income determination*. New York: Academic Press.

Wright, E. O. (1980). Class and occupation. *Theory and Society*, 177–214.

Wright, E. O. (1985). *Classes*. London: Verso.

Wrightsman, L. S. (1987). *Psychology and the legal systems*. Monterey, CA: Brooks/Cole.

Younger, R. D. (1963). *The people's panel: The grand jury in the United States, 1834–1941*. Providence, RI: Brown University Press.

Zeigler, D. H. (1978). Young adults as a cognizable group in jury selection. *Michigan Law Review, 76*, 1045–1110.

Zeisel, H., & Diamond, S. (1976). The jury selection in the Mitchell-Stans conspiracy trial. *American Bar Foundation Research*, 162.

Table of Cases

Akins v. Texas, 14, 82, 91–92, 166
Alexander v. Louisiana, 11n, 35n, 101, 102, 105, 115n, 190n
Apodaca v. Oregon, 37n, 113
Atlas Roofing Co. v. Occupational Safety and Health Review Commission, 113
Avery v. Georgia, 14, 93–94, 97

Baldwin v. New York, 113
Ballew v. Georgia, 113
Batson v. Kentucky, 15, 20, 55, 68, 155, 162n
Bradley v. Judges of Superior Court for Los Angeles County, 78n
Brown v. Louisiana, 113
Burch v. Louisiana, 113
Bush v. Kentucky, 82

Carter v. Jury Commission of Greene County, 9, 15–16, 78n, 98–99, 166
Carter v. Texas, 82
Cassell v. Texas, 14–15, 93
Castaneda v. Partida, 78n, 79n, 82, 105, 106, 115n
City of Mobile, Ala. v. Bolden, 11n, 35n, 190n
Coleman v. Alabama, 97
Colgrove v. Battin, 113

Duren v. Missouri, 11n, 35n, 43, 107, 109–110, 190n

Eubanks v. Louisiana, 95
Ex parte Virginia, 82

Fay v. New York, 27, 86, 111–113
Furman v. Georgia, 80n

Glasser v. United States, 96, 107–108, 110

Hale v. Kentucky, 90
Harris v. People of California, 11, 28, 29, *see also* Harris trials, in Subject index; People v. Harris
Hasegawa v. Maui Pineapple Co., 139
Hernandez v. Texas, 17, 78n, 82, 104–105, 115n, 165
Hill v. Texas, 15
Hollins v. Oklahoma, 90
Hoyt v. Florida, 108, 109, 115n

International Longshoreman and Warehouseman's Union v. Ackerman, 78n

Johnson v. Louisiana, 28, 37n, 113
Jones v. Georgia, 97–98, 101

McGartha v. California, 80n
McKiever v. Pennsylvania, 113
McMartin trial, 11, 120, 193–217, 217–220n, *see also* McMartin trial, in Subject index

Neal v. Delaware, 82
New Jersey v. Long, 50
Norris v. Alabama, 88, 89–90, 103

Patton v. Mississippi, 15, 93
Patton v. Missouri, 15
People v. Breckenridge, 11n, 35n
People v. Estrada, 11n, 35n, 190n
People v. Graham, 11n, 36n, 190n
People v. Harris, 11n, 36n, 37n, 43, 144, 145, 160, 172, 190–191n, *see also* Harris trials, in Subject index; Harris v. People of California
People v. King, 11n, 35n, 190n

People v. Lewis, 11n, 35n
People v. Murphy, 53
People v. Newton, 9–10, 11n, 35n, 69, 72–74, 215
People v. Sirhan, 11n, 35n, 190n
People v. Taylor, 78n
People v. Wheeler, 11n, 35n, 190n
People v. White, 11n, 35n, 190n
Peters v. Kiff, 11n, 35n, 84, 102–103, 190n
Pierre v. Louisiana, 90
Plessy v. Ferguson, 88
Press-Enterprise Co. v. Superior Court of California, 6

Reece v. Georgia, 94–95, 97
Rose v. Mitchell, 15, 36n, 84, 103–104, 113

Sandoval v. Superior Court for Los Angeles County, 78n
Scott v. Sanford, 82, 86–87
Sims v. Georgia, 98, 101
Smith v. Texas, 15, 91, 92, 96, 115n
State v. Cage, 190n
State v. Guirlando, 78n
Strauder v. West Virginia, 9, 14, 16, 82, 86–87, 88, 107, 155, 163n
Swain v. Alabama, 95–97, 101, 108, 154

Taylor v. Louisiana, 11n, 35n, 45, 78n, 108–109, 190n
Test v. United States, 107
Thiel v. Southern Pacific Company, 96, 110–111, 112, 190n
Thomas v. Texas, 88–89, 91
Turner v. Fouche, 9, 16, 99–100

United States v. Fernandez, 165
United States v. Fujimoto, 78n
United States v. Maskeny, 107
United States v. Mitchell, 70, 72–73, 216

Whitus v. Georgia, 97, 98, 101, 115n
Williams v. Florida, 27, 97, 113
Witherspoon v. Illinois, 146
Woodson v. North Carolina, 80n
Woody v. Brush, 82

Index

Absolute disparity, 101, 105, 107
Age, 43
  economic excuses and, 127, 129, 134, 139
  excuses and, 55, 56, 64, 65, 67
  master files and, 48, 50
  McMartin trial and, 205, 207, 208, 210
  qualified-juror files and, 55, 56
  scientific *voir dire* and, 157
  source lists and, 47
American Bar Association (ABA), 46, 68
American Nazi Party, 6
Asians, 20
  Harris trial and, 145
  McMartin trial and, 208, 210
  residential mobility of, 22
  scientific *voir dire* and, 145
  verdicts and, 7–8
Assembly Bill No. 1454, 30, 52
Atkins, L.C., 91–92
Attica Prison rebellion trial, 215
Authority-class position, 121, 123, 124, 125, 126, 127, 134–135, 137

Bill of Rights, 9, 142
Black, Hugo LaFayette, 91, 92, 94
Black Panther Party, 9, 20, 73, 158
Blacks, 13–16, 18, 20, 21, 78
  capital punishment and, 20, 28
  cluster-sampling methods and, 166, 174, 176, 177, 189
  excuses and, 55, 56
  exemptions and, 68
  gerrymandering and, 30, 32, 33
  grand juries and, 82, 84, 89, 90, 92, 95, 98, 99, 103
  judicial discrimination and, 29
  jury challenges and, 43
Blacks (*cont.*)
  jury impanelment lists and, 60
  jury panels and, 65, 68
  master files and, 42, 48, 51
  McMartin trial and, 205, 207, 208, 210
  Newton trial and, 73–74
  qualified-juror files and, 53, 54, 55, 56
  rape trials and, 74–75
  residential mobility of, 22, 23, 24, 25, 48
  scientific *voir dire* and, 143, 144, 150, 151–153, 154, 155, 156, 157, 161
  source lists and, 42, 45
  Supreme Court rulings affecting, 81–83, 86–104, 109, 110, 111, 112
    before 1880, 86–87
    between 1880–1934, 88–89
    between 1935–1948, 89–91
    between 1965–1967, 95–97
    cross section criterion and, 91–95, 96
    institutional racism and, 97–100
    as jury forepersons, 103–104
    statistical indices in, 100–102
    white defendents and, 102–103
  verdicts and, 5–7
  voir dire and, 69, 70, 95, 96–97
Blue-ribbon juries, 26–27, 86, 111–112
Buckey, Peggy Ann, 195, 196, 211
Buckey, Peggy McMartin, 11, 193, 194, 195, 196, 197, 199, 200–204, 211, 212, 213, 214
Buckey, Raymond, 11, 194, 195, 197, 199, 212, 213, 214

California Code of Civil Procedures, 30, 187, 190
Capital Cities—ABC, 211

Capital punishment, 20, 93, 161
  Harris trial and, 144, 145, 146, 147–148, 150, 154
  judicial discrimination and, 28, 29
  Newton trial and, 73
  for rape, 74
Census lists, 46
Census tracts
  cluster-sampling methods and, 168–170, 172, 174, 177, 178–180, 182, 183, 184, 187, 189, 214
  gerrymandering and, 30, 32, 43
  jury impanelment lists and, 58, 60
Challenges for cause, 68–69
  in McMartin trial, 198
  in scientific *voir dire*, 154, 159
Chanel, Pat, 159
Chicago Seven trial, 216
Child care responsibilities, 64, 66–67, 128, 137, 215
Children's Institute International, 211
Chin, Vincent, 5, 7–8
Chi-square statistics, 44
  in cluster-sampling, 173, 174, 177, 179–180, 183–184, 185, 187, 189
Choa, Andrew, 72–73
City directories, 47
Civil Rights Act of 1875, 14, 81
Civil trials, 3, 8
  Supreme Court rulings affecting, 84–86, 113
  voir dire in, 69
Clergy, exemptions for, 67
Cluster-sampling methods, 165–190, 214
  computer-generated graphics analysis in, 173–174
  covariance structure analysis in, 173
  description of, 168–170
  empirical model in, 170
  policy implications of, 187–189
  residential segregation and, 166–168
Cognizable groups, 43
  cluster-sampling methods and, 165
  Hispanics as, 104
  scientific *voir dire* and, 160, 161
  socioeconomic factors and, 111
The Common Sense Book of Baby and Child Care (Spock), 158
Communist Workers' Party (CWP), 6
Comparative disparity, 101, 105, 107
Computer-generated graphics analysis, in cluster-sampling, 173–174
Constitution, U.S., *see* specific amendments to
Covariance structure analysis, in cluster-sampling, 173
Cross section criterion, 5, 165, 166
  in McMartin trial, 197–198
  source lists and, 44–45
  Supreme Court rulings affecting, 91–95, 96, 107–108, 109

Daily Breeze, 196
Daily News, 212
Davis, Angela, 69, 158, 216
Davis, Danny, 197
Death penalty, *see* Capital punishment
Department of Motor Vehicles lists, *see* Driver registration lists
Desegregation of schools, 16
Dicker, Cathleen, 195
Disabilities, economic excuses for, 136
Discriminant analysis, in McMartin trial, 202–203
Distance requirements, 30, 44, 58, 60
  cluster-sampling methods and, 170, 173, 177–178, 180, 188
  economic excuses and, 119–120, 136
  excuses and, 64
DMV registration lists, 19, 46–47, 50–51, 76, 166
Due process clause of 14th Amendment, 94, 102
Duncan socioeconomic index, 127

Ebens, Ronald, 7–8
Economic excuses, 119–140
  authority-class position and, 121, 123, 124, 125, 126, 127, 134–135, 137
  extralegal variables in, 135
  human capital factors and, 124, 125, 128, 137, 139
  hypotheses on, 124–125
  juror characteristics and, 128
  juror qualifications and, 123–124
  labor-market position and, 121, 123, 124, 125, 126, 127, 134, 137–138, 139
  legal variables in, 124–125, 128–129, 135–136

Economic excuses (*cont.*)
organizational structure and, 121, 123, 124, 126, 129
structural approach in, 121–123, 124, 125
Education
cluster-sampling methods and, 173
economic excuses and, 137
excuses and, 65
McMartin trial and, 205, 207–208, 210
scientific *voir dire* and, 158–159, 160
voir dire and, 71
Egan, Joques, 159
Emancipation Proclamation, 81
Empirical model of jury selection, 170
Employment
authority-class position in, 121, 123, 124, 125, 126, 127, 134–135, 137
exemptions and, 67–68
labor-market position in, *see* Labor-market position
organizational structure in, 123, 124, 125, 126, 129
residential mobility and, 21, 23, 24–26
English language proficiency
economic excuses and, 135, 137, 139–140
qualified-juror files and, 53–54
scientific *voir dire* and, 157
Entman, Robert M., 199
Equal protection clause of 14th Amendment, 9, 87, 100, 102, 104, 105, 111, 155
Excuses, 111, *see also* Economic excuses
jury panels and, 64–66, 67
qualified-juror files and, 53, 55–56
Supreme Court rulings on, 109, 111
Exemptions, 124
jury panels and, 64, 67–68
qualified-juror files and, 53
Supreme Court rulings on, 108–109

Factor analysis, in McMartin trial, 202, 203–204
Federal and Uniform Jury Selection Act of 1968, 187–188
Federal Jury Selection Act of 1968, 44, 45–46, 51–52, 63, 86, 114, 165
Fifteenth Amendment, 14, 81
First Amendment, 212
Fourteenth Amendment, 14, 73, 81, 88, 89, 90
due process clause of, 94, 102
Fourteenth Amendment (*cont.*)
equal protection clause of, 9, 87, 100, 102, 104, 105, 111, 155
Fourth Amendment, 212
Frankfurter, Felix, 93
Fuller, Melville, 89

Gender, cluster-sampling methods and, 170, 173, 180, *see also* Women
Gerrymandering, 4, 43–44
in structural approach, 18, 29–34, 35
Gits, Dean R., 197, 212
Goodness-of fit chi-square values, 44, 177, 179–180, 183–184
Grand juries, 14, 15, 16, 39, 82, 84, 89, 90, 95, 103
cluster-sampling methods and, 165
cross section criterion and, 92
distance requirement and, 44
institutional racism and, 98, 99
in McMartin trial, 195, 213
socioeconomic factors affecting, 112
voir dire and, 71
Greensboro trials, 5–7, 8

Harlan, John Marshall, 108
Harper, David, 73–74
Harris trials, 11, 28, 29, 43, 155, 156, 160, 172
background of, 144–145
defense jury-selection strategies in, 145–146
jury profile in, 147–148
Markov chain and, 150–154
scientific *voir dire* in, 148–150
Harrisburg Seven trial, 70, 159, 215
Hillside strangler trial, 68
Hispanics, 13, 16–17, 18, 19
capital punishment and, 20
cluster-sampling methods and, 172, 174, 176, 177, 183, 184, 185–187, 189
distance requirement and, 44
economic excuses and, 137
excuses and, 55, 56
exemptions and, 68
gerrymandering and, 30, 32, 33
Harris trial and, 145, 150
jury challenges and, 43
jury impanelment lists and, 60
jury panels and, 65, 68

Hispanics (*cont.*)
master files and, 42, 48, 51
McMartin trial and, 205, 208, 210
qualified-juror files and, 53–54, 55, 56
residential mobility of, 22–23, 24, 25, 48
scientific *voir dire* and, 145, 150, 157
source lists and, 42, 45
Supreme Court rulings affecting, 82, 83, 86, 104–107, 109
verdicts and, 9
Home ownership, 22–24, 45
Hughes, Charles Evans, 89
Human capital factors, 17
in economic excuses, 124, 125, 128, 137, 139
Hung juries, 29

Illness, excuses for, 64, 67
Impanelment lists, *see* Jury impanelment lists
Inclusiveness standard for source lists, 46
Income, *see also* Socioeconomic factors
excuses and, 64, 65
McMartin trial and, 208
residential mobility and, 23
scientific *voir dire* and, 160
Interval number, 48

Jackson, Robert Houghwout, 112
Johnson, Judy, 194
Judicial discrimination, 18, 26–29, 34
Jury box, 40, 71–75
Jury challenges, 43, *see also* Challenges for cause; Peremptory challenges
Jury duty fees, 123, 139
Jury forepersons, 15, 71–74, 84
Supreme Court rulings affecting selection of, 103–104, 113
Jury impanelment lists, 40, 56–62, 172
Jury panels, 40, 63–68
in McMartin trial, 205–208
Jury qualification criteria, 40
cluster-sampling methods and, 177
economic excuses and, 123–124
gerrymandering and, 33
qualified-juror files and, *see* Qualified-juror files
Jury qualification questionnaires, 40, 54–55, 64, 76, 120
in McMartin trial, 199–200
Jury Selection and Service Act of 1968, 44, 47, 57, 67, 190
Jury selection procedures, 39–78
geographical area and population in, 40, 42–44
jury box stage of, 40, 71–75
jury impanelment lists in, 40, 56–62
jury panels in, 40, 63–68
jury qualification questionnaires in, 40, 54–55, 64, 76
master files in, 40, 42, 47–51
qualified-juror files in, 40, 51–56
source lists in, 40, 42, 44–47
voir dire in, 40, 68–71, 76
Jury summonses, 39, 61–62, 63–64, 76
Jury System Improvement Act of 1978, 56
Juveniles, 113

KABC-TV, 195
Kaufman, Charles, 7–8
Kaufman, Irvin, 45
Key-man selection, 39, 52, 57, 95, 105
King, Rodney, 10
Kissinger, Henry, 159
Ku Klux Klan, 5–6

Labor-market position, 4, 215
economic excuses and, 121, 123, 124, 125, 126, 127, 129, 134, 137–138, 139
excuses and, 55–56, 64, 66
residential mobility and, 21, 22, 34
scientific *voir dire* and, 160
source lists and, 45
Lawyers, exemptions for, 67
League of Women Voters, 107
Lincoln, Abraham, 81
LISREL maximum-likelihood estimations, 173
Little, Joan, 70
Logit regression
on economic excuses, 126, 129
in McMartin trial, 202, 203
Los Angeles Times, 195, 197, 211, 212

MacFarlane, Kathleen, 211
Marital status, economic excuses and, 134, 137
Markov chain, 150–154
Marshall, Thurgood, 103
Master files, 40, 42, 47–51, 120, 126, 199
Maxwell, Boyce, 7

McConahay, John B., 199
McMartin, Virginia, 195, 196, 211
McMartin trial, 11, 120, 193–217
background of, 194–195
comparision of eligible/impaneled jurors in, 205–208
importance of race screening in, 208–210
juror profile analysis in, 200–204
jury selection in, 197–198
media and, 195, 196, 197, 211–214
pretrial publicity/influence on public opinion in, 198–200
pretrial publicity/political motives in, 196–197
verdict in, 210–211
Media
Greensboro trials and, 6
McMartin trial and, 195, 196, 197, 211–214
Meese Commission, 193
Michols, James, Jr., 103
Mitchell, James E., 103
Mitchell, John, 72–73, 216
Mobility, *see* Residential mobility
Multiple-regression analysis, in McMartin trial, 202
Murphy, William Francis, 92, 107–108, 111

National Women's Rights Party, 107
Native Americans, 44, 69, 158, 208
New Catholic Left, 159
Newsweek magazine, 196
Newton, Huey, 9–10, 69, 72–74, 215
Nitz, Michael, 7
Nixon, Richard, 72

Occupation, *see* Employment
One-day-one-trial scheme, 55
Organizational structure, 123, 124, 125, 126, 129
Organization of Chinese Americans, 8

Palermo, Barbara, 212
Penalty phase, *see* Sentencing
Peremptory challenges, 15, 68, 69–71, 166
in Harris trial, 146, 148–150
in McMartin trial, 198
in Newton trial, 73
in scientific *voir dire,* 146, 148–150, 154, 159
Supreme Court rulings affecting, 97

Philibosian, Robert, 196, 211
Police officers, exemptions for, 67, 123, 128
Pounder, William, 211
Prima facie discrimination
blacks and, 90, 92, 93, 97, 100, 102, 103, 104
Hispanics and, 105
women and, 109, 110
Public Law No. 92–269, 48, 49

Qualification questionnaires, *see* Jury qualification questionnaires
Qualified-juror files, 40, 51–56

Raidor, Bette, 211
Raidor, Milan, 211
Random selection, 13, 39
cluster-sampling vs., 165, 166, 168, 169, 182, 184, 187, 189
cross section criterion in, *see* Cross section criterion
jury impanelment lists and, 57
master files and, 47, 51
source lists and, 44–45
Supreme Court rulings affecting, 95
Rape trials, 74–75
judicial discrimination and, 29
Supreme Court rulings affecting, 90, 93, 94, 95
Recalcitrants, 4, 21, 22, 34, 200
Reconstruction, 14, 88
Reece, Amos, 94–95
Reed, Stanley Forman, 92
Registered-voters' rolls (ROV), 17, 18–20, 35, 44–47, 70, 76, 108, 109
master files and, 50–51
residential mobility and, 21
residential segregation and, 166
Supreme Court rulings and, 95
Rehnquist, William Hubbs, 110
Reiner, Ira, 195–196
Representativeness standard for source lists, 46
Residential mobility, 4
economic excuses and, 128
jury panels and, 64
master files and, 48, 49
qualified-juror files and, 54
source lists and, 45
in structural approach, 18, 21–26, 34

Residential segregation, 166–168
Richelieu, Frank, 197
Rosenzweig, David, 197
Rubin, Lael, 197
Rule of exclusion, 18
Rules of Civil Procedures, U.S., 27

Sanford, John F.A., 87
Satz, Wayne, 195, 211
Scientific *voir dire,* 141–162
  bias research in, 156–160
  in Harris trial, *see* Harris trial
  Markov chain and, 150–154
  in McMartin trial, 120, 198, 210, 214, 215–217
  social significance of, 154–156
Scott, Dred, 86–87
Scottsboro Boys case, 157
Selective-service lists, 47
Sentencing, 21, 71–72, 145
Sequestration, 72, 119, 159–160, 215
Seventh Amendment, 3, 83, 113
Shaw, David, 212
Silent Shame, 193
Sixth Amendment, 3, 27, 29, 42–43, 45, 83, 113, 142, 212
"60 Minutes," 212
Slaughter-House trial, 86–87
Socioeconomic factors, 4, *see also* Income
  cluster-sampling methods and, 170, 173, 180
  economic excuses and, 135
  excuses and, 111
  in structural approach, 18, 23, 34
  Supreme Court rulings and, 110–113
  voir dire and, 71
Source lists, 40, 42, 44–47, *see also* specific types
Spock trial, 70, 157–158
Stans, Maurice, 72–73, 216
Stare decisis, 46
Statistical indices, Supreme Court use of, 84, 100–102, 106–107
Stevens, Glenn, 196
Stone, Harlan Fiske, 92
Strong, William, 88
Structural approach, 13–35
  economic excuses in, 121–123, 124, 125
  gerrymandering in, 18, 29–34, 35
  judicial discrimination in, 18, 26–29, 34
Structural approach (*cont.*)
  procedural anomalies in, 18–21, 34
  socioeconomic factors in, 18, 23, 34
Subscribers' lists, 47
Summonses, *see* Jury summonses
Supply-side determinants, structural approach in, 17
Supreme Court, U.S., 81–114, *see also* specific cases of, in Table of Cases
  blacks and, *see* under Blacks
  cross section criterion and, 91–95, 96, 107–108, 109
  economic discrimination by, 110–113
  guidelines followed by, 83–86
  Hispanics and, 82, 83, 86, 104–107, 109
  statistical indices used by, 84, 100–102, 106–107
  women and, 86, 107–110

Tax rolls, 47, 93–94, 97
Taylor, Anna Diggs, 8
Telephone subscribers' lists, 47
Thirteenth Amendment, 14, 81
Time magazine, 196
Timnick, Lois, 197
Tokenism, 82, 83
Travel requirements, *see* Distance requirements
Tso, James, 8
Twenty-mile rule, 30, 58, 60
"20/20," 196

Unanimity rule, 28–29, 113
Undeliverables, 4, 18, 21–26, 34, 199
Urban, Walter, 212
Utility company lists, 47

Verdicts, 5–8, 71
  in McMartin trial, 210–211
Vesco, Robert L., 72
Vietnam Veterans against the War trial, 215
Vietnam war, 157, 158, 159
Vinson, Frederick Moore, 93
Voir dire, 10, 40, 68–71, 76, 166, *see also* Scientific *voir dire*
  economic excuses and, 120, 121
  in McMartin trial, 120, 198, 210, 214, 215–217
  Supreme Court rulings affecting, 95, 96–97

Warren, Earl, 104–105
Watergate trial, *see United States v. Mitchell,* in Table of Cases
Welfare recipient lists, 47
White, Byron Raymond, 95–96, 101, 104, 109, 110
Williams, Aubry, 94
Women, 13, *see also* Gender
  economic excuses and, 128, 137
  excuses and, 55, 65, 66–67, 109
  exemptions and, 67–68, 108–109
  grand juries and, 112
  Harris trial and, 153–154
  jury challenges and, 43
  McMartin trial and, 205, 208, 215
Women (*cont.*)
  qualified-juror files and, 53, 55
  residential mobility of, 23
  scientific *voir dire* and, 153–154, 157–158
  source lists and, 45, 47
  Spock trial and, 70, 157–158
  Supreme Court rulings affecting, 86, 107–110
  voir dire and, 70, 71, 142
Workers Viewpoint Organization (WVO), 6
Wounded Knee trial, 215

Z-test statistics, 84, 106
  in cluster-sampling, 174, 183, 184–187, 189

GPSR Compliance

The European Union's (EU) General Product Safety Regulation (GPSR) is a set of rules that requires consumer products to be safe and our obligations to ensure this.

If you have any concerns about our products, you can contact us on ProductSafety@springernature.com

In case Publisher is established outside the EU, the EU authorized representative is:

Springer Nature Customer Service Center GmbH
Europaplatz 3
69115 Heidelberg, Germany

Batch number: 10844675

Printed by Printforce, the Netherlands